Scanderbeg (Italian engraving 1540)

SCANDERBEG

Harry Hodgkinson

Edited by

Bejtullah Destani & Westrow Cooper

With an introduction by

David Abulafia

The Centre for Albanian Studies

First published 1999 by
The Centre for Albanian Studies
Distributed by
Learning Design, English Street, London E3 4TA
Tel: 020 8983 1944 Fax: 020 8983 1932
e-mail: info@learningdesign.org website: www.learningdesign.org

ISBN 1 873928 13 0

Printed and bound in the Republic of Ireland by
Colour Books Ltd,
105 Baldoyle Industrial Estate, Baldoyle, Dublin

Contents

. . . .

Acknowledgements

The Centre for Albanian Studies would like to thank the following people for their assistance and encouragement:

Elsie Ayrton, Ada Clarkson, Dorothy and Eddie Lunt.

Patricia Nugee, for generously allowing us to reproduce her print of Scanderbeg, Zakaria Erzinçlioglu, Philip Logoreci, Peter Rennie, Ihsan Toptani, Noel Malcolm, Justin Elliot, Eddie McParland, Graham Carder, Tony Wisewell, Ferid Hudhri, Evelyn FitzHerbert, Nicholas Oliver, Avdyl Gula, Alexander Duma and Hilmi Zogjani.

Bejtullah Destani
Centre for Albanian Studies
London
September 1999

About the Author

. . . .

HARRY HODGKINSON

Harry Hodgkinson was born in Blackburn, Lancashire in 1913. From the age of 16 he started writing for The Blackpool Times, Yorkshire Observer and Bradford Telegraph.

In 1936 he walked from Charing Cross to Jerusalem and published stories from his travels in Christian Science Monitor, The Times and The Guardian. He was employed by Naval Intelligence at The Admiralty and worked under Ian Fleming, in charge of Albania and Yugoslavia.

After the war he was adviser to The Director of Naval Intelligence regarding the Soviet satellite states. In 1954 he published 'Adriatic Sea', and in 1955 'Tito between East and West'.

He was in correspondence with Edith Durham for many years and received some sixty letters from her.

From 1985 he was the Chairman of the Anglo-Albanian Association. He left many unpublished manuscripts about the Balkans.

Harry Hodgkinson
Journalist, writer, Naval Intelligence Officer and Balkan expert.
Born 15 March 1913; died London 2 October 1994

French engraving of the beginning of XVIIth century

Introduction by David Abulafia

. . . .

SCANDERBEG: A HERO AND HIS REPUTATION

SCANDERBEG is not merely a dominating figure in the history, and historical consciousness, of the Albanians, but a figure of commanding significance in the history of fifteenth-century Europe. His career serves as a timely reminder that what occurs in the Balkans has great bearing on the future of western Europe as well.[1] It is therefore surprising at first sight that during the twentieth century he has attracted rather little attention from scholars, at a time when the serious study of the fifteenth century confrontation between Christians and Turks has reached new levels: one thinks of the work of Franz Babinger on Mehmet the Conqueror,[2] of Paul Wittek on the rise of the Ottomans,[3] of Cemal Kafadar on the sense of Turkish identity,[4] alongside excellent studies of Scanderbeg's contemporaries and allies, notably Alfonso the Magnanimous, who has been the subject of a major biography by Alan Ryder.[5] In part this reflects the isolation of Albania from the rest of Europe for much of the second half of the twentieth century, though it should be remembered that also in Hoxha's despotic state Scanderbeg was cultivated as a national hero both at Kruja, in the museum dedicated to his memory, and in Tirana, where neither Lenin, Stalin nor Mao could usurp from him the name of the city's major square, nor deny his statue a prominent place among the city's monuments.

During this century, he has not lacked historians, but they have found the material challenging for reasons that will become plain. Bishop Fan Noli wrote his *Historia e Skënderbeut* in 1921, but it required extensive revision before appearing in English as *George Castrioti Scanderbeg* in 1947.[6] Athanas Gegaj published an important study of *L'Albanie et l'invasion turque au XVe siècle* in 1937.[7] Most recently the scholarly world has fallen greatly into the debt of Alain Ducellier, whose superb study of *La façade maritime de l'Albanie* has transformed our understanding of the history of the Albanian coastline up to the time of Scanderbeg.[8] Perhaps, indeed, it has been this area of Albanian history that has fared best in recent decades, as our understanding has grown of the relations between the Albanians and their neighbours, including the Venetians who dominated the waters of the Adriatic, and the kings of Naples who dominated the opposite shores, and often tried to dominate Albania as well.[9] However, our understanding has not been improved by the dogmatic Marxist-Leninist historical writing that dominated Albania in the age of Hoxha. While exalting Scanderbeg as a national hero, historians also characterised the period as one of feudal oppression, whether by local landlords or by Turks.

A consistent problem for those trying to write about Scanderbeg has been the need to assess the material provided by the priest from Shkodër, Marinus Barletius, author of the *De vita et Moribus Georgii Castrioti* of 1504.[10] Near enough in time to Scanderbeg's career to have the benefit of precise knowledge, Barletius' book is also a work heavily influenced by the humanistic concerns of Renaissance admirers of classical antiquity. Barletius' image of Scanderbeg is therefore highly reminiscent of that of ancient Greek orators exhorting the Athenians to resist the Persian invaders who are about to overwhelm their land: for the Persians under Xerxes, read the Turks under Mehmet II; for Themistocles, read Scanderbeg. The influence of Barletius can be seen most powerfully in Nelo Drizari's *Scanderbeg, his life, correspondence, orations, victories and philosophy*, of 1968, who takes Barletius as his major source and offers resounding translations of speeches attributed to the hero:[11]

> It is not that I have brought liberty to you, but here I have found liberty. Scarcely had I set foot within our country, scarcely had your ears heard the sound of my name, but that all of you made haste to meet me... It is not I who has given

> you this Nation and superiority. It is not I who has given you this city. It is you who have given them unto me. It was not I who put arms into your hands. I found you ready in arms. I found you everywhere bearing the signs of liberty in your hearts, in your faces, in your swords, and in your lances.[12]

To say that historians have not found it easy to distinguish Barletius' ringing exhortations from the genuine words of Scanderbeg is not to imply that they have been careless or gullible. There are genuine difficulties in establishing the details of Scanderbeg's career, particularly since his own archives, which must have existed, are no longer to be found. However, we can make some progress towards establishing a Scanderbeg archive of our own. Scholarship on the subject of Scanderbeg has benefited from the publication of documents relating to his career preserved in Italian archives. Since the mid-fifteenth century sees the creation of the first network of diplomatic representatives, with the courier systems carrying messages between seats of government that such a system generated, it is not surprising that there are frequent references to Scanderbeg in the correspondence of the dukes of Milan, the kings of Naples and the marquises of Mantua, among others.[13] Much of this material has been made available for scholars in an important article by Sulejman Meço.[14]

There are also letters from Scanderbeg himself, for example a letter sent to the rebel prince of Taranto in southern Italy, Giovanni Antonio del Balzo Orsini, in October 1460, against whom the king of Naples, Ferrante (or Ferdinand) I was unleashing a force of Albanian stradiots under Scanderbeg's command; this correspondence was translated by Drizari, and the original texts can be found (with photographs of some of the documents) in Meço's article.[15] In this letter we can hear the voice of Scanderbeg clearly, advising the prince that he has a great obligation to Ferrante and to Ferrante's father Alfonso of Aragon, who had done much to support him when Kruja was under siege from the Turks.[16] Nor was Scanderbeg unaware of the classical past: he mentions in the same letter how Pyrrhus of Epirus had once caused great harm to the Romans in Italy, and he says that 'if our chronicles do not lie we are called

Epirotes.' We have the sense that, like the prince of Taranto and the king of Naples, his court was open to the influence of the revived classical culture of Renaissance Italy. He urges the prince to understand that the major threat is in fact that of the Turks. It was better to pursue peace within Italy, and to stand together against the Turks, than to keep alive quarrels which would only make the Turkish advance more invincible. In fact, Ferrante owed his kingdom to Scanderbeg, who recognised the obligations that he had incurred towards Ferrante's father and helped clear the south east of Italy of rebels.[17] His coming to Italy excited great interest, and in Milan and Mantua the rulers of the Renaissance states marvelled at his arrival.

Reading the archival documents, there can be no doubt that Scanderbeg had already attained the reputation of a hero in his own time. Nor, of course, is there much doubt that his reputation alone could not win him his wars. The failure of most European powers, apart from Naples, to give him support, accompanied by the failure of Pope Pius II's plans to organise a great crusade against the Turks, meant that none of his victories against the Turks permanently undermined Ottoman power in the Balkans.[18] What is noticeable about his victories is that in the long term they did not displace the Turks from the region; indeed, in the short term, they actually attracted Turkish armies into Albania. By 1500 the Ottomans understood that this area needed to be brought under tighter Turkish authority; they consolidated their hold on the sea shore, loosening the Venetian grip on the coastal towns and setting off a renewed struggle for the Straits of Otranto and the Ionian Sea, which would culminate seventy years later in the battle of Lepanto.[19] The time was past when they would rely on local satraps drawn mainly from the resident Christian nobility. For it was clear that, once the Turks had reached the Adriatic, the threat to western Europe was profound. Already in 1480/1 Mehmet II had captured Otranto on the heel of Italy, massacring its male population, and making real what Scanderbeg had been warning the west would happen.[20] Meanwhile, the stream of Albanian settlers in southern Italy, coming no longer to help the king of Naples against his foes, but to settle in Christian territory away from Turkish rule, grew more persistent, resulting in the formation of Albanian villages which were already visible in the records of the early sixteenth-century government of Naples, and which have persisted in some cases until today.[21] This was not simply a struggle that concerned Scanderbeg's Albanian subjects, but one which involved all of Christendom.

Scanderbeg's major legacy was to be as a source of inspiration to those in subsequent centuries who saw in him an exemplar of the Christian struggle against the Turks. Paulus Jovius began his eulogy of the Albanian hero with the remark that no Christian prince or emperor had ever compared with Scanderbeg in the vehemence with which he resisted the Turks: *Nemo Christiani nominis princeps aut imperator Georgio Castrioto vehementius atque felicius arma Turcarum exercuit.*[22] In reality, he belonged to the smallest of the three major confessional groups in present-day Albania, and his elevation to the role of a national hero for Muslims, Orthodox and his own Catholics is a modern phenomenon (not to mention his role as a hero in the Communist period); but in the search for a national hero at the time that Albania became an independent nation, he was the obvious choice, the potent foe of the Ottoman Empire from which, four and a half centuries later, the Albanians at last extricated themselves.

Harry Hodgkinson's engaging book is an attempt to move closer to the historical personage, and to set him in the dramatic landscape of Albania itself. Scanderbeg's English language bibliography in fact goes back to the sixteenth century; Gambini's study of Scanderbeg was translated from Italian and appeared in London in 1562;[23] Jacques de Lavardin's history of Scanderbeg was translated from French, and was published in England in 1596.[24] Thus the hero was being acclaimed far from the waters where the struggle with the Turks was at its peak. Since then publications on Scanderbeg in English have largely consisted of works by Albanian writers, notably those by Noli and Drizari referred to earlier (though it would be wrong to pass by Gibbon's comparison with Alexander the Great and, of course, Pyrrhus of Epirus).

Hodgkinson's book does not claim to be that definitive work of scholarship that is still required. But it is informed by a love of Albania, and a sense therefore of place. It aims to stand in the well established English tradition of elegantly written, readable historical works aimed at a wider audience, a tradition in which the history of the Byzantine and Balkan world has been well represented by such figures as Sir Rennell Rodd, William Miller, Sir Steven Runciman and, most recently, Donald Nicol and John Julius Norwich. Yet while several of these authors have graphically described the fall of Constantinople to the Turks in 1453, rather less attention has been paid to the continuing battle against the Turks in the western Balkans, and its implications for the history of neighbouring regions such as Italy. This book represents another stage in the uncovering of the remarkable career of a fifteenth-century figure whose heroism was lauded by contemporaries, and whose military skills were feared by his foes. As King Ferrante of Naples said when advising the duke of Milan of Scanderbeg's arrival in southern Italy in 1461, 'his arrival will add not a little *opinione et nervo* to our affairs.' [25] He was a figure who (literally) towered over many of his contemporaries.

Dr David Abulafia
Cambridge University, March 1999

NOTES

1 N. Malcolm, *Kosovo. A Short History*. London, 1998. Provides a masterly reminder that if we ignore the earlier history of the Balkans we are unlikely to make much sense of the present either.

2 Franz Babinger, *Mehmed the Conqueror and his time*, transl. R. Manheim, ed. W.C. Hickman, Princeton, NJ, 1978.

3 P. Wittek, *The Rise of the Ottoman Empire*, London, 1938.

4 C. Kafadar, *Between Two Worlds. The Construction of the Ottoman State*, Berkeley/Los Angeles, 1995.

5 A.F.C. Ryder, *Alfonso the Magnanimous, King of Aragon, Naples, and Sicily, 1396-1458*, Oxford, 1990.

6 F.S. Noli, *George Castrioti Scanderbeg (1405-1465)*, New York, 1947.

7 A. Gegaj, *L'Albanie et l'Invasion Turque au XVe siècle*, Louvain, 1937.

8 A. Ducellier, *La Façade Maritime de l'Albanie.* Durazzo et Valona du XIe au XVe siècles, Thessalonika, 1981.

9 See, for example, Pëllumb Xhufi, *Shqiptarët Përballë Anzhuinëve (1267-1285)*, Studime Historike (1987), pp. 199-222; D. Nicol, *The Despotate of Epiros*, 2 vols., Oxford, 1957 and Cambridge, 1984.

10 Marinus Barletius, *Historia de Vita et Gestis Scanderbegi Epirotarum Principi,* Rome, 1510[?], and other contemporary editions.

11 Nelo Drizari, *Scanderbeg. His life, correspondence, orations, victories and philosophy*, New York, 1968.

12 Drizari, *Scanderbeg*. p.3

13 V. Ilardi, *Studies in Italian Renaissance Diplomatic History*, London, 1986; and, for an older view, G. Mattingly's classic *Renaissance Diplomacy*, Boston, MA, 1955, or later editions.

14 S. Meço, *Dokumente për Historinë e Skënderbeut*, Albania (journal of the *Comité national-democratique 'Albanie Libre'*), Rome, 1970, pp. 89-177.

15 Meço, *Dokumente,* pp. 124-6; Drizari, *Scanderbeg*, pp.61-4

16 See e.g. Barletius, 1510 edition, f. cxxi^{r}, f.cxxiii^{r}, f.cxxv^{r} (lib.IX); and Paolo Giovio, *Commentarii della cose de Turchi, di Paulo Giovio, et Andrea Gambini, con gli fatti, et la vita di Scanderbeg,* Venice, 1541, f. 22^{v}-27^{r}; also *Gli illustri et glorioso gesti et vittoriose imprese, fatte contra Turchi, dal sign. Giogio Castriotto, detto Scanderbeg*, Venice, 1584, c. 40-46, cap. 22.

17 David Abulafia, 'From Ferrante I to Charles VIII', in *The French Descent into Renaissance Italy, 1494-5. Antecedents and effects*, ed. David Abulafia, Aldershot, 1994, p. 6; also the comments by Alan Ryder, 'The Angevin bid for Naples, 1380-1480', *The French descent,* p. 67.

18 David Abulafia, 'Ferrante I of Naples, Pope Pius II and the Congress of Mantua (1459)', in *Montjoie. Studies in crusade history in honour of Hans Eberhard Mayer,* ed. B.Z. Kedar, R. Hiestand and J. Riley-Smith, Aldershot, pp. 235-49.

19 David Abulafia, 'From Ferrante I to Charles VIII', p.23; Carol Kidwell, 'Venice, The French invasion and the Apulian ports', *The French descent*, pp.295-308

20 *Otranto 1480. Atti del convegno internazionale di studio*, ed. C.D.Fonseca, Galatina, 1986, 2 vols.

21 British Library, MS Egerton 1905, ff.111^{v}-125^{r}, a document of 1508, reporting the number of hearths in Albanian, Greek and Slav *(Schiavoni)* communities; see also A. Ducellier et al., *Les Chemins de l'exil. Bouleversement de l'Est européen et migrations vers l'Ouest à la fin du Moyen Age*, Paris, 1992, for Albanianand Slavic settlement in southern Italy

22 Paulo Giovio, 'Elogiorum Georgius Castriotus Scanderbechus Epiri Principis', from Giovio's *Elogia virorum literis illustrium*, Basle, 1577, p. 144; facsimile (with Albanian and Italian translations) in Paulus Jovius (1483-1552), *Skënderbeu në pesëqindvjetorin e vdekjes*, E Boton Balli Kombëtar në Mërgim, Rome, s.d.

23 Andrea Gambini, *Two very notable commentaries, the one the originall of the house of Ottomanno, written by Andrew Cambine, and thother of the warres of the Turcke against George Scanderbeg,* London, 1562.

24 Jacques de Lavardin, *The historie of George Castriot, surnamed Scanderbeg, King of Albanie*, London, 1596.

25 I should like to record my gratitude to Patricia Nugee, who generously allowed me time with her collection of books on Scanderbeg when it was on show at the University Library, Cambridge, in 1996; several of the volumes from that exhibition are mentioned here. I also owe an inestimable debt to Bejtullah Destani for his provision of books, journals, pamphlets and photographs of manuscript material on the life of Scanderbeg.

Prefatory Note

No biography of Scanderbeg has been published in England since 1596, and a couple of hundred years ago the lack was already being noted by General Wolfe, who wrote to a friend that 'if a tolerable account could be got of the exploits of Scanderbeg, it would be inestimable.' In fact, no full-length account of his career has appeared anywhere that is not wholly or partly based on the original panegyric written for anti-Muslim propagandist purposes by an Albanian monk around 1500. The partial exception to this is the Albanian Orthodox Bishop Fan Noli's George Castrioti Scanderbeg (New York, 1947), a labour of love and scholarship which has a unique place among the hundreds of volumes dealing directly or indirectly with the subject.

Fan Noli brought together for the first time most of the basic documents and references. The more important are quoted textually at considerable length, though in the original Italian, French, Serbian, etc., and without translation. He also provides copious notes and a history and critical appreciation of the bibliography of Scanderbeg, so that the actual narrative account of Scanderbeg's life is little more than a factual summary of events, and occupies less than 60 of his 240 Pages.

Bishop Fan Noli's work is invaluable to any later biographer, however, for he was the first to erect signposts in the tangled undergrowth of mediaeval Albanian history. Albania has attracted a number of scholars, but fate seems to have decreed that they should have wretched luck in the attempt to finalise their work. The great authority on the customs and legal lore of the northern mountains, for example, was a Father Gjecov, who after collecting this for 25 years was shot by the Yugoslavs after the first world war. Three scholars of the old Austro-Hungarian empire planned to publish five volumes of documents on Albanian history, but their work ended with the second volume, and this brought them only to 1407, when Scanderbeg was two years of age. One, the Hungarian Ludwig von Thalloczy, was killed in a train collision. Another, Constantin Jirecek, a Czech, died in 1918 when still only in his sixties.

The third, the Croat Milan von Sufflay, who was a generation younger than they were, was killed by a Serb fanatic in 1928, having completed only one chapter of a projected history of Albania. This transfer of violence from the life of the subject to that of the scholar has resulted in a number of valuable but fragmentary books of specialised interest; and the present biography is an attempt to display for a wider public some of the riches which these pioneers discovered.

A complete bibliography would be merely a reprint of Fan Noli's, and so none is attempted here; but on important or controversial points the relevant reference is quoted in the Notes to the various chapters.* One or two additions should also be made to Fan Noli's list. He does not mention a biography published in wartime Italy by Alessandro Cutolo, which makes use of a certain amount of new material from the Venetian archives. Since he wrote, the 'History of Mehmet the Conqueror' by Kritovoulos, which gives a lively account of the later Albanian campaigns from the Ottoman point of view, has appeared in an admirable English translation by the late Margaret Hasluck. Mrs Hasluck lived in Albania before the war and set herself to love and understand the traditional life of the northern mountains. She produced a monument to herself in her posthumous 'Unwritten Law in Albania' (Cambridge University Press, 1954).

Those who wish to know more of the human and social background to the Scanderbeg story should not omit her book, nor the late M.E. Durham's 'Some Tribal Origins, Laws and Customs of the Balkans' (Allen and Unwin, 1928). The present writer owes a deep debt to both Miss Durham and Mrs Hasluck, not only for their writings, but for their encouragement in studying Albanian life and history and for the stimulation of their knowledge, enthusiasm and kindness.

Harry Hodgkinson
London 1959

*The Notes to each chapter appear at the end of this volume.

A Note on Spelling

Though Scanderbeg is spelt with a 'k' in modern Albania, the more usual form is by now too well established elsewhere to be disturbed. As it is even used by Bishop Fan Noli, himself one of the most distinguished Albanians of modern days, any change might appear somewhat pedantic.

Places and persons in the Balkans have often possessed several names, according to the language momentarily in the ascendant. Thus the town which the Albanians now call Durres began life as the Greek colony Epidamnos and subsequently became the Roman Dyrrachium, the Byzantine Dyrrachion, the Serbian Drac and the Venetian Durazzo. The principle adopted here has been to retain the version familiar through general and continued use: most people know where Durazzo is, even though its own inhabitants have a different name for it.

In one case three different names have been used for a single city, according to the historic context - Constantinople for the capital of the eastern Roman Empire; Istanbul for the Ottoman capital; and Byzantium for the centre of a universal religion and culture.

Where familiarity or historical significance do not suggest the spelling in this way, the current usage of the language most nearly concerned has been followed. Thus the Macedonian Skopje appears, rather than the Serbian Skoplje, and the great Serbian emperor is spelt Dusan, not Dushan.

As to pronunciation, the inverted circumflex in Serbo-Croat adds an 'h' to the sound of the letter concerned: zh, ski, ch; the acute accent adds a somewhat softer 'h' to the 'c' on which it appears; 'j' is 'y' and 'c' is 'ts.' In Albanian, 'c' is 'ts' unless it has a cedilla underneath, when it is 'ch'; 'ë' is an 'e' narrowed almost to vanishing point, and 'gj' has a 'zh' sound: the port of Shëngjin (St. John), for example, is pronounced Sh'nzheen.

(HH)

Coat-of-arms of the Castriot family
(an Italian engraving of the XVIth century)

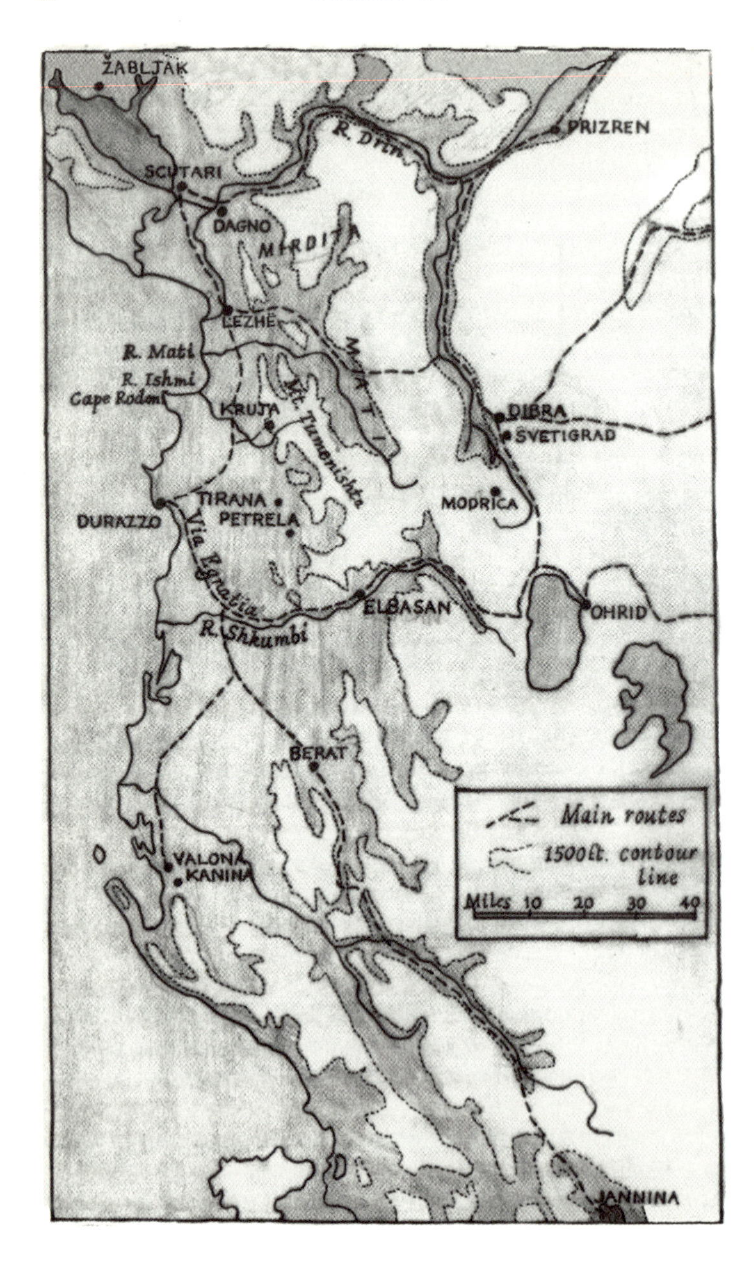
ŽABLJAK
PRIZREN
R. Drin
SCUTARI
DAGNO
MIRDITA
LEZHË
R. Mati
R. Ishmi
Cape Rodoni
MATI
KRUJA
Mt. Tumenishta
DIBRA
SVETIGRAD
MODRICA
TIRANA
DURAZZO
PETRELA
Via Egnatia
ELBASAN
OHRID
R. Shkumbi
BERAT
Main routes
1500 ft. contour line
Miles 10 20 30 40
VALONA
KANINA
JANNINA

Chapter One

. . . .

Europe's Oldest Society

When the Turkish armies first came to Europe to win for themselves the lands that the Byzantine emperors were no longer strong enough to rule, they quickly digested the succulent flesh of the Balkans: the rose-heavy valleys of Bulgaria, the Serbian plum orchards and the olive groves of Greece. When nothing remained but the bare shell of mountains to west and north, they looked around for further conquests and, having captured Constantinople, the seemingly impregnable capital of the eastern world, they turned their attention to Rome, historic centre of the western world. As a stepping stone in this direction, they needed to become masters of Albania, and of the narrow straits separating their Balkan conquests from Italy.

In Albania they were opposed by a mountain chieftain called Gjergj Castrioti, nicknamed Scanderbeg, or the Lord Alexander. His assets were meagre: a fortress that lay like an eagle's nest on the sheer side of a mountain, never more than twenty thousand armed men, and a touch of genius in waging guerrilla cavalry operations. Yet, under the inspiration of his leadership, these were enough to hold the mightiest army of the world at bay for a quarter of a century, saving not only his own country from defeat, but with it the peninsula of Italy and perhaps the remainder of Western Europe. When, after his death, the Turks finally flooded through the mountain passes to the Adriatic coast, it was too late for them to go further. Their impetus was spent, and their opponents were masters of the sea.

So long as the Turks remained a formidable military power, the story of Scanderbeg was familiar to educated Europeans, and almost three hundred years after his death General Wolfe, the hero of Quebec, could speak of him as a commander who 'excels all the officers, ancient and modern, in the conduct of a small defensive army'.[1] This is a vast claim, especially from such a master of warfare; and the achievement it celebrates was all the more remarkable in view of the conditions under which the Albanian leader worked. His people were few in number, and they had never formed a politically organised nation under their own rulers. They were a group of clans and tribes, accepting no government from above, but regulating their affairs by means of an intricate and traditional social code that had come down unbroken from the days before written history began.

These spare, hardy, underfed highlanders of northern Albania, who produced Scanderbeg and then followed him into battle, have chosen for themselves a national totem from the birds of the mountain peaks. In their own language they are not Albanians or Illyrians or Epirots, or any of the names that foreigners have given them in the past couple of thousand years. They are simply Shqiptars, or Sons of the Eagle. They too see themselves as untamed, uncaged and fearless. As to human ancestors, they believed they are descended from the ancient Illyrians, who occupied the Balkan land mass while the Greeks were creating their dazzling and quarrelsome cities in the clear air of the tideless coast.

These same Illyrians, as the Albanians never tire of reminding themselves, produced an Alexander to subdue Asia; a Pyrrhus who crossed over to Italy to fight the Romans; a series of emperors, Diocletian among them, who staved off the collapse of the Roman empire; and finally in Constantine the man who founded the second and more enduring Rome.

The language of the Albanians, which comes down from pre-classical days, is weighty evidence in favour of their claim.

But even more compelling is the pattern of ideas and social customs by which they ordered their lives before Scanderbeg was born, and by which they continued to order them unchanged from his day until a generation or so ago. These men of our own times, like those whom Scanderbeg led to war, still carried on a taboo against working in iron, for instance, which leads the imagination back to the time, two and a half millennia ago, when the new technique of iron smelting, based on the rich mines of Bosnia, broke down the old heroic, aristocratic Bronze age society with which Homer has made us so familiar. Both Serbs and Albanians, we are told by a visitor earlier this century, could make copper pots or cut up old petroleum canisters and fashion tin pots and other articles of them—copper and tin are of course the components of bronze—but 'no one who valued his reputation' could hammer iron.[2] That was left to the gypsies, who had no reputation to value.

Corralled in their hills for generation after generation, these Balkan islands of tribal Quixotes fought back against the intrusion of iron with scorn, the last weapon of a vanquished ruling class. They preferred even poverty to compromise. A French traveller in Bosnia in 1807, after the iron mines had been reopened there, pointed out that not a single Serb would work in them: of two thousand workers, one third were Catholics and two thirds gypsies. And exactly a hundred years after this, a guide who took a number of Montenegrin mountaineers for a walk round London reported: 'We stopped outside a large hardware shop in the Brompton Road, and the two men examined every tool and pot in the window. They then glanced inside. I shall never forget their contempt when they saw that the men behind the counter were not, as they expected, 'crni cigani' (black gypsies) but English. 'What', cried the elder in horror, 'Englishmen making and selling iron things! ... I had rather see my son dead than see him sink so low as this! The English! By God, they are no better than Black Gypsies'; And until we arrived at Whitehall and saw the Horse Guards, nothing would make him modify his opinion that the English are a 'pogan narod' (unclean or depraved race)'.

Invading religions, like invading armies, never completely captured the citadel of the Albanian soul. Even whilst nominally accepting Christianity or Islam, the vestiges of the earlier pagan faiths remained. The new ideas were accepted for the sake of peace with the dominant power of the moment but as they were imposed from without, they touched no deep spring of feeling in the people themselves. They were just strong enough to shrivel the old mythologies, so the ancient beliefs could not be quickened into new life, but remained as a mere set of rules to be applied without regard for common sense or humanity.

For example, it had been agreed over the centuries that a wife could be divorced if she proved unfaithful, for otherwise the offended husband, bound as he would be to kill her to avenge his honour, might find himself involved in a blood feud with his wife's brother or her lover's family. Where the tribe had been converted to Roman Catholicism, and the Church had been strong enough to enforce its ban on divorce, this gap through the hedge of revenge was closed. A cuckolded husband had now to kill his wife or accept the dishonour, he was caught between two worlds, in which it was at once religiously a sin to divorce an offending wife but socially a virtuous action to murder her.

The old laws of the mountains, though they endured longer than any other system of authority in Europe (and probably still command the loyalty of the older Albanian highlanders) remained essentially the law that the great Greek tragedians grappled with and transformed: a law whose sanctions come into operation mechanically, like a natural phenomenon, without regard for the motive of the offender or the gravity or triviality of the offence. On occasion, it could even be the abettor of flagrant injustice. Its guiding principle was that blood must be shed to pay for blood, and that it must be shed by the person closest to the last victim. Thus it followed by an inhumane logic that anyone who killed his near relation—a son, father, uncle, brother and so forth—had committed no crime because he could not be expected to avenge the murder on himself. In these cases, the victim had merely had 'ill luck' to die in the way he did.

There were even certain inducements to such crimes. A man was allowed to marry his brother's widow, so if he fell in love with a sister-in-law he 'could not always resist the temptation to make her a widow. The victim's blood was lost in spite of the murderer's motive, and the fratricide married the widow and suffered no disability except some loss of face'.[3] Here we are dealing not with prehistory but with the twentieth century, and specifically with Scanderbeg's own village nearly five hundred years after his death.

'At Kruja in 1930 when the authorities sought to punish a man who had murdered his brother during a quarrel, the widow swore that the pistol had gone off accidentally when her brother-in-law was trying to wrest it from her husband, who had threatened suicide. Having thus prevented the authorities from taking action, the widow made no effort to keep the true story of the murder quiet, but repeated it every day during the month when the women met for the ceremonial 'keening'. She was also openly commended by the public for preventing the government from shaming her husband's family by arresting the murderer.'

These women of our own day who met for the ceremonial keening, and approved this record of murder and lying, who are they but the Furies that the ghost of Clytemnestra called up to avenge her, when she in her turn had been killed by her son Orestes for killing her husband Agamemnon? They, like the women of Kruja, cared nothing for the reasons which had led her, her victim or her son to commit their several crimes; they knew and cared only about what actions were sanctioned and what prohibited, and could not rest until a transgression had been avenged. Indeed, if we look at the Oresteia[4] in the light of what we now know of Albanian tribal custom, we may gain a clearer view of how the central problem would have appeared to its first audiences, whom Aeschylus was trying to convince that divine law must at length acknowledge the demands of human justice.

The trilogy opens, as everyone knows, with Agamemnon returning from the Trojan War and being killed by his wife Clytemnestra; the question which then arises is who, if anyone, shall avenge the murdered king. In modern Albania there would have been no difficulty: it would have been the task of her husband's brother. 'He had the right to do so, woman though she was, for a question of honour was involved, and for questions of honour women might lawfully be put to death'. On these grounds the duty belongs to Menelaus, but so far as the play is concerned Menelaus does not exist: there is a perfunctory and necessary reference to him in the first chorus, but even here Aeschylus does not mention the word 'brother'.

Orestes thus remains as the head of his family and the nearest relation of the victim, and so it is for him, if anyone, to see that the customary law is carried out. But, to return to Albania, 'her son by the dead man could not kill the murderess because matricide is not allowable. He must avenge his father but he must not kill his mother, and so must decide which of two irreconcilable duties to discharge.

Under the old dispensation there can be no compromise between those contradictory demands, as Aeschylus shows in the last few lines of human recriminations in the Eumenides trial scene, before first Apollo and then Athena enter the discussion. Orestes and the Furies finally argue one another to a standstill. Clytemnestra did kill her husband, say the Furies; but that is not so serious, for a husband and wife are not blood relations. And neither is a son of the same blood as a mother, comes Orestes' reply. It is complete checkmate between them, and the gods have to step in.

This passage has caused much trouble to editors of Aeschylus. The argument that a husband is not a blood relation of his wife, says one, is 'a mere quibble like Portia's pound of flesh without blood', and another finds it 'a weak argument, for it plainly dishonours the marriage-bond'. The idea that only a father is a real parent is an 'astonishing argument'; the suggestion, which has Apollo's support, that the mother is only a nurse, 'cannot possibly make a clear appeal to any audience'. The real question, however, is not whether they would convince a twentieth century audience, but whether the arguments were familiar to some tens of thousands of Greeks over two thousand years ago.

Or, for that matter, to the Albanian mountaineers of our own days. To them, as to their ancestors, the mother is merely a receptacle through which the father's blood is passed to a new generation; to them, as to the Furies, the husband and wife are not biologically akin. So it comes about that though the tribes always had a prohibition on marrying 'their own blood,' the Christian Churches have had the greatest difficulty in trying to make them recognise that they should extend the prohibition to the maternal side of the family. Not so long ago this view prevailed even further afield: there is the story of the 17th century Serbian robber chief Iliga Smiljanic who swore 'blood brotherhood' with his maternal uncle Vuk Mandusic in order to establish a relationship between themselves which, according to modern ideas of biology, already existed.

In blood brotherhood[5], which may be sworn for a political or family alliance, or for less estimable reasons, there is a token and symbolic exchange of blood. Each of two people pricks his finger and lets a drop of blood fall on a piece of sugar that the other one then eats.

The Roman Catholics never recognised this ceremony and left people to carry it out as they would in the old pagan ways, while the Orthodox tried to Christianise it, so that the couple might together take Holy Communion in which their own blood was mingled. The origin of the custom was very probably the practical need to create a binding relationship in a tribal society where occasions of conflict were so frequent. But it was much more than a social formula. The literal transmission of blood was regarded as the basis of relationship, and the blood brother was henceforth subject to the same prohibitions in the choice of wife as though he had been a son of the same mother.

So we are not dealing with what one critic has called the 'quaint subtleties' of Aeschylus, but with ideas that are hardly yet dead in the Balkans and from his use of them seem to have been much alive behind the rational facade of classical Athens. And why indeed should we ever have supposed that this master of construction, who never fails to produce the effect he wants, should suddenly lose control of his art at the most critical point of his trilogy, when he must command general assent if he is not to ruin in advance the cause of the new conception of justice and mercy that he is celebrating?

So, too, in an Albanian and Balkan background, the mystery falls away from that time-honoured *pons asinorum* of Sophoclean criticism, the outburst of Antigone just before she is led away to be walled up and left to die. Antigone, it will be remembered, had two brothers, Eteocles and Polynices, who fought for the mastery of Thebes and killed each other in doing so. Eteocles was defending his power, Polynices challenging it with foreign help; and Creon, their uncle, on assuming power in Thebes, decided to teach an unforgettable lesson to would-be traitors. He issued an edict that on pain of death the body of Polynices should be left unburied for the dogs to eat. Antigone wilfully disobeyed, was sentenced, and at one point broke out into this explanation of why she had acted as she did:

> *O but I would not have done the forbidden thing*
> *For any husband or for any son.*
> *For why? I could have had another husband*
> *And by him other sons, if one were lost;*
> *But, father and mother lost, where would I get*
> *Another brother?*[6]

This has long been a stumbling block. Goethe thought it a motive 'which is quite unworthy of her and which almost borders on the comic'. And a modern translator says that these lines, 'possibly a spurious interpolation, are rejected by some editors as being both logically and psychologically inappropriate'. He is prepared to accept it on the supposition that Antigone, in her last despair, gives utterance to 'an inconsistent and even unworthy thought'.

Another critic regards the story as self-evidently absurd—'the grotesqueness of it cannot be blinked'—but thinks that 'the topsy-turvy dialectic' of the argument made a strong appeal to Sophocles' fancy, and he 'succumbed to the temptation to thrust it in' rather, one presumes, as a jackdaw flies off with whatever takes its eye. But he inserts it, not just in an odd corner, but at the most dramatic moment of a tense and tautly constructed play. The critic can only suggest that the interpolation was so short 'that it would never really have time to jar;' rapidly and passionately spoken, the spectator would not in effect know what Antigone was talking about. This is to get rid of a difficulty in the character of Antigone by introducing an absurdity into that of Sophocles, who insists on having his little joke, not despite but *because* no one will be able to see the point of it!

If one regards Antigone as a modern Protestant liberal defending private conscience against royal tyranny, then her outburst is bizarre and her motive will indeed seem 'unworthy,' to use Goethe's lofty rebuke once more. But in fact from the very first moment she is not a rebel but a traditionalist, defending old social habits against government reforms as did the woman of Kruja in 1930, though with less success. She is concerned with one concrete problem: the need for the customary funeral rites, which she alone can now carry out and which, as we know from Oedipus at Colonus, she had promised her brother to perform if he died in the attack on Thebes. So:

I will bury my brother
And if I die for it, what happiness!
Convicted of reverence—I shall be content
To lie beside a brother whom I love.

This feeling, and the 'grotesque' explanation she later gives for her action, would until recently have been taken as self-evident by the mountaineers of Albania, Montenegro or Serbia, though unfortunately for classical scholarship none of them ever took up Sophoclean criticism. Had they done so, their difficulty would have been to know when to stop quoting examples to prove that Antigone, far from undergoing some momentary aberration, felt as countless thousands of Balkan sisters have felt towards their brothers both before her time and since; as Scanderbeg's sisters, for example, felt for him and he for them even after they had married. There is, for example, a Serbian poem translated by Bulwer Lytton about a white handkerchief, scented with rose and amber, that Omer Bey's wife finds in their bedroom.[7] It had been given to Omer Bey by his mistress, but he said it was a wedding gift from his sister, the wife of Zekir Bey. His wife did not believe him, and there and then she got out of bed and sat barefoot by the light of a taper, writing to ask his sister if this were so, and implicitly putting a curse on Zekir Bey if the truth were not told:

Long live they husband, naught ail him,
May'st thou never have cause to bewail him!

Madame Zekir wept when she received the letter. If she told the truth there would be trouble between her brother and his wife. If she told a lie, she might cause the death of her husband. So she told a lie.

Then the letter she laid in her breast
And she pondered with many a sigh,
'I choose of two evils the least,
If my husband must die, let him die'
Since the choice lies 'twixt one or the other
Any husband a woman may spare,
But a sister that injures a brother
Does that which she cannot repair.

Another translator[8] takes a Serbian poem about the wife of the Hospodar Gjergj, who finds that her 'three treasures' are missing when the warriors come home from a battle. These are her husband, the best man at their wedding (this link was thought to be particularly close, and carried the same marriage prohibitions as consanguinity) and 'her dearest brother'. She mourns for them, after a different fashion for each:

For her brave lord she cuts her tresses,
For her best man she wounds her cheeks,
And for her brother puts out both her eyes,
and each action has its own symbolism:
She cuts her hair, it grows again;
She wounds her cheeks, the wounds do heal,
But none can heal those hurt blind eyes,
Nor yet her heart for her lost brother.

Even in less heroic ways, the mountain woman would make sacrifices for her brother, as in the case of Ike, wife of the Montenegrin guide of Edith Durham, who roamed the Albanian and Montenegrin highlands before the First World War and preserved much lore that would otherwise have been lost.[9] Ike had a brother called Marko who, being unmarried, had no human beast of burden to carry water for him, knead bread, do his mending and work on the land. So she did all for him, as undeterred as he was himself by the storming, cursing and beating she used to receive from Krsto her husband. 'I could not let him degrade himself by carrying hay', she said, and explained her refusal to obey her husband very simply: 'A woman's brother comes before all".

To show that this was not intended as a mere figure of speech, Edith Durham mentions an old ballad in which: 'The sister begged the brother to sup with her: "Come, O my brother and sup with me!" "I cannot sup with thee, O my sister. Last night was I in the wine-shop—and I fell a-quarrelling with some

Turks. I slew one—a mother's only son. Neither gold nor silver will the Sultan accept. He demands head for head—either my head or one of my kin. None have I that can take my place. So tomorrow I shall die." And again spoke the sister to the brother: "Four grown sons hath thy sister. One will I give to the Sultan in place of thy head, O brother." And she gives up her youngest born, sending him off to his death with the pretext that "thine uncle summons thee to his wedding to be bride-leader to the maiden."

Even death does not sever the link between brother and sister. Among the Albanian exiles of Southern Italy there is a poem about a woman who had nine sons and one daughter.[10] The daughter, Garentina, married into a family a long way off, and the mother only agreed to part with her on a promise from one of her sons, Constantine, that he would go and bring his sister back whenever she was needed for a family feast or an occasion of mourning. But there came a terrible year in which all nine sons were killed in battle, and when All Souls Day came round the mother went to the church, lit candles and reminded the dead Constantine of his promise. When night came he rose from his grave, the tomb turned into a spirited horse with trappings of black, and the ring that had closed it became a silver spur. He finds his sister dancing at a public festival and tells her she must come home. She does not question this at all but immediately leaves her home and children and rides back with him. "There is mould on your shoulders," she says. "No, that is just smoke from the rifles." "Dust drops from your hair." "No, it is your eyes that are blinded by dust from the road." "The shutters of our house are closed." "That's for protection against the north wind." At the church, Constantine tells her to go on alone, as he wishes to enter and pray. He has fulfilled his promise, and his sister has been restored to her family; but their mother takes her for an illusion sent to announce her own forthcoming death, and the two women die in their shared misery.

And there is another story, from the Catholic Mirdite mountains of Albania. 'A Mirdite woman was given in marriage to a Christian Scutarene. Her brother was a daring outlaw who harried the Turks, and they set a price upon his head. So daring was he that he would come to the town by night to visit his sister. Her husband, sorely tempted by the promised reward, betrayed his brother in-law to the Turkish officials. One night, when he had entered and, as is customary, given up his weapons, the Turkish guards rushed in and killed him. His sister mourned bitterly, but did not suspect her husband's treachery until the night when she found him counting a bag of gold. Then the truth flashed upon her. She charged her husband with her brother's death, and he could not deny it. Frightened, he tried to calm her terrible wrath. Sooner or later, said he, her brother was sure to be caught, if so foolhardy as to visit the town. Someone would have had the reward. "Why not we, as we are so poor?" He spoke of all they could buy with the money, and she spoke no word. He thought he had convinced her, and lay on his bed and slept. But for the Mirdite woman there was no sleep. She sat far into the night, and ever her brother's blood cried to her; and at night she rose and took her brother's *handzhar*—the heavy sword he had so often wielded well. She stood over her sleeping husband, swung up the sword, and in her brother's name struck off her husband's head. Then she stood by her two young sons, and here she wavered. But the call of her brother and her tribe was stronger than mother-love. "Seed of a serpent," she cried, "ye shall never live to betray my people." And them, too, she slew, and with the bloody *handzhar* in her hands fled from the town to the Mirdite mountains, where she was hailed as a hero; for she had avenged her brother and cleansed the honour of the tribe.

The man who told this story said "It is the greatest tale in all the world; even the old Greek tragedies do not surpass it." Indeed, it was from such material as the Mirdite woman that Antigone was fashioned. The assumptions which, to the perplexed confusion of modern scholarship, led the Greek sister to her doom, were still alive in the Albanian mountains more than twenty centuries later. And this is hardly surprising since there, alone in Europe, the tribal organisation of the Illyrians was preserved until well into the twentieth century; and that organisation recognised kinship through descent on the male side only.

Biologically the woman, in an inelegant phrase used in the mountains, was 'a sack for putting things in'; her body was needed (housework apart) only to transmit children who owed nothing to her genetically. If a husband died, the widow naturally returned to her father's family, with whom her emotional links had probably never been weakened.

The original tribal system had not remained throughout Albania. In the coastal plains of the centre, which were more accessible to foreign control and where the fertile land made surpluses of wealth possible, a feudal system sprang up; local landlords held large estates in return for acknowledging the particular ruler of the moment, and accepting his religion. In the south, where the hill country was less rugged and isolated, towns sprang up, the Orthodox Church could exert its influence, and an elementary form of division of labour broke down the old self-contained subsistence farming economy. In the north, however, geography was against any major change. From the jumble of hills overlooking the river Shkumbi up to the tortured peaks of the 'Accursed Mountains' high up on the Montenegrin frontier, a typical cross-section of Albania from west to east would look rather like a two-rise lock on a canal. There is a short swampy stretch by the sea, then the first range of mountains just behind Kruja, covered with oaks and rising to 3,000 feet or so. Behind this is a first level of well-populated plateau, narrow in places but often wide enough, or easily connected with other level districts, to form a fairly large geographical unit, as in the areas known as Mati and Mirdita. To the east of this rises another range of mountains rising up to nearly 6,000 feet; then comes another level of plateaux in the Dibra area, and the next range of mountains rise to around 9,000 feet and mark the frontier of Macedonia. The pine woods go to within about two thousand feet of the summit; beyond that is nothing but scree, bare rock and treeless pasture.

In the more remote folds of the highest mountain ranges to the north and east the tribal system could be seen at its purest. The isolation here was extreme: two neighbouring valleys, for example, might be a day's journey from each other. In such conditions a tribe, having once found a valley of its own, would jealously guard its frontiers and prevent invasion by another. The tribe consisted of everyone descended from a common male ancestor: a man might know who his father's fathers had been for twenty generations, but his mother's relations he neither knew nor cared to know beyond two. All who were known to have common descent were 'brothers' and 'sisters', and could not marry; but there was a great deal of intermarriage on the female side, as this was thought to have no biological significance at all.

In theory, of course, it should have been impossible to find a wife or a husband within the same tribe, if relationship on the male side was forbidden. In practice, however, the rule was less rigid.

For one thing, even the preternaturally long memories of the Albanians could not remember family trees quite for ever, though there was nothing unusual in a twentieth century mountaineer tracing his descent to the fourteenth century, when the continuity had been broken by a series of migrations. Again, such migrations caused by wars, famines or natural disasters, and the smaller movements resulting from private individuals sent into exile or escaping from justice, gave as it were a genetic aeration to the stagnant waters of tribalism. And while the idea of kinship remained in principle, the larger and more accessible tribes organised themselves in 'groups' between which marriage was usually permitted. The 'group' might be based on any convenient distinguishing mark such as religious belief, where this differed from its neighbour's; geographical convenience; or common loyalty to some leading personality. In later times, if not earlier, the 'group' had a military significance and represented a unit that fought together, and the name that is used for it—bajrak—is the Turkish word for a military standard.

In the more open plains, there would be enough land, both arable and pasture, for several tribes to live. Here outstanding individuals, families or groups, especially if they were good fighters, would assume the headship of such geographical groups, accumulating wealth with which to support their authority in the form of flocks of sheep and goats. Thus, for example, the several tribes living in the plateau area of the Mati (a name that assumed the form of Emathia in Renaissance times, and presumably derives from the Albanian word mathë, great) became known collectively as the men of Mati; and because of their pre-eminence in numbers and reasonably central position, their leader at least twice in the country's history became the leader of the Albanians as a whole, once in the fifteenth and once in the twentieth century.

Leadership depended on social pre-eminence, and so the same families maintained their authority for generations and even centuries; but heredity was qualified so far as individuals were concerned by the need to choose the best man for the job. The rights of the head man of any family, whether eminent or obscure, did not necessarily pass to the first-born. At each vacancy there was a conclave of male members of the family, whose vote decided the succession. In the case of the greater families, the new head must be acceptable not only to his immediate kinsmen but to the several thousand people who would have to accept his interpretation of the law and follow him into battle. He thus owed his position to his own qualities of character as well as his descent; and if he still harboured ideas of tyranny he was further held in check by a council of elders who saw that the ancient customs were observed and knotty problems arbitrated, and a general assembly of all the male members of the tribe or unit, whose opinion had to be taken on vital questions like peace and war and punishment of capital offenders.

The natural transition for such leaders would have been to

leave the upland plateaux with their fighting men and conquer the more pacific remainder of Albania, forming a national army and sustaining both it and their government on the revenues from the prosperous plains. This in effect was attempted by Scanderbeg and achieved for a short period by King Zog; but unfortunately the plains and coastline were only too accessible to foreign powers immensely stronger than the Albanian mountain chieftains could ever hope to be.

The local leaders were not able to chase the Romans or Byzantines or Turks from the plains and wrest the ports from the Greeks or the Venetians; but none of these in turn had the power to subdue the mountains and impose their own civilisation on the people who lived there. So the heads of the tribal groups in the north found themselves between two worlds: the tribal organisation and habits of thought to which their deepest loyalties belonged, and the feudalism which their nominal conquerors wished them to assume, and which had its attractions in terms of prestige and wealth. The result was an uneasy compromise. There was the minimum of dealings with the foreigner, though his ideas and habits and much of the paraphernalia of his way of life percolated among them, as with the ubiquitous cups of coffee that the highlanders drink whenever they can. And, by way of reaction against this process, the maximum encouragement was given to the old laws and customs of this society without a State; for as there was no formal government and no single religious faith to preserve a common identity, only these could assure the tribesmen of the continuity of the traditions they valued. So it happened that after the Turkish conquest the old unwritten law of the mountains was codified by one of the leaders who accepted the new regime;[11] and in this established but still oral form it acted as a further defence against the written law of the conqueror.

In such conditions, an entire series of assumptions and beliefs and practices was retained. We have seen the intense, and as it now seems misguided, idea of the relationship between brother and sister retained in its original freshness from the time of Sophocles. We have seen the biology of Apollo and the Eumenides still taken for granted among the mountain tribes. Christianity and Islam were neither of them strong enough to instil the insights of Judaism, the sense of a moral responsibility to a holy God, into these inaccessible and elusive mountaineers. They were willing to change their faith, intermarry, assume different names to suit the various religions they professed publicly or believed in secretly, but the ease with which they did so shows how little any of these really commanded their loyalty. Their fundamental beliefs remained pagan. 'The district had neither church nor mosque', we are told of a remote hill village not far from Elbasan at the beginning of this century. 'Every inhabitant had two names: a Christian name, under cover of which he refused military service; and a Moslem one, under which he refused to pay poll-tax.' The head man of the village, though religion was for him no more than a political convenience, was not without his means of discovering what the divine powers intended for man. After 'a noble banquet of roast lamb, stewed fowl, cheese, milk, and maize-bread,' this inheritor of the techniques of the ancient soothsayers 'picked up the fowl's breast bone and held it against the sun. He carefully traced all the lines made by the marrow, and said gravely: "One of us five will die within a fortnight...' Such is the belief in bones in Albania that I believe men have died from sheer terror when their death has been read. Thus, an only son—well known to a friend of mine from Djakova—was at a family feast. He picked up a fowl's bone, looked at it, and threw it down with a cry. His father asked what was the matter and the youth said: "In three days you will bury me." His horrified father picked up the bone and saw the reading was only too true. He cried out in grief: "In three days we shall bury thee." The poor lad blenched and sickened. He could not eat, gave up hope, and died. "When he saw in the bones he must die," said the Djakovan, "he died."[12]

Tattooing has also been preserved among the women of

northern Albania, as it has even more notably in parts of Bosnia, thus preserving two mountainous islands for a custom that was common to the Thracian, Illyrian and Celtic tribes of the Balkans before the Christian era. Herodotus says that it was a sign of noble birth, and Cicero speaks of 'a barbarian ... punctured with Thracian signs.' These were stars, suns with rays and geometric designs; or even animals, like the one noted on the arm of a bacchante attacking Orpheus on a vase in the Louvre. Gunpowder has replaced soot as the medium rubbed into the needle pricks to make the designs: circles and crosses, rayed suns and moons, and traditional patterns that go by such names as 'the ear of corn', 'fern twigs' and 'the fir tree'. An original ritual significance for the custom is suggested by the fact that the women who do undergo the ordeal do so at puberty, at certain specified times of the year—St. Joseph's Day, Lady Day and Palm Sunday.

Among such survivals from the past, none has been more persistent or commanded deeper loyalty in the north than the legal system that has served these isolated communities for countless centuries. As no national state emerged, so there could be no permanent police apparatus for settling disputes; and in view of the tribal organisation of society, the responsible unit has always been the family and not the individual. Each separate family had to take justice into its own hands, not indiscriminately, but on the basis of commonly accepted ideas of what was due in any particular situation. Thus, to take an extreme offence, a murder created a debt of blood and the executioner was the nearest relative of the dead man. Here is the origin of the so-called 'blood feud' or 'vendetta', which is not the creation of blood-lusting barbarians but on the contrary, the first infusion of a spirit of law into a society not yet rich or complex enough to organise the external forms of law. What gave the blood feud its murderous and near insane atmosphere of massacre was the invention of the rifle. Hitherto, the avenger had been compelled to rely on his own skill and courage, and justice must often have been long delayed. Firearms, once introduced, became as necessary and valuable an extension of the highland Albanian as are his four legs to the centaur. The victim could now be assassinated at long range, or even when sitting at his own hearth among his family. Consequently, men under blood ceased to move around, and the economic life of the mountains was slowed down (and the hard farm work done by the women increased); but at the same time the course of the feud was speeded up, and with it the number of victims on either side who might have to pay for the original offence. This might have sprung from some seemingly innocent cause. Two men walking along the road together, for example, might have jostled each other accidentally; the tempers of two armed men, each thinking he had been insulted by the other, might have ended in a shot, from which ripple after ripple of revenge would have radiated out into the future. In one of the northern valleys around 1890, a man refused to give the reward (a single cartridge) he had promised to a shepherd for finding a lost lamb. Incensed, the shepherd killed him. This happened on Easter Sunday, when all the local people were gathered for the festival, and within an hour fourteen men of the two families concerned lay dead in expiation of the original insult.

Such a lethal practice came near to destroying the society it had been intended to preserve. Under the influence of the outside religions, Christianity and Islam, not to mention plain common sense and the normal human inertia which, more than cowardice, had no doubt always tempered the full rigour of the blood feud, exceptions were introduced into the old customs. Cases were agreed in which it would be possible to compound blood for a fine or banishment, and where these loopholes existed they began to be generally used. A most elaborate protocol emerged, detailing when and where revenge might and might not be taken: for example, an injured party might, under the influence of 'boiling blood', kill any member of the offender's family within the first twenty four hours. However, after that period, even the most heated blood was held to have cooled down, and vengeance could be taken only on the specific man responsible for the initial offence.

Naturally, blood feuds between families did not exhaust the possible crimes. There were offences against society itself to consider, such as tampering with water rights or rights of way, or some particularly atrocious act—murder of a guest, for example, or an elder of the tribe—and here society, in the form of the tribe or village, found itself involved in a blood feud against an individual or a family. And since there were no paid or permanent officials to carry out the relevant sentence, the work had to be undertaken by society as a whole.

Thus in the Mirdite tribe of Fan there occurred 'an amazing case of wholesale justice' in February 1912. One family 'had long been notorious for evil-doing—robbing, shooting, and causing trouble to the tribe. A gathering of all the heads condemned all the males of the family to death. Men were appointed to lay in wait for them on a certain day and pick them off; and on that day the whole seventeen of them were shot. One was but five and another but twelve years old ... Such was the belief in heredity that it was proposed to kill an unfortunate woman who was pregnant, lest she should bear a male and so renew the evil.' (Three shots were fired at her and missed; she was finally saved by another man of the tribe who took her under his protection).

In conditions like these, coupled with the poverty of the countryside, it goes without saying that every house was in its way both a fortress and a prison. The ordinary peasant's house could scarcely have been simpler in its architecture. It was no more than a small square room with walls of stone taken from the nearest stream, then bedded in mud and bound together by horizontal beams every three feet or so. There were no windows for an enemy to shoot through, let alone to enter by; and the doorway was as low as possible, with a thick door that could not easily be broken down from outside. The roof had to be of stone slabs, because with thatch or boards the family could have been roasted alive by an enemy. For further protection there was no chimney. The fire of logs was kept in place by a ring of stones in the centre of the room, and such smoke as did not drift around the room to irritate the eyes of the family rose, unimpeded by any ceiling, to escape in its own time through the gaps between the stones of the roof.

'The furnishings were in keeping. They consisted of a three-legged stool or two, a box or pile of bedding but no bedsteads, a rough shelf with a frying-pan and a few platters and pots, a big metal jug for boiling water, an earthenware pot for holding drinking water, a round dining table on stumpy supports about ten inches high, a flour-bin, a pan for mixing bread, perhaps a pan for baking it, and nothing for washing—the nearest stream served for that—a few satchels of home-dressed wool and a distaff hung on the wall, and a hen stared at the company from her nest under the eaves. The only ornaments were yellow maize-cobs, rosy pomegranates, and strings of onions or garlic, all hanging from the tie beams. At meal times a cat took up a vantage point under the dining-table, to filch what it could.'

This was the simplest house, in effect no more than a kitchen. As the family grew, more rooms would be added and the completed settlement surrounded by a stone and timber farmyard wall. Where, however, a family was numerous, or had more enemies, or where land was scarce, it was the custom to build a kulle, or tower, in which the new rooms took the form of an extra floor, so that two- or three- storey fortress houses became a familiar sight. These had the advantage that even if an enemy penetrated to the ground floor, where the livestock and stores were kept, the family could go upstairs, pull up the ladder after them and close the trap door. Here, too, it was possible to have the luxury of small windows on the upper floors, thus relieving the preternatural gloom of life in the one storey settlements; and in more recent centuries these windows might be glazed in the case of the richer families. Beyond these towers there was one further stage: the castle, like that of the Castriotis at Kruja, though this would not normally be built by an Albanian. The castles were the work of past invaders who used them to restrain and overawe the tribes. When a foreign ruler was forced out by a rival, local families would move into the vacated castle—although usually only until the next conqueror arrived on the scene.

The basis on which life was physically maintained was as ancient and restricted as everything else in the northern mountains. There is enough arable land, well provided with springs, to allow subsistence farming in the plateaux and on the lower mountain slopes. The main crop is maize, and the staple diet of bread and porridge is helped out with eggs, occasional fowls, lamb and kid. The flocks graze in summer on the higher mountain pastures, and they find winter grazing in the woods and copses, or have their diet supplemented where necessary by oak leaves stripped from the trees in autumn. These woodlands have been the salvation of the northern Albanians. They allow comparatively large numbers of animals to be kept alive during the bitter winters; they provide a framework for the buildings and fuel for heating and cooking; and the roots act as a natural reservoir from which the rain is gently channelled off into an intricate network of small streams which assure the maize crop of the large volume of water it needs. The tree, which civilisation has hacked down for its own—mainly warlike—purposes in Dalmatia and Greece, leaving behind arid and desiccated land and bare mountains, has here mediated between man and nature from time immemorial, preserving by its wood, its shade, the nutriment of its leaves and the very obstructiveness of its roots, the conditions of continued life and so the very fabric of the most ancient surviving society in Europe—the society which so suddenly and unexpectedly awoke under a leader of genius half way through the fifteenth century and held the greatest empire of the world at bay for a generation.

Chapter Two

. . . .

Emperors, Despots and Chieftains

The rough and lonely mountains of Albania throw a protecting arc around the green coastal plain, like tiers of a classical theatre pierced here and there by the narrow gangways of high, snow-swept passes. This, it would seem, is a land isolated by nature from outside interference. But the appearance of security is deceptive: from the rise of the Roman Empire until the collapse of the Ottoman, it was free only for a single generation five hundred years ago.

Long after the worldwide empire of the Romans had collapsed, the concept remained alive. Even throughout the Middle Ages, it seemed the normal and natural method of government. As God was thought to have given spiritual authority throughout the world to his Church, so it was accepted that the Emperor held a divine mandate in secular affairs. Each of these powers was indivisible in theory, but only too obviously divided in practice between Rome and Constantinople; and thus neither half of the old empire could refrain from trying to conquer the other half when it felt strong enough. When this sanctified self-interest launched an army to west or east, it naturally followed the shortest and easiest route between the two capitals. This was from Rome down the Appian Way to the heel of Italy, then across the forty mile strait of Otranto to Durazzo, and so eastward along the Egnatian Way to Thessaloniki and Constantinople. So the

Albanian ports and mountain passes, especially Durazzo and the main route inland, were essential to the plans of either side, as a bridgehead for an army marching east or a base for a navy sailing west.

Any history that Albania might have enacted for herself was thus drowned in the flow and counter-flow of foreign armies, until the sequence was interrupted at the beginning of the thirteenth century. Then, more than eight hundred years after its collapse, Henry VI of Germany, son of the crusading Emperor Frederick Barbarossa, had the ambition to revive the universal Roman empire. He acquired the kingdom created in southern Italy by the Normans, who had just shown by their conquest of Durazzo and then Thessaloniki that the Byzantines could easily be conquered by a resolute army from the west. But Henry died, and it was at the instigation of the Venetians as paymasters that the army of the Fourth Crusade was deflected to the capture of Constantinople in 1206. As this was done for commercial advantage rather than imperial conquest, the attack did not recreate the universal empire but merely broke the eastern half into fragments. Instead of a weak Greek empire, a still weaker so-called 'Latin' one was set up in Constantinople. Ambitious crusaders created smaller realms of their own here and there, and various former subjects—Serbian, Bulgarian and Greek—began to govern independently of both the victorious westerners and the exiled Byzantines.

In north western Greece the illegitimate son of a former governor, related by blood or marriage to three Byzantine imperial families, proclaimed himself Despot of Epiros and took the name of Michael Angelos Komnenos Doukas.[1] His capital at Arta was the only remaining centre of Greek rule in the Balkans, though many of his subjects were themselves Albanian. His rule extended to the Egnatian Way which cuts Albania into two; and here his neighbour was the Albanian family which controlled the country north of Elbasan, the Albanon or Albanopolis of the Byzantines from which the north, and later by extension the whole of Albania, took its name. Their stronghold was the fortress of Kruja, which overlooked the coastal plain with its back firmly against the wall of mountains and could at any time menace the imperial highway itself. In 1207, presumably because Constantinople could no longer defend it, a chieftain of the name of Demetrios had possessed himself of Kruja, and had begun to carry out what was in effect a tentative foreign policy for a small sovereign state in the making. He married a daughter of the ruler of the new and rising kingdom of Serbia, and together with Michael of Epiros he signed treaties with the Adriatic trading republic of Ragusa, allowing its citizens free access to their territories. This was a gesture of defiance by the Albanian and Greek neighbours against encroachments by Venice on their coastal areas. At first Venice preserved the fiction that she had taken over Durazzo and the isle of Corfu in the name of the new Latin empire, but she quickly assumed direct control over them and tried to extend her rule over other towns and strategic points on the coastline of Albania and north western Greece.

Thus for the first time, instead of the political lines of force moving from west to east across an inert Albania, a new and tentative north to south grouping had been created, intent on preserving what were in effect emergent Serbian, Albanian and Greek nations from erosion by Latins of the west or Byzantines from the east. The urge to a separate identity was particularly marked in the Albanian Demetrios. Though he described himself as panhypersevastos and great archon, sonorous but far from sovereign titles probably bestowed by his royal Serbian father-in-law, he was evidently aware of the dangers of political and cultural assimilation if he retained the Orthodox religion of his two neighbours, for in 1208 he asked the Pope to send a legate to his court to instruct him in the Roman Catholic faith. In the same year, however, the Archbishop of Durazzo died, and when the Venetian governor seized the Church revenues and estates in and around the town, Demetrios and his Greek ally did the same in the surrounding countryside, so that at one time it looked as though the Albanian chieftain might be converted and excommunicated simultaneously. The overtures continued for over forty years, and even in 1250 Pope Innocent IV could be encouraged at news of 'the heartfelt desire of the Bishop of Albanon to be joined to Rome'. But by this time the Byzantines, under the emperor Gjon Vatatzes, were restoring their authority in the Balkans, and they could offer more tangible rewards than the Vatican. They wished to retake Durazzo and the Albanian coast; but they could not hold those in peace without the friendship of the Albanians on the north flank of the road from Elbasan to the sea. So in 1252 they allowed Kruja to become a vassal state within the empire, and its inhabitants both within and without the town were completely freed from imperial interference. Thus Kruja became not only a physical stronghold but a symbol of political independence for the Albanians. Such it remained until the western half of the Balkans fell to the rising Serbian empire.

Serbia had for long been ruled, under the authority of the Byzantine emperor, by a series of *zupans*, or barons, each with his own small area of influence. When the empire fell, one of these families imposed its sovereignty on the rest and began to expand its rule outside the strictly Serbian areas. This was the Nemanjas of Ras, now Raska, in the Ibar valley who enjoyed a combination of talent and good luck. They were near enough to the main centres of Byzantine civilisation to appreciate and adopt the outward signs of its greatness: the ambitious buildings, the vigorous frescoes, the glittering ritual of church and court, and the subtly ambitious diplomacy. Their lands were fertile and centrally placed for exerting influence among other Serbs. They were rich enough in minerals to be able to strike a gold, silver and copper currency. This annoyed the Venetians, whose coins were used as a model (Dante speaks of finding in hell 'That man from Raska/Who badly forged Venetian coins')[2] but it financed a profitable foreign trade and paid for mercenary armies which brought first independence, then primacy among their neighbours, and finally foreign conquest.

Almost more important, at least to us who enjoy their artistic legacy, was the personal quality of the Nemanjas, who combined ambition, energy, and practical talent with a profound sense of the transience of human glories, and so alternated in that insatiable Slav fashion between action and contemplation, between absorption in worldly affairs and complete detachment from them. The first great figure in the dynasty was Stefan Nemanja, who left his throne near the end of the twelfth century, obtained a ruined monastic building at Hilandar on Mount Athos, endowed it and filled it with Slav monks. Among them was his son Sava, who now received him into the monastic life, and later returned home as head of the Serbian Orthodox Church, crowning two successive kings, and being finally canonised as a national saint.

The energy and piety of this family encouraged a flowering of art and architecture on the old Byzantine stock comparable with the parallel Renaissance in Italy.[3] In three centuries of independence fifteen hundred churches were built, and ten thousand frescoes painted in them. Of these, enough have survived to astonish our own century with their humanity, freshness and sheer technical ability. Warring against Byzantium and yet imitating it, the Serbian rulers took its arts as their model, but modified them by elements from across the Adriatic. Thus architects from Dalmatia raised the cupolas and half domes of the east on Italianate walls of polychrome marble or stone and decorative brick. And under the impulse of the Slav temperament, movement and emotion were breathed into the traditional subjects of Byzantine art, and eventually this freedom overflowed the strictly religious subject-matter; monarchs assumed the timelessness of saints, and saints the heroic gestures of warriors. In the series of frescoes at Mileseva and Sopocani realism, humanity and a restrained but highly emotive use of colour were carried further than anywhere else in Europe in the second half of the thirteenth century. Declining in quality but dazzling by their scope, the story of the Nemanja frescoes is carried to its conclusion with the thousand pictures commissioned by the last Serbian emperor to celebrate his country's imperial greatness in the church of Decani, on the north-eastern frontier of Albania.

Albania naturally fell to such a powerful, self-confident and brilliant civilisation, for there was no means of organising a national resistance in a tribal, materially poor society, different though the Albanians were from the Serbs in race and religion. Conditions during this period in 'Abbanie where the people are devout and obedient to the Church of Rome' are described by a Dominican monk, Father Brocardus,[4] who prepared a handbook for the Valois family in 1332, in the hope that it would be of use to future crusaders to the Holy Land. Two nations lived in northern Albania: the 'Albanoi' or Albanians in the countryside and the Latins in the larger towns like Scutari or Ulcinj. ('Latins' is a vague term to cover the conglomerate populations of these Adriatic towns, who liked to think of themselves as inheritors or even direct descendants of the original inhabitants in Roman days). 'The power of the Latins', says Brocardus, 'is enclosed within the circuit of the cities which are theirs, though they have some vineyards and fields without the cities' and some of them even lived outside the walls. The Albanians, who 'have a language quite other than the Latins' and are more numerous than they, 'could put into the field more than 15,000 men on horseback, well fitted to wage war in the manner of their country, valiant and good fighters.' Both peoples were Roman Catholics, but they had separate bishoprics, the Latins five and the Albanians four, all nine of them under the jurisdiction of the Archbishop of Bar. Because of their religion they were 'harshly oppressed under the intolerable and very hard servitude of the Slavs. Indeed they are a downtrodden people; their clergy is lowered and humbled, their bishops and abbots often imprisoned, their nobles disinherited and imprisoned, their churches, both cathedrals and collegiate, are dispersed and deprived of power, their monasteries and priories lost and destroyed.'

This was the other side of the picture of Serbian greatness.

The orthodox Church was indeed favoured as an instrument of imperial power. Whole districts were given to it, with the monopoly of corn milling. When great churches like that at Decani were being built in or near Albanian districts the local people were made to contribute towards it; some by tribute in kind (there is a case of four thousand silk cocoons a year being asked from one man), some by providing free transport for the goods they needed, and some by forced labour imposed as needed on a group of *katuns*, or cantons, the groups of families through which the highland Albanians traditionally regulated their relationship with the outside world.

Brocardus had stressed the number of fighting men and their courage because he hoped to induce his patrons to use them to free Albania from the Serbs. With their help, and that of the Latins, he thought that a thousand French horsemen and five or six thousand infantry could conquer the country 'at their ease'. His prophecy was never put to the test; perhaps fortunately for the house of Valois, for almost as he was writing, the greatest conqueror among all the Nemanjas, Stefan Dusan, came to the throne and extended his power from Belgrade in the north to the Gulf of Corinth in the south, from the Adriatic in the west to within modern Bulgaria in the east, and conquered the whole of Albania except for Durazzo. Dusan was proclaimed Emperor and Autocrat of the Serbs and Greeks, the Bulgarians and Albanians, and it seemed a natural and inevitable step for him to go on and conquer and carry on the now moribund empire of Byzantium, moving his capital from Skopje to Constantinople.

Such a plan seemed to be forced on him as much by self-defence as by ambition. During his reign an entirely new force had appeared in Europe, vigorous and intrusive but still capable of being held in check. The Ottomans, named after their founder Othman, were one of a series of small Turkish migrations which leap-frogged over each other across Asia Minor; and they created for themselves a small kingdom just across the Sea of Marmara from the Byzantine capital. Influenced by it, even marrying into its imperial family, and influenced also by the more delicate Persian perceptions in art and architecture transmitted by their predecessors and neighbours the Seljuk Turks, the Ottomans built themselves a capital of domes and cypresses, gardens and running waters at Bursa. It seemed that they had come to the end of their wanderings and might be content to remain there, their rulers falling victims to over-refinement and their *ghazis*—the ascetic, fanatical Muslim horsemen who had carried them to triumph—decaying in the enjoyment of the spoils of war.[5] It was to these neighbours and relations that the Byzantine emperors turned for help in keeping Stefan Dusan within bounds. Twice they came to Europe, and twice they returned to Asia Minor; but the third time, in 1354, they decided to stay and started to dig trenches to defend themselves on Gallipoli. Only Dusan was strong enough to evict them, and he could keep them out of Europe only if he were also master at Constantinople. He got together an army, and had he succeeded the Roman Empire might still be in existence today, but ruled by Greeks and Slavs. However, in the midst of his preparations to march and his negotiations for help from Venice and from the Pope, he died of a fever in 1355 at the age of only forty-six.

So it was not the Serbs who marched against the Turks, but the other way round; with Dusan dead, the balance of advantage swung to the newcomers. Serbia did not yet exist as a national state. Her political and military successes had been due to the unusual quality of her rulers, and without them she relapsed into a collection of local and mutually jealous *zupans*, each ruling over his own section of the populace. To the Turks, in contrast, a particularly able ruler was a bonus, not a necessary condition of survival: their society, and especially their army, was organised to act almost of its own accord, with the minimum of reliance on personal genius. As their empire expanded and became more stable, it had less need of impulsive cavalrymen such as the *ghazis*; and as its territory was the result of conquest, it need consider no local warlords with ancient rights, fortified castles and private armies. Instead the Turks recruited a standing army from among their own people, who were given land enough to live on in peacetime and regular pay when called up. This gave the Sultans an effective and sizeable force owing undivided loyalty to themselves: a force which could be trained and fought as a single unit, and not as a confederation of allies with differing aims and a necessarily more parochial conception of warfare. When the empire expanded further, and began to take over wide stretches of south-eastern Europe, these *Yeniçeri* or 'New Troops'—the Janiffaries of western historians—were augmented by Christian boys taken prisoner in the wars. Four out of every five of these remained the property of their captors, but the fifth was handed over as a slave to the Sultan. He was set to work, often with a Turkish farmer in Anatolia, until be spoke Turkish and was at ease in Muslim life. Then be joined the army, where he invariably proved as loyal and courageous as his Turkish-born counterpart.

With this formidable—and for the times unparalleled—weapon, the Ottoman Turks conquered the south eastern Balkans and transferred their capital from Bursa to Adrianople in 1361. The Serbian *zupans* who had relapsed into anarchy since the death of Dusan, were now briefly frightened into uniting again to complete the work that he had begun. They advanced through what is now Bulgaria in 1371, but were defeated at Tchermen on the Maritsa river. A few months later Stefan Ures V, the last member of the Nemanja family, died and there was no one to assume even nominally the empty title of emperor. Some of the Serbian rulers in Macedonia became vassals of the Sultan, others living further to the north prepared to resist him. But each had to decide in the light of his own interests, for there was no longer any central authority to which he might look for initiative and support.

In Albania the death of Stefan Dusan and the disintegration of his empire caused great hardship, especially in the mountains. It removed an unquestioned and peaceable, albeit stern, system of rule which had encouraged trade and also found employment as soldiers for the endemic surplus male population. A decade of great migrations had taken place in the 1360s, when first fighting men and later their families moved into Greece to take service with the local princelings, such as the Duke of Athens and the despot of Mistra, and to colonise waste lands in Attica and Boeotia. Among those who stayed behind were the Balsha family, Serbian in origin but Roman Catholic in religion, who had administered part of the Nemanja empire. They now began to take over most of Dusan's former possessions and sought to bring the separate Albanian chieftains into their plans of family aggrandisement. They acted in effect as sovereign princes, though at first claiming only the grandiloquently modest title of 'magnificent barons of Maritime Slavonia', and they had the help of the small but rich republic of Ragusa, who saw in them an ally against the pretensions of the larger and still richer republic of Venice.

Moreover, the Balshas were in a position to control a number of trade routes inland through the river valleys of northern Albania, especially the one to Prizren, where the Ragusans maintained one of their main warehouses for the Balkan trade. This route started at the monastery and customs house of Obeti, a few miles up the Boyana river towards Scutari, and then passed under the fortress of Dagno and along the Drin river on the thirty-hour trek to Prizren. Five such routes started at various points on the Adriatic, and caravans of two or three hundred packhorses, with boxes and sacks lashed to their angular wooden saddles, regularly wound their way under armed escort through the narrow mountain valleys. They carried up silk and satin from the looms of Italy to delight the Serbian nobles and their wives, and supplies of salt (in which the Ragusans had a complete trading monopoly) for curing their winter food. On the return journey the caravans brought down timber and metals, skins and wool, cattle, and food of all kinds including dried fish from Lake Scutari. The trade was hazardous in unsettled times, but the rate of profit was high, and the chiefs who lorded it alongside the route usually welcomed it as a valuable source of revenue in tolls and other financial sweeteners. Venice, who in the normal course of events would have stepped in to take the southern Adriatic coastal towns for herself, was in no position to check the Balshas. She was engaged in a war of life and death against her main trading rival which led in 1382 to the all-but-fatal siege of her own lagoons by the Genoese fleet.

A final attempt to rally Serbian power was made in 1389. One of the more northerly of the Serbian rulers, Lazar Hrebeljanovic, who claimed no more than the title of *knez*, or lord, formed a league to prevent the Turks from advancing further into the Balkans. Albanians, Croats, Bulgarians and Hungarians joined him on the plain of Kosova—the 'field of blackbirds'—on 15 June 1389. This was the saddest day in the history of Serbia. Changed already from a fact to an idea, she was now transformed by defeat into a legend. A truncated realm was allowed to remain under the title of despotate, and with a ruler who acknowledged the sovereignty of the Sultan, and this preserved a shadowy existence for some decades more. But the real Serbia lived on only in the songs of the ballad makers, who built around the experience of Kosova a cycle of epic poems which, sung to the accompaniment of the one-stringed *gusle*, kept alive the memory of imperial splendour while at the same time exploring the significance for the nation of its crushing defeat.

Lazar came to be regarded as a ruler who, true to the spiritual insights of his Nemanja predecessors, had deliberately chosen death for himself and destruction for his state rather than accept a kingdom at the hands of the Sultan.[6] "Shall I choose an earthly empire rather than an everlasting crown?" he asks in anguish, and by his answer binds the Serbian people for centuries to come to choose honour, if need be with death, rather than a life of shameful 'capitulation'—capitulation defined as including what many nations would be content to regard as the necessary compromises called for from the weak in their relations with the strong. Lazar's choice is applauded by the songwriters, even though the immediate suffering it brings to his people is so great that one of them can speak of a young woman so possessed by sorrow that a young green pine tree would dry up and shrivel at her touch.

There was now no power in the Balkans capable of withstanding the Turks. But in eastern Asia Minor, at the other end of their empire, they shortly found themselves confronted by an army of a calibre beyond any they had yet encountered. Timur the Lame, or Tamerlane, emerging from the plains around Samarkand, broke into the Middle East at the head of his wiry cavalry. The Sultan Bajazet attempted to stop him and was beaten at Angora, the modern Ankara, in the heart of Anatolia. He was treated with courtesy at first, but after an attempt at escape was confined in a cage, which is the point at which Marlowe's Tamerlane cries:

'There, while he lives, shall Bajazeth be kept;
And, where I go, be thus in triumph drawn.'

The Ottoman empire appeared to have vanished as surely as its Serbian vassal, and in Albania the Balsha family assumed dynastic pretentions, the reigning prince calling himself Balsha III. They occupied Vlora and Berat and captured the town of Scutari as their capital, though the Venetians still held out in the citadel. Durazzo, walled and almost surrounded by sea, resisted them; but the Albanian family of Thopia, who had for some time occupied it as vassals of the Angevin rulers of Naples, thought it prudent to safeguard their inland estates by switching allegiance to the Balshas while keeping the town firmly in their own hands. In fact, if not in intention, the Balshas were taking the first steps towards creating an independent nation of Montenegrins and Albanians, putting considerable pressure on the local chieftains to fall in with them. The Ragusans continued to help, giving them honorary citizenship and acknowledging them as princes of Albania. But the Ragusans prudently stopped short of the service the Balshas most wanted, which was the offer of skilled shipbuilders to help in driving the Venetians away from the Albanian coast.

The Venetians, however, had no intention of being driven away. Now that Serbian power had collapsed and their own had revived through the defeat of the Genoese, they were determined to pick up as many useful strong points down the coast as they could, especially near the Strait of Otranto where the trading lifeline from the Adriatic to the Levant was most vulnerable. It was no part of Venetian policy to stand by and see the creation of a neutral or hostile nation state, ideally endowed by geography, to exert pressure upon her. She brushed aside the Balshas' impotent threat to incite the Turks against her (in any case she had signed a comprehensive treaty of peace and commerce with Bajazet, and was herself better placed to call for Turkish help if ever it should be needed) and in the summer of 1409 Balsha was induced to call off the war and sign a treaty abandoning most of his coastal conquests.

In the meantime, life had begun to stir once more in the Ottoman Empire. Tamerlane, who had left the Middle East to make war on China, died suddenly at the beginning of 1405 and the four sons of Bajazet—Suleiman, Isa, Musa and Mehmed—bestirred themselves to recreate their father's empire. This first involved making war on each other. Suleiman had been allowed to rule over Rumelia, the eastern portion of the Turkish possessions in Europe, in return for acknowledging the new conqueror as his overlord. Mehmed, without any such acknowledgement, had managed to maintain some rudimentary authority in the mountains around Amasya and Tokat in north central Anatolia. Isa now took over the family's historic capital at Bursa, and Musa was soon to be found looking after Mehmed's interests in Thessaly and Macedonia, the most westerly provinces of the broken empire. Between these four a war of attrition now began. Mehmed conquered Bursa, Isa escaped into Europe, borrowed an army from Suleiman, returned and was defeated and killed. Suleiman now crossed into Asia to avenge the defeat of his forces and drove Mehmed back beyond Ankara. At this point Musa, with Serbian support and not impossibly with that of Gjon Castrioti and on behalf of Mehmed, attacked Rumelia while his brother was away. The first time he was defeated; but in 1410, after about three more years for preparation, he renewed the attack and was completely successful. Musa, now the master of the former Ottoman possessions in Europe, declined to give them up to Mehmed. He felt so sure of himself that he undertook the luxury of a punitive expedition against the Serbs, whom he blamed for his first defeat by Suleiman, presumably because they did not give him enough support. He also decided to insist on the payment of tribute to himself by the Byzantine emperor, which would have been a notable act of recognition. But the ambassador sent to collect it came to terms with Mehmed, and when he did reach Constantinople he arranged, not the collection of tribute, but an alliance between Mehmed and the emperor. So in 1412, when the outraged Musa gathered his army in front of Constantinople to avenge this insult, Mehmed slipped across the Hellespont and joined contingents of local allies at Nis in Serbia. He then marched south east and defeated his brother to the east of Sofia. Musa was captured while escaping and strangled in the victor's camp. After a gap of ten years, the Ottoman empire was thus again united under a single ruler. And one of the first acts of the new Sultan, Mehmet I, was to extend the frontiers of the Serbs who had sided with him and helped him to victory.

Once again, it appeared, a Serbian kingdom might be rising to some degree of power in the Balkans, this time in wary alliance with the weakened Turks rather than in opposition. The Serbs reoccupied the battlefield where their greatest national humiliation had taken place, and when in 1421 the last Balsha in the direct male line died, they advanced into Montenegro, becoming neighbours of the Venetians around Scutari and of the Albanians along the river Drin and in the neighbourhood of Prizren. The main obstacle to their advance was not yet apparent:

in the year that the Balshas collapsed, the talented and tireless administrator Murad II became Sultan and began the systematic reorganisation of the empire as an instrument of conquest.

At this point the leading families of Albania, both the mountain chieftains of the north and the territorial magnates of the centre and south, possessed a greater freedom of action than perhaps ever before or since. Some of them already had lengthy pedigrees and their degree of importance and sphere of influence were well known and recognised; but one family, the Castriotis, had risen in two generations from almost complete obscurity to a state of rough and insecure equality with the others.[7] Pal Castrioti owned a couple of villages called Signa and Lower Gardhi on the eastern fringe of the Mati territory, but his son Gjon, in the period of transition after the collapse of Dusan's empire, extended the family lands as far as the Adriatic. And it was Gjon's youngest son Gjergj, later to be known as Scanderbeg—the Lord Alexander—who became the national hero of Albania.

Chapter Three

. . . .

A Family in Search of a Sovereign

THE TERRACE OF PASTURE and beech woods that the Albanians call Mount Scanderbeg was the coastline of the Adriatic at some faraway point in geological time, but now it lies between five and fifteen miles away from the sea and three thousand feet above. It is the westward rampart of the wilder mountains that billow upward, peak beyond peak, to the north and east; and towards the summit of one plunging spur, where the olive groves come to an end amid a few final yards of scrub and bare limestone, the ruins of the fortress of Kruja stand like the abandoned nest of some great bird of the cliffs. Kruja was a fortress before the classical Greeks set up their colonies nearby, and until the perfection of artillery it was virtually impregnable against all attackers, forced as they were to approach it from the plains below. To its great physical strength was added the moral authority of its acknowledgement as a free city by the emperors of Byzantium.

Somewhere around 1400, at what exact date and by what precise means we do not know, Gjon Castrioti became the lord of Kruja; possibly soon after the disaster of Angora had removed the oppressive attentions of the Turks, and almost certainly with the approval of the Balsha family, the supreme overlords of northern Albania. He now held a wedge of the territory from the coast to the frontier of Macedonia, and could put into the field a couple of thousand fighting men or more. As such he became an eligible ally to the other landed families of Albania, with whom he was able to make a series of well-chosen dynastic marriages thanks to the prolificacy of his wife. She seems to have belonged to the Musachi: they were the most powerful family in the south, controlling Berat and the fertile coastal area which had been the granary of Albania since classical times. She bore him nine children. Four were sons—Stanisha, Reposhi, Constantine and Gjergj. Whilst they could be expected to lead his armed men into battle for either family honour or foreign payment, the five girls could equally advance the family interests at the altar. Mara married a Crnojevic; they were Serbs living at Zabljak on Lake Scutari who eventually turned themselves into the first Montenegrin royal family. Angelina married an Arianiti; they held the fortress of Kanina overlooking Vlora Bay and had the prestige of a distant relationship with several bygone Byzantine imperial families. Helena, or Yolla, married another Musachi. Zaharia married a Balsha, whose power and princely pretensions were already well–established. Castrioti had no daughters to spare for his modest neighbours and fellow mountain chieftains like the Dukagjini and the Zahari. All his matches were with the great landed magnates who possessed strong fortresses, large estates, and aristocratic lineages with a glimpse, however far and fleeting, of the imperial purple.

Like Demetrios of Kruja two hundred years earlier, he also began to follow a foreign policy of his own, independently of the Balshas. In 1407, when the Venetians forced the local overlords to sue for peace, Castrioti brought himself to the notice of Venice by asking her to intercede with the Pope on behalf of the Bishop of Kruja, whose position was threatened by a proposal that the See of Kruja be incorporated within that of Lezhë, which was now a Venetian town. This would have reduced the number of Albanian Sees to the advantage of the Latin ones; Castrioti was thus making a national gesture as well as defending his personal prestige.[1]

Towards the end of 1409 Castrioti made a further approach to the Venetians, declaring that his son (possibly Stanisha, the eldest, who might now be in his teens) had been taken hostage and that he was under daily pressure to allow the Turks to use his territory to make an attack on the Venetian possessions in Albania. He had no wish to accede to the Turkish demands, both for religious reasons and because of his affection for Venice, and thus requested the right of refuge if the Turks proved too strong for him. He was very willing that he and his people should serve the Republic if suitable provision could be made for them. If Venice were unable to do anything for him, he felt he would be right to plead justification should it prove that he had to bow to the superior strength of the Turks and obey them.

The Venetians do not appear to have rated this Turkish threat very highly, as we might expect in view of the collapse of Ottoman power at Angora seven years earlier; and the reply was distinctly cool, even by their calculating and unimpassioned standards. They did not commiserate with him on the news about his son. They thanked him for his goodwill and kindly feelings toward themselves and advised him to do nothing for the present that could lead to trouble with the Turks. He—good and dear son as they regarded him—could rest assured that if ever the occasion arose for action in his and their combined interests, they would always be ready to help him. They were ready to act on his complaints regarding certain officials in Durazzo, Scutari and Lezhë, but were unyielding on the main point: they declined to take Gjon Castrioti under their political protection or to hire his unemployed soldiers and give him a private allowance.

It is not at all clear how this initiative should be interpreted. It certainly cannot be taken at its face value, for the Turks were too weak to have thought seriously of ousting the Venetians from the Balkans, or even to have forced Castrioti to give them a son as a hostage. The only danger to Venetian possessions in Albania came from Balsha III, who alternated between signing treaties of peace and launching fresh warlike attacks. In 1410 he did in fact attack Scutari again, and many years later Gjon Castrioti was to admit to the Venetians, what we should have suspected in any case, that he had been at that time under pressure to help the Balshas. It might, however, have been tactless or even dangerous to say so openly when they were the strongest power in Albania; and as the Balshas had already vainly threatened to call in the help of the Turks if Venice would not give them the territory they wanted, Castrioti may well have calculated that though he spoke of 'Turks', the Venetians would understand that he was in fact offering them an alliance against the Balshas.

Castrioti was not merely playing a game of Machiavellian intrigue. In his new domains he had the problem of providing for a large surplus male population, whose only accomplishment, given the sparsity of land in the mountain valleys, was in making war. Some larger and richer power had to be found to employ them, and so allow them to be fed and clothed. Castrioti had perhaps 2,500 fighting men to look after in this way if he were not to see them starve or emigrate, and his own personal authority disappear with them. The Balshas were only a glorified version of his own family—strong and dangerous, but in no position to solve his economic troubles. The only powers who could do that were Venice or, in normal times, Turkey. Either might support him against the other, or alternatively might be induced to buy frontier peace from him. The idea of coming to terms with the Turks had as yet by no means the stigma of deserting the Christian cause that it came to have a generation later. As yet, the bitterest feeling in the Balkans was between Roman and Orthodox Christians themselves, with the Muslims as the possible ally of either. And, nominally at least, many of the Balkan rulers had acknowledged the Sultan as overlord since his victory at the battle of Kosova in 1389.

The course of the Ottoman civil war that followed the collapse of Timur's empire showed that some of these local rulers were induced to contribute forces on behalf of one or other party. Nothing could have been more natural than that Gjon Castrioti and other chieftains on the western marches of the empire, would also be asked, or that promises of territorial expansion would be made in the event of victory. In 1409, when he wrote to the Venetians, the final encounters of the civil war were already in preparation. He now had nine children, of whom Gjergj, the youngest, was probably four years of age,[2] so it would have been entirely possible for him to send his eldest son Stanisha as the nominal head of a family contingent, but entirely of his own free will and in the hope of favours to come.

There is, however, no means of knowing whether such a contingent was ever sent, or whether it was even offered or requested. Even if it had been, Castrioti could have derived little immediate advantage from it. For though the Turks at last found a new Sultan, it was many years before they could restore their old authority, and in the meantime the Serbs began to cherish the hope of re-establishing their former power. Castrioti accommodated himself to the change. In 1407 he had been struggling to preserve the Roman Catholic bishopric of Kruja, but by 1419 this political weathercock was being accused, along with the Balshas, of persecuting Roman Catholics in the interests of the Orthodox Church.

Two years later again the last in the direct male line of the Balshas died, and while this removed a dangerous local rival, it exposed Albania more directly to its new neighbour, the Despot of Serbia. By the beginning of 1422 the Despot, Stefan Lazarevic, was ready to make his own the old Balsha claim on Scutari and the Albanian coastline. Either pressure or self-interest suggested to John Castrioti that it would be just as well if his family were associated with these Serbian ambitions in case they should succeed. At the same time it was equally advisable to keep on good terms with Venice, in case they should fail. So he wrote to the Venetians again, saying that he had been forced to send one of his sons to join the Despot, but that he would much prefer to see Scutari owned by the Venetians than by the Serbians.[3] He was willing to give what help he could in defending it, and would like to be recognised by Venice in the way the Thopia family had been when they, and not the Castriotis, were her neighbours in

Albania. So one Andrea Marcello was told to go to Lezhë and, disguising himself as a merchant, cross the frontier and have an interview with 'Lord Gjon'. He was to salute and do him honour 'with necessary and pertinent words', and to say that Venice had always regarded him as a very dear friend and intended to go on doing so. Venice was quite sure that he had sent his son to the Despot's service with the very best intentions, but did not find it necessary at the moment to accept his offer to help Scutari, though if the occasion should arise it was taken for granted that he would be willing to carry out his promise.

Information had been received that the Despot was raising an army, and should Marcello hear that it was in fact destined for the siege of Scutari, he should call on Gjon Castrioti to give evidence of his kindly feelings for Venice by withdrawing his own forces from the Serbian camp. If possible, the said Lord Gjon might have his attention drawn to the dangers in which he and his fellow chieftains would stand if the Serbs should come to predominate in Albanian affairs: this theme should be embroidered with 'such relevant words and reasons' as the ambassador's discretion might suggest. If these secured what was wanted, well and good; but if not, and if the conversations made clear that some promise must be made 'for his honour', then Marcello could offer one hundred ducats[4] and two suits of clothing for a year. If in fact it was found that no troops had been sent to join the Serbians, and that Gjon Castrioti did not intend to take a subsidy from them, then the hundred ducats and the clothing could be made an annual obligation, subject to the promise to give aid to Scutari as necessary. If Marcello should discover that troops had in fact been sent to help the Despot of Serbia, then in order to induce Castrioti to withdraw them, he was empowered to offer up to two hundred ducats a year and two suits of clothing. It occurred to the thrifty Venetians that their local officers might have come to an agreement with Castrioti before the envoy arrived: in that case nothing was to be offered, he was merely to be told that Venice hoped he would keep the promises he had made. There was thus a graded scale of rewards, ranging from nothing for a genuinely disinterested friend to a modest maximum of two hundred ducats and two suits for a cynical political horse–trader. It is small wonder that the Balkan chieftains could become so adept at exploiting, and inflating, their nuisance value, and calculating just how far they dare go in playing off their greater and richer neighbours against each other.

The few ducats so carefully counted out by the Serene Republic were evidently not inducement enough for Castrioti to desert what then seemed the winning cause of Serbia. For in 1426 he and his four sons, Stanisha, Reposhi, Constantine and Gjergj, gave two villages to the Serbian royal monastery at Hilandar.[5] That this land–hungry, shrewd and ambitious man should have made such a sacrifice to ingratiate himself and all his male children in the good opinion of the Serbs and their national Church, is the clearest indication of where he thought the balance of power in the Balkans now lay. Serbia had again reached the Adriatic not far from Scutari and her frontiers now marched with those of the Albanians. And within a year of this display of Castrioti piety, the old Despot had died, and the new one, Gjergj Brankovic, was bent on making an alliance with the Hungarians and pushing back the Turks still further to the south and east. The course of the future seemed assured.

This apparent revival of Serbia was based on the temporary eclipse of the Turks rather than any accretion of power to herself. She was stronger only because the enemy was weaker. Nothing had been done to lessen the feudal weaknesses of Serbia, whereas Turkey needed only a period of unity and good administration to become quickly as formidable as she had been before her defeat by Tamerlane. Her idea of a standing army loyal to the monarch was superior in time of war to that of a federation of forces bought or bullied from semi–independent rulers like the Castriotis and their Slav equivalents. Her government was carried on by highly talented nonentities who served the Sultan without any parochial or family interests; hence it was cohesive, and not divided by sectional jealousies. And since 1421 the Turks had found in Murad II the administrative talent they needed. He reorganised the empire, and before the end of the decade was planning to make good the losses of a generation, and even to surpass the old frontiers.

Murad's attention was at first drawn more particularly to the city of Thessaloniki in the south. This splendid trading centre, the second greatest in the old Byzantine empire, found itself isolated in the midst of a reviving Ottoman empire, and could hope for no help from the enfeebled rulers of Constantinople. The Turks were waiting for it to fall to them like a ripe fruit when in 1423 the local ruler, finding that he could no longer defend it, offered it to the Venetians. They accepted it, along with the obligation to pay an annual tribute to the Sultan. The Turks were indignant at being robbed of their prize, but for the moment they were not prepared to fight for it.[6]

As they fully intended to challenge Venice for possession sooner or later, however, they naturally sought to prepare as much trouble for her as they could until they were ready to act. What could be more natural than to embarrass her by a diversion at a particularly sensitive point: the entrance to her own Adriatic Sea? For that the neutrality, if not the active help, of the owners of Kruja was necessary. So in August 1428 we find Gjon Castrioti writing once more to the Venetians to say that the Sultan has been asking him for help against them 'every day' since they had occupied Thessaloniki. He recites his claims on Venetian goodwill. He has been faithful to them ever since the Battle of Angora, despite the attempts of Balsha to incite him against them. When the Despot of Serbia wished to move against Lezhë, he was warned that it must be over the dead body of Castrioti's own realm. He has uncomplainingly endured the wrongs he has suffered from local Venetian officials. This time he sends letters he has received from the Turks to confirm his story, and adds that he has already warned the local Venetians that the Turks are preparing to attack them. In these letters the Sultan seems to have been claiming old Gjon's adhesion by right, for he is referred to as 'my overlord', which suggests that he had begun to receive an annual payment of tribute.

If the Sultan, angered at being refused help, should attack him, Castrioti asked the right to retire with his men on to Venetian territory. He also asked for material help and for the right to fly the standard of St. Mark, the patron saint of Venice, on his fortresses. This last demand, which was tantamount to an offer to accept Venice as sovereign power and would automatically embroil Turkey and Venice in war should Castrioti be attacked, was neglected by the Venetians in their reply. They merely said they were sure that he would be able to resist the Turks, that he might withdraw into their possessions at need, and that if necessary help would be offered him. He had also drawn attention to the position of a son 'who has become a Turk and a Muslim', presumably his eldest son Stanisha, who married a Muslim woman and had a son called Hamza by her. If the Sultan should order this son to attack his father or pillage Venetian territory, Castrioti trusted that he personally would not be held responsible, thus seeking in advance the right for his family to be sure of choosing the winning side by fighting with impunity on both. 'The Senate is of the opinion that the father is in a position to give orders to his son', was the laconic comment on this veiled threat.

Gjon Castrioti was able to secure two concessions from the Venetians, however. Two local chieftains, Vukovic and Zaharia, were quarrelling over which of them should control the Ragusan trade route up the Drin river, and he asked the Venetians to suggest to Ragusa that she would be better advised to use a route from Lezhë through his own territory. This demand, 'although against the interests of the Republic', was granted for one year. He also secured the right, granted to him at the death of Balsha but not always honoured locally, to buy salt tax free from the Venetian stores at Durazzo. Wherever she could, Venice maintained saltpans as a state monopoly, and she could wield immense influence among smaller neighbours like Castrioti by deciding under what conditions they should be allowed to buy the salt they needed to preserve their food for the winter. This time, however, Castrioti was able to strengthen his request for salt on the agreed terms by sending with his envoy a letter from the Turks offering him the chance to buy his salt at Vlora. To add weight to this implied threat, whilst giving an appearance of goodwill, he told the story of two brothers called Djuras, chieftains who had been refused the right to buy salt by the Venetian authorities at Kotor. They sent a representative to the Sultan to ask if he would supply them, but Castrioti had intercepted him and sent him back home with a message that his masters should wait to see the result of the present approach to Venice. The Venetians not unnaturally approved this conduct and said they would see that all obstacles he complained of at Durazzo were removed.

Gjon Castrioti had been forced to turn to Venice to try and balance Turkish pressure because his Serbian allies had failed him. In 1427, only a year after his compromising gift to Hilandar monastery, Murad II claimed that Serbia belonged to him by rights as the true heir of Lazar II. In reply the new Despot, Gjergj Brankovic, offered to pay tribute and supply troops, to break up an incipient alliance with the Hungarians, to give his daughter Maria as wife to the Sultan with a considerable dowry of Serbian land. After a certain amount of fighting Serbia was once again reduced to a small and powerless state, living in an uneasy twilight between independence and vassalage and of no help to any Albanian who wished to resist Turkish pressure. Gjon Castrioti's reaction to the coming clash between Turkey and Venice was thus to sit tight and wait for the storm to blow itself out.

Since Thessaloniki was first handed over to the Venetians, the Turks had increased their demands for tribute threefold, and this had always been paid for the sake of peace. Early in 1430 still more was demanded, and when the Venetians demurred the Sultan attacked the city and entered it after a short campaign on 29th March. It was devastated and largely depopulated: a warning to all who resisted the revived power of the Ottomans. Murad was freed by this victory for more wide-ranging attacks. He himself occupied Janina in north western Greece, the capital of the Despotate of Epirus; and another army, under his general Izak Bey Evrenoz, moved into Albania against the chieftain who had dared to refuse help when the Sultan demanded it. 'This is our news' reported a letter of 18th May from the Ragusan Senate to one of its representatives in Bosnia, where a possible Turkish attack was also being feared: 'As we wrote earlier, the Turk took Salonica, and having done so ordered some of his men into Morea and some against the territory of Gjon Castrioti ... and according to report, Gjon was trying to come to an agreement with them. We cannot say what happened subsequently, as our ships have not yet arrived from there'. 'The only news we have'—and this was ten days later—'is that the Turks ... have occupied all Gjon Castrioti's land and razed all his fortresses to the ground, except for two which they have equipped for themselves. Part of the land has gone to the Turks and part has been left with the said Gjon.'[7] By June it was known that the Turks had also laid waste the countryside to the north of the Castrioti lands: the Dukagjini and Crnojevic areas and Venetian territory right up to Scutari itself. For Gjon Castrioti the patient work of a lifetime was undone. Robbed of Kruja and Svetigrad, he passed from being a valuable ally and a potential national leader to a single tribal chieftain among many, shorn of some of his land and holding the remainder through the good graces of the Turks. Penned up in his mountain valleys, he might cause trouble as an occasional cattle raider, but his political influence would be negligible. He had sought to build up his own authority by balancing between two great powers, and now became a mere vassal of one of them. The former ally of Orthodox and Roman Catholic rulers now accepted the obligation to send forces to serve with a Muslim army whenever they were needed.

Albania as a whole was not yet decisively lost, however. The Turks did not occupy and administer it permanently. Their power lay in their army alone, and this had to thread its way through the narrow mountain passes, at which point it was extremely vulnerable to any guerrilla leader of courage and ingenuity. In 1433 Gjergj Arianiti, of Kanina, showed what might be possible by trapping a force which Izak Bey Evrenoz was bringing from Janina through the Kuvelesh mountains to the heart of Albania. Using swift, lightly–armed cavalry, he surprised and defeated an army much larger than his own. This unexpected news of victory against the Turks sent a wave of optimism through the dispirited courts of Christian Europe. The victor was offered the protection, more honorific than practically useful, of the Pope, the Emperor and the King of Naples. In Byzantium it was recalled that one of his great grandmothers had been a Comnena, a distant relation of the former reigning family of that name but enough to serve as an omen that the dying empire might still undergo a miraculous revival.

Encouraged by these national successes, the Castrioti family began tentatively to climb back upon the fence. In or around 1438 Gjergj, the youngest son, and the Scanderbeg of later days, received a gift of land from the Turks, and presumably undertook to come to their help in war whenever they should ask him. But in the same year he and his eldest brother Stanisha became honorary citizens of Venice and Ragusa. While having no immediate alternative but to accept the Sultan as their overlord, they were evidently willing to show their secret sympathy with his enemies and ready perhaps to consider taking part in the concerted preparations then being made, under the inspiration of Pope Eugenius IV, to clear the Turks out of Europe once and for all as soon as a favourable opportunity arose. Hungary was now the most immediately threatened of all the major powers, for the Turks had reached the Danube, leaving Serbia prostrate behind them.

So it was to Budapest that the Pope sent as his legate Cardinal Cesarini, a diplomat and classicist in his early forties, to organise what was in effect a religious crusade against the

Muslims. Cesarini assembled a force of about 25,000 men under the leadership of Ladislav, King of Hungary and Poland; the Serbian Despot, Gjergj Brankovic; and the ruler of Transylvania, Gjon Corvinus-Hunyadi, who had already beaten the Turks several times on his own territory. This force crossed the Danube in 1443, choosing a time when the Ottoman empire was once again largely preoccupied with troubles in Asia Minor. Early in November it reached the area of Nis, in southern Serbia, where it was confronted by the local Turkish commander and his auxiliary forces, among them according to legend a group of Albanians under Gjergj Castrioti. The Turks were defeated, the Hungarians marched on to the south, and the Albanian rode home as fast as he could to regain possession of the fortress of Kruja.

Chapter Four

. . . .

BIRTH OF A LEGEND

NATIONAL HEROES CANNOT be bound by the mere facts of history, for they must go on serving their country as symbols even when they have ceased to be living leaders. Some incident in their careers is singled out, or invented where necessary, to illuminate the virtues most coveted by their people. Gjergj Washington and his little axe proclaim the desire to keep public morality at the same level as private. Bruce and his spider teach pertinacity in the face of uncongenial nature. Alfred burning the cakes is the English ideal of the amateur, adept only at saving his country in her extremity. And the Serbian story of Lazar's choice between an earthly and a heavenly kingdom is an attempt after the event to give spiritual meaning to a military defeat which might otherwise have dissolved the national spirit entirely.

The Albanians have a more elaborate story than any of these about their national hero, and most people who have heard it will first have done so in Gibbon's persuasive cadences. 'Unable to contend with the Sultan's power', this version begins, Gjon Castrioti, the ambitious chieftain of Kruja, 'submitted to the harsh conditions of peace and tribute; he delivered his four sons as the pledges of his fidelity; and the Christian youths, after receiving the mark of circumcision, were instructed in the Mahometan religion, and trained in the arms and arts of Turkish policy.'[1] The three elder brothers were 'confounded in the crowd of slaves' and lost their lives, probably by poison; but the fourth brother Gjergj, 'who, from his tender youth, displayed the strength and spirit of a soldier,' won the favour of Sultan Murad II and was called by the Turks Iskender Bey, or Scanderbeg—the Lord Alexander—in flattering reminiscence of Alexander the Great and as 'an indelible memorial of his glory and his servitude.' He was made a general and given five thousand horse and 'served with honour in the wars of Europe and Asia,' but though brought up as a Muslim from his ninth year, he 'dropped the mask of dissimulation' when close on his fortieth year and, after the Turkish defeat at Nis, 'proclaimed himself the avenger of his family and country.'

This dramatic version coincides only with the more prosaic account given in the previous chapter in the incident of the seizure of Kruja. Gjon Castrioti did indeed submit to hard conditions from the Turks, but not until his youngest son was 25 or more years of age. After the battle of Angora in 1402 the practice of setting aside one slave in five for the Janissaries had to cease: the Turks were more concerned not to be taken, than to take slaves. The empire collapsed and the Ottoman court became an iron cage in the baggage train of a conqueror a year or two before Gjergj was born; and the devsirme, or 'collection', of Christian boys for the Turkish army by travelling commissions in time of peace, was introduced by Murad II. He came to the throne in 1421, when Gjergj Castrioti was certainly 16 and probably 18 years of age, and it was applied first in the eastern Balkans and only later in Albania and the other Christian provinces.

This discrepancy between the probabilities of history and the narratives of historians, from Gibbon in the eighteenth century to Toynbee in the twentieth, must evidently be resolved; and the first task is to trace the traditional story to its origin. This proves to be an Albanian monk who under the latinized name of Marinus Barletius[2] wrote a life of Scanderbeg about the end of the fifteenth century. Barletius was much younger than his subject, whom he did not know personally; but much of his information came from men who had known and fought under him. It is to Barletius we owe the main elements of the story; that Sultan Murad II took Gjergj Castrioti away in the ninth year of his age; that three of the four brothers[3] were poisoned; that Gjergj rose to great authority and was called Scanderbeg for his prowess in war; and that he forced the Sultan's secretary to write an authorisation for him to occupy Kruja after the Turkish defeat at Nis.

Only two of these items are open to documentary proof, and both can be shown to be false. The three brothers were not poisoned at all, for one at least ended his life peaceably in an Albanian monastery. And Murad II did not ascend the throne until 1421 when, as already mentioned, Gjergj Castrioti was a young man and not a child. (An earlier writer than Barletius, the Neapolitan humanist Giovanni Gioviano Pontano,[4] who probably met Scanderbeg personally in Italy, but whose testimony seems to have been overlooked until recent times, does in fact say that he had certainly reached adolescence when he became a hostage). It could perhaps be argued, as Gibbon does, that Barletius has made a mistake in the name of the Sultan. But this explanation contradicts the spirit as well as the letter of his book. He does not introduce Murad's name casually, for it is an essential part of his story that this particular ruler is seeking a personal revenge for an act of treacherous ingratitude. Barletius is under the impression that Murad was a very much older man than Scanderbeg; that he acted somewhat as a foster father towards him and was outraged as a man and not just as a ruler by the final defection; and that Murad was 80 years of age when he led his armies into Albania, when he was in fact only in his fifties and very little older than his opponent. And, finally, if Murad II was not the Sultan in question, it is hard to see who else could have been. Scanderbeg was born in 1403 or 1405, during the period of collapse of the Ottoman empire; and, as has been shown, his father felt at liberty to pursue an independent policy towards his neighbours for a quarter of a century after this. Gjon

Castrioti and his four sons made their gift to the Serbian monastery on Athos when Gjergj was over twenty, and this incident is almost conclusive proof that the family was then still living united at home and felt no fear at possible Turkish reprisals. Not until 1430 was the family attacked and defeated by the Turks; and that was in the ninth year of Murad II's reign, not the ninth year of Gjergj Castrioti's life.

The traditional story is not only historically improbable; it is psychologically incredible. It can easily be shown that the Christian boys who in later centuries were taken from their homes and brought up as Turks were quite as loyal and vastly more energetic than the Muslims among whom they lived. Having no family concerns to divide their attention, they devoted themselves wholly to the Sultan's interests and administered his empire for him with a zeal, devotion and talent long unrivalled anywhere else in Europe. If Scanderbeg had revolted as and when he is supposed to have done, his would have been a unique aberration, and the natural question is to ask why this one Albanian, from among so many, should have acted so thoroughly out of character? Gibbon came near to asking this question, and would probably have found it necessary to recast his story had he done so. Scanderbeg, he points out, 'had imbibed from his ninth year the doctrines of the Koran: he was ignorant of the Gospel; the religion of a soldier is determined by authority and habit; nor is it easy to conceive what new illumination at the age of forty could be poured into his soul.' If indeed it is true that a man's perceptions atrophy at the age of forty (or did so in the eighteenth century) that is all the more reason for Gibbon to crown this list of impressive objections with the rational conclusion: therefore, this account is palpably untrue. Unfortunately, instead of looking at Scanderbeg with the detached eye of a seeker after truth, he assumed once more his congenial role of hammer of the faithful, and could not resist the opportunity of giving aid and comfort to their enemies. 'In the eyes of the Christians,' he says loftily, 'the rebellion of Scanderbeg is justified by his father's wrongs, the ambiguous death of his three brothers, his own degradation, and the slavery of his country; and they adore the generous though tardy zeal with which he asserted the faith and independence of his ancestors.' Gibbon then continues with the reasons, quoted earlier, why Scanderbeg could not or should not have become a Christian in middle age, and finally sums up against him on the grounds that a man must revolt against oppression as soon as he feels it—even as a child, presumably, at the court of the strongest monarch in the world—or forfeit his right to do so for ever. 'His motives would be less exposed to the suspicion of interest or revenge, had he broken his chain from the moment that he was sensible of its weight, but long oblivion had surely impaired his original right; and every year of obedience and reward had cemented the mutual bond of the sultan and his subject. If Scanderbeg had long harboured the belief of Christianity and the intention of revolt, a worthy mind must condemn the base dissimulation, that could only serve to betray, that could promise only to be forsworn, that could actively join in the temporal and spiritual perdition of so many thousands of his unhappy brethren.' This is cold-hearted pleading for a verdict, not interpretation of a character from within, and had Gibbon pondered the discrepancies of his story and pursued a little further the sources open to him, he might have presented Scanderbeg as a human being instead of a magnificent monster. And he might have shown Edward Gibbon in the same light, instead of exposing him as an apologist for tyranny, granted only that it is exercised long enough, and against Christians.

Gibbon is not alone, for the changeling slipped by Barletius into the cradle of historical fact has been weaned and reared to flourishing manhood by successive historians.[5] By dint of quotation and cross reference, footnotes and commentary, the fantasy has assumed the status of truth, from which all kinds of conclusions are to be drawn. How has this come to happen? The easiest answer is to take a parallel from Homeric studies, where a poetic interpretation of historic events has been subjected to the same literal commentary as though it were a contemporary chronicle written by scholars taking part in the actions they are describing. Barletius, the Homeric prose-writer of Albania, was an artist who felt deeply about his subject. As an Albanian, he reverenced in Scanderbeg the greatest of his fellow-countrymen. In true Renaissance style, moreover, he saw in him the classical hero reborn, and edited or created for him actions worthy of—and on occasion purloined from—the great narrators of antiquity. As a Roman Catholic, hating the Turks with a bitter intensity, and still hoping that his country might be freed from them, he wrote as though they had always been the object of a deep crusading hostility on the part of the Albanians and had never, for example, been regarded as a potentially useful ally in negotiations with Venetians or Serbians. And, finally, he collected his material among largely illiterate tribesmen, who remembered what concerned themselves or their families with penetrating clarity but for whom the impedimenta of scholarship—the names and dates of monarchs, the size of their armies, the policy that governed their actions—lay lightly on them. They were men who cast their accounts of a notable event in the form of a ballad, not of a government despatch; and when after the lapse of a generation or so the story came to be written down, these ballads had already prepared the form in which it was to be presented.

Barletius' biography is the *Iliad* of the Albanian war against the Turks, with the hostage theme performing the same function as the rape of Helen in the earlier and greater work. Each provides a cause for the action readily comprehensible and acceptable to a popular audience. Without the action of Paris, the Trojan War would sink to a predatory invasion of Asia Minor, unworthy to be celebrated; and if Gjergj Castrioti had not been carried away against his will before he had been able to make his own decisions, then his struggle would have seemed to Barletius a dynastic and national one only, and not a dedicated religious crusade able to shame and inspire Christian Europe to go and do likewise. Gjergj Castrioti must be the perfect knight and the

Sultan the dark foil, and this simple confrontation immediately turns the life of the hero into epic drama disguised as biography. The affronted Scanderbeg, robbed of home, lands and religion by Murad II, is able in the fullness of time to re-establish himself in all of them. The Sultan finally dies within sight of the fortress he once stole from the boy, trying in vain to win it back by a display of overweening force. It is this theme of David destroying Goliath after having first been trapped by him that warms Barletius' heart and makes his narrative pulsate with patriotic fervour.

In fact, as we well know, Murad II did not die in the midst of his failure to take Kruja. He died in his capital of Adrianople, and of apoplexy, probably brought about by over-eating. But the two events were only a few months apart, so it is tempting to see them as cause and effect and to suppose that he really died of chagrin; and when that point has been reached the poetic justice of killing him in Albania becomes too tempting to miss. And as Scanderbeg revolted at the age of about forty, his opponent, the man who took him away as a child and feels as a foster father betrayed, must be a generation older. So in Barletius' story Murad has to be somewhere around eighty when he comes to Kruja. He directs operations with the skill, energy and steadiness of a man twenty or thirty years younger—anything less than this would fail to pay tribute to Scanderbeg's own military genius—and only at the moment of failure does he suddenly realise his age. Then, like a dying prima donna in a romantic opera, he rallies his forces for a lusty peroration, and so dies.

Yet the fact remains that this great monarch did himself take over from his generals the task of trying to destroy a minor princeling, and brought with him troops and train on a scale not seen in Albania since Roman times. This suggests that Barletius may be right in underlining the theme of personal rancour on Murad's part. If the story of kindness towards a young hostage has to be abandoned, some other motive for it needs to be found. And Barletius seems unwittingly to provide it. For in fact he does not quite say, as Gibbon assumes him to have done, that Gjergj

Castrioti spent his time at the Turkish court or with the Turkish army until the disaster of Nis impelled him to desert the Sultan and return to his homeland. At two points in the narrative it is clearly implied that he was already in Albania in or around 1438, five years before the fateful battle, in the possession of lands already given to him by the Turks. Thus his gesture of independence was a simple repudiation of the Sultan's overlordship at the first possible opportunity, and not calculated treachery to an almost lifelong friend and benefactor.

The character created by Gibbon does not correspond even to the evidence available in his principal source; and we now further know, as he did not, that in 1438 both Gjergj Castrioti and his brother Stanisha became citizens of Venice (and of Ragusa)[6], which shows that they were strong enough to be worth Venice's friendship and free to seek it. Though holding lands from the Sultan (and therefore, one may be sure, binding themselves to send contingents to fight for him when required) they already hoped to secure liberty of action by looking for other protectors, and resuming the old balance of power policy that had served their father so well until the eve of the final disaster. There was, however, one moral weakness in Gjergj's position. He was the youngest of the four sons, and so any lands he held came to him not by hereditary right but as a personal tribute from the Turks. Their authority alone legitimised his, and if it were to be withdrawn or rejected, he could rely only on force and strength of character to preserve his possessions from other claimants, his own elder brothers included. Hence the necessity, when the legend came to be created, of quietly poisoning these three and blaming it on the heathen Turk. And hence perhaps some at least of the fury and indignation of the Sultan when defied by a minor satrap of his own creation.

There remains one small obstacle in the way of abandoning the hostage story altogether, and that is the name the Turks are supposed to have given Gjergj Castrioti: Scanderbeg, the Lord Alexander. It was for long an Albanian custom, especially among conformists to Islam who remained secretly Christian, to have two names, one for each confession. There is no reason to suppose that this practice had not been adopted already in the fifteenth century, and no one would stand more in need of protective colouring than a young man bearing the aggressively Christian name of Gjergj. Alexander, or Leka, has always been a popular Albanian name, since all Albanians believe they are descended from the ancient Illyrians and number Alexander the Great among their ancestors. If the Turks, and not the Castrioti family, did link the two Alexanders, they may even have done so ironically after hearing him and his followers talking so much of their distinguished lineage, much as Marco Polo was always called Marco Millions on his return home because of his habit of dragging in whenever he could a reference to the teeming wealth of China.

As to the title of 'Bey' or 'Beg', there existed from the very beginning of the Ottoman empire a class of local potentate known as the *Dere Beys*—'Lords of the Highland Glens'—a feudal fringe composed of men who had been awarded lands formerly belonging to the nobility of the Byzantine empire. They were obliged to supply so many horse and foot in time of war as auxiliaries for the regular army. Gjon Castrioti was in effect dispossessed of his lands as a Christian and allowed to have them back, less the strongholds of Kruja and Svetigrad as a, possibly Muslim, *Dere Bey*. This was not the most heroic beginning for a national hero, and so in their patriotic enthusiasm the ballad makers quickly improved on the literal facts, producing a reckless Quixote who, having been given the finest training that a great empire could offer, rounded upon it for the sake of a point of family honour.

But the real story is an even finer one: that of a young man who saw his patrimony destroyed and who, in the act of taking his revenge, found himself committed to a national cause rather than a personal one. He accepted the tragic consequences of that association and rose in the process to a courage more moral than physical, causing him to submerge his own private and family interests in those of a nation as yet unborn.

As a result, that nation has remodelled the circumstances of his life to match and justify its own experience since his death, and in Barletius' story it found malleable material. After his death, the Albanians came under Turkish rule for four and a half centuries, and most of them accepted the religion and civilisation of the conqueror. Nor did they merely remain inert under an alien government. Many rose to the highest positions, for in its great days there was little or no racial discrimination in the Ottoman empire. Indeed, at one point in the seventeenth century, after a period of chaos, 'the empire was once more clamped together by the ferocious rigour'[7] of an Albanian, Mehmet Koprulu, whose family provided prime ministers for twenty years and 'enabled the Ottomans once again to play a vigorous and menacing role in south-eastern Europe, and to strain the defences of the western world.'

Yet at the height of their triumphs the Albanian pashas and vizirs remembered their national origins. They helped each other to rise in the hierarchy; and as the empire decayed in the eighteenth century they retained the resolution to carve out principalities for themselves. An Albanian, Mehmet Ali, founded modern Egypt; another, Ali Pasha, was at the same time trying to form a kingdom out of Greeks and his own fellow-countrymen. And when finally the Ottoman empire, in its last stages of decay, proved unable to defend Albania against her neighbours, it was an old Muslim aristocrat who raised the flag of independence on the day Scanderbeg had done so more than four and a half centuries earlier. So at length the legend had created its own truth.

Scanderbeg, like these later Albanians, was thus required to have undergone the twin experience of conforming to foreign rule while keeping his national feelings intact. As for the circumstances of his life while doing so, these as they appeared to the imagination of later generations are perhaps best described in an account of the Ottoman Court shortly before it did in fact come under the rule of the Koprulus. The writer is a young muezzin who attracted the attention of the Sultan as Gjergj Castrioti is supposed to have done a century and more earlier. He was Evliya Chelebi,[8] grandson of Mehmed the Conqueror's standard–bearer at the conquest of Constantinople, and he was taking part in a service in Santa Sophia at which the Sultan Murad IV was present. On his father's advice he began to show how clever he was by beginning to repeat the whole of the Quran from memory. The Sultan did not wait to make quite sure the boy could accomplish this feat, but soon capitulated by sending him a gold-embroidered cap and bidding him come to the imperial loggia in the mosque. He was there and then chosen, not merely as a page, but as a *musahib* or 'intimate companion', and so joined those who acted as equerries, private secretaries and members of the sovereign's own personal circle. Murad gave him a present of 'two or three handfuls of gold coins—six hundred and twenty three pieces in all' and next day he began his course of studies at the palace: calligraphy, music, grammar and recitation, not to mention 'a number of complimentary phrases and ceremonies which I was to observe when in the emperor's presence.'

He was taken to the Privy Chamber, 'a large domed room, with a high throne in each corner. There are numerous windows and balconies, fountains and basins, and the floor is paved with variegated marbles ... All of a sudden, the Emperor made his appearance like the rising sun, by the door leading to the Inner Harem. He saluted the forty pages of the Privy Chamber and all the favourites who returned the salutation with prayers for his prosperity. The Emperor having seated himself with great dignity on one of the thrones, I ran forward and prostrating myself kissed the ground in front of his feet. At that moment, by God's inspiration, there came to my mind some complimentary verses which I repeated without the least fear or hesitation.' The Sultan asked for something else and Evliya, unabashed, asked him whether he wanted poetry or religious chant or something in any of the seven languages and seventy-two branches of knowledge he was versed in. The Sultan rallied him on his boastfulness, but he did not give way and even ventured on a simple pun, at which the monarch 'slapped his knees with his hand and burst into such a fit of laughter that his face became quite red; then, addressing Emirgune, his favourite musician, he said: "what do you think of this young devil?"

Then the Sultan called for music. Evliya sang a number of songs, one of them composed by his own former music master in honour of a favourite royal page who had been murdered by rebels when carrying a message from the Sultan to one of his pashas. When he heard it, the Sultan took out his handkerchief and asked who had taught him a song he had forbidden to be sung in his presence. He had learned it, said Evliya in a flash, from two of his father's slaves, who had since died in the plague.

"What a sly lad," exclaimed the Sultan. "He quotes the authority of the dead so as not to compromise the living." He then added: "Long mayest thou live" and bade me continue my performance.' And Emirgune the musician reminded his royal master that the veins of those who had shed the innocent blood had since been opened. Indeed they had, agreed Murad. To avenge his favourite and his brother he had caused the heads of three hundred thousand rebels to roll in the dust. "May Allah prosper all your undertakings!" piously replied Emirgune.

This crust of hothouse luxury and opulent refinement, thinly stretched over a volcano of personal danger and hysterical cruelty, was the vision which sprang to mind when later generations of Albanians thought of Scanderbeg's youth and pictured him treading his delicate path to fame and ultimate freedom. They were proud that one of their own could be subtle enough to survive and succeed in such an atmosphere; they were even prouder of the fact that he maintained his highlander's integrity at the same time, dealing with guile and intrigue on their own terms, and yet uncontaminated by them.

It is not easy for a biographer to forego such a story: long pages of warm, romantic prose dwelling upon the temptations and dangers of the Ottoman court at Adrianople,[9] and moving in leisurely fashion from the council chamber and the languid harem to the battlefield and back again. The story must seem less dramatic when set all the time in the bare highlands of Albania, though it gains in coherence as well as truth to historic fact. It explains why Gjergj Castrioti could defy the Turks with such light-hearted self-confidence, which he is unlikely to have done had he really known from within the organisation, sense of purpose and size of their armies. What he did after the battle of Nis was precisely what one would expect from a local chieftain of little experience, witnessing the defeat of a peripheral force and assuming that he had seen a national disaster. And the prosaic story removes an implied slur from his character. The more the legend emphasised his prowess in the Sultan's service, the more it accused him of responsibility for the death of many fellow Christians in battle. Of the attempts to resolve this difficulty, Gibbon not unjustly says that 'we may smile at the art or credulity of the historian, who supposes that in every encounter he spared the Christians, while he fell with a thundering arm on his Mussulman foes.' Now at length we may take the complacent smile from our faces.

Chapter Five

. . . .

THE ATHLETE OF CHRISTENDOM

'IN THE CONFUSION of a defeat, the eye of Scanderbeg was fixed on the Reis Effendi, or principal secretary; with a dagger at his breast, he extorted a firman or patent for the government of Albania; and the murder of the guiltless scribe and his train prevented the consequence of an immediate discovery. With some bold companions, to whom he had revealed his design, he escaped in the night, by rapid marches, from the field of battle to his paternal mountains. The gates of Croya were opened to the royal mandate; and no sooner did he command the fortress than Gjergj Castrioti dropped the mask of dissimulation, abjured the prophet and the sultan, and proclaimed himself the avenger of his family and country. The names of religion and liberty provoked a general revolt: the Albanians, a martial race, were unanimous to live and die with their hereditary prince; and the Ottoman garrisons were indulged in the choice of martyrdom or baptism.'

Such is the dramatic account that Gibbon, with admiring disapproval, gives of Scanderbeg's actions immediately after the Hungarian army had defeated the Turkish at Nis in November 1443. The same story was taken by Longfellow[1] and given still more romantic flourishes in the ineffable jogtrot verse of Tales of a Wayside Inn:

In the darkness of the night
Iskander, the pride and the boast

Of that mighty Othman host,
With his routed Turks takes flight.

He is going nowhere in particular, but merely rides on through the night and gazed at 'the fateful stars'. Suddenly, for no specified reason,

. . . he smote his steed with his staff
And smiled to himself, and said:
"This is the time to laugh."

But before he has time to do so,

There came a scribe of the King
Wearing his signet ring,

who upbraids Scanderbeg for deserting the Turkish army and, using the family name for the purposes of rhyme, declares:

'This is the first dark blot
On thy name, George Castriot!'

Unabashed, George replied that the war belonged to God, and who were they to withstand 'the wind of His lifted hands'.

Then he bade them bind with chains
This man of books and brains,

who was ordered to write, and seal with his ring, an order to the Governor of Kruja to surrender the city to the bearer. The scribe objects that he will assuredly lose his head if he does so. His captor indicates without a word that the penalty will be no less if he does not:

Then swift as a shooting star

The curved and shining blade
Of Iskander's scimitar
From its sheath, with jewels bright,
Shot, as he thundered: 'Write!'

The scribe writes. The Pasha of Kruja, when shown the writing of the King, bowed his head and was silent for a time. Then, instead of asking Scanderbeg how it came about that the Sultan could be in both Asia Minor and Nis at the same time, meekly handed over the keys, pronouncing a few suitable words of resignation to a higher will:

'Allah is just and great!
I yield to the will divine:
The city and lands are thine;
Who shall contend with fate?'

In both these versions of the story there is an element of frantic haste. Gjergj Castrioti escapes 'by rapid marches' and drops 'the mask of dissimulation' the moment he is in command of Kruja. But the battle of Nis was fought on 3rd November; and according to Albanian tradition, his family flag with the two–headed black eagle on a red ground was raised on the 28th November. The two places are about a couple of hundred miles apart by the most likely route, so that Scanderbeg galloped home at a steady eight miles a day. He could have done better on foot. We must therefore be prepared to accept, and ready to explain, the fact that Scanderbeg may have been back at home for a fortnight before declaring his independence of the Turks. The simplest explanation may be the most reasonable: he may have waited to make sure that the Turks were really well and truly in retreat towards their capital at Adrianople before making his challenge. And he would be well aware that by the last week in November the snow begins to fall and choke the high passes into Albania. If no punitive army had been sent against him by then, none could survive before next spring at the earliest.

The weather, then, probably determined the date of his formal defiance. At the same time, there is every reason to suppose that he rode home with great speed: a resolute leader, with at least a few hundred well-equipped fighting men, and armed also with the knowledge of the Turkish collapse, was in a strong position to ensure his own and his family's future. It can be taken for granted that he made the best use he could of those assets. Both ambition and prudence dictated a policy of speed and courage: he could at one and the same time carve himself a principality and neutralise the possible handicap of having gone to the help of the defeated army. He could act while the other chieftains were hesitating, uncertain of the result.

What then of the threat to the imperial secretary; or even, according to Gibbon, his murder? It hardly needs to be said that there is no sort of documentary evidence for such an incident. It is equally true, of course, that there is no evidence that Gjergj Castrioti ever took a contingent of troops to help the Turks at Nis. There is, however, an inherent probability that someone from his family did, in view of their relations with the Turks since 1430, and the obvious need to assemble all the forces possible to withstand this major Hungarian attack. Moreover, had the Castriotis been neutral—even more, had they decided to join in the Christian crusade and send forces to fight against the Turks—his biographer would not have omitted this example of family piety. On the contrary, he evidently feels that there is a case to answer in the circumstances surrounding the fall of Kruja.

Writing around 1500 of events still clear in the public memory he could not overlook the fact that his hero was present on the wrong side at Nis. We may presume he was there because the Turks had called on him to discharge a straightforward feudal obligation to the Sultan; but Barletius dared not bring himself to suppose anything so compromising, for what he wished to show were Scanderbeg's Christian principles. Thus he used, even if he did not invent, the story of almost lifelong capture at the Turkish court. Equally the spirit of the story of the royal scribe is simple: Scanderbeg re-entered Kruja as master with what the governor took to be a valid authorisation. If he had to fight for it, that would certainly form part of the legend, as further proof of his hostility to the Turks and Islam. Since he had not, it must have been clear to every Albanian that he secured the vital document either by force, fraud or subterfuge on the one hand, or on the other as part of a political bargain with the Turks. As between these two possibilities, only one was possible to a pious biographer in 1500. Bullying and chicanery alone were compatible with the picture of Scanderbeg as a fanatical hater of the Muslims; nor were they entirely without their attractions to a generation fed on the ideal of the crafty but disinterested *Prince*. So the traditional story, being exactly what we would expect from anyone writing under such circumstances, has nothing more to commend it than its usefulness. It may be true, but there is not a jot of evidence to substantiate it.

At the time, however, there was no reason whatever why a shrewd Albanian family, particularly one which had suffered so severely for its rashness in refusing help to the Turks once before, should not have negotiated with them on the eve of this vital campaign. They had recently supported both branches of Christianity, and one if not all of them had lately turned Muslim, so it is vain to look for religious faith as their guiding principle. If Gjon Castrioti had been involved, and not his youngest son, we could have been fairly sure in the light of his record that he would have been conducting negotiations all round the compass: with the Pope's representatives, the Venetians, probably the Serbs and Hungarians, as well as with his nominal sovereign, the Sultan.

To the Christians he would have explained how he was acting under duress, but would prove his friendship on the battlefield. And he would have sought to wring concessions from the Turks in such a time of emergency, pointing out the danger in which he stood from their enemies and the vital need to hold Kruja if his lands were to be defended for the Sultan.

Unfortunately we do not know whether Gjon Castrioti was now alive or dead. The fact that overtures were made to Venice by his sons in 1438 may mean that he had just died then; and this would explain why Gjergj Castrioti should receive a grant of land from the Turks—presumably part of his father's possessions—in that year. We do not know what negotiations, if any, were begun by Scanderbeg before the battle of Nis, but it is hard to believe that the son of such a father was not fully alive to the dangers and opportunities of the forthcoming battle. The entire campaign was intended to turn the Turks out of Europe; and it must be assumed that the Albanian chiefs, with their nominally Christian traditions and their very real love of power, were approached to help in tightening the net around the doomed empire. It would have been entirely in character for the Turks, faced with this threat, to hint that they might return Kruja to the Castriotis in return for their military support, well knowing they could claim to have been misunderstood if they won the war.

A Castrioti would have been able to estimate an offer of that kind at its true value, and capable of insisting on possession first, and assistance afterwards. For there would have been a real risk in denuding the Castrioti lands of their fighting men without such a guarantee: in case of defeat local rivals or foreign troops might capture Kruja and the surrounding district before they had a chance to return home and defend their own. All this is necessarily speculation; but it remains true that at Kruja alone is the fortress said to have been handed over to him, and at all the other fortresses in Albania he had to fight for possession. Had he threatened an official secretary with death, he could quite as easily have ordered him to write the names of these as well. It may well be that in the moment of defeat, in return for a safe conduct for their garrison, the Turkish authorities gave Scanderbeg authority to take over Kruja, calculating that he would be prepared to defend it against their enemies in his own interests, whatever his future relations with themselves. This seems the most reasonable explanation, and the most honourable to all parties concerned. It would explain why the governor of Kruja should yield his charge without a fight, and why Barletius should feel bound to introduce a story which exposes his hero as a bully but acquits him of what had then become a much graver charge, that of collusion with the enemy of Christendom.

Hardly less remarkable than the ease with which he occupied Kruja is the way in which, having turned Christian again, he secured the all-important support of the Roman Catholic Church. Although fresh from the battlefield, where he had fought on the wrong side, he returned home not a prodigal, but the leader of the national and Christian cause. Under this combined impetus he quickly captured a line of minor fortresses to the east of Kruja, including Petrela near Elbasan and was halted only when he reached the eastern frontier with Turkey and tried to take the eastern counterpart of Kruja, the strong point of Svetigrad.

Albania was cleared of Muslims, for those who did not escape were given the choice of baptism or butchery: a harsh alternative that reflects no credit on anyone concerned, but was for centuries afterwards a measure to which Balkan peoples tended to resort in times of danger and high emotion in dealing with minorities associated with a larger outside power that might one day seek to crush and assimilate them. Scanderbeg was not personally cruel (though his character was certainly not unsuited to the asperities of the times) but he seems to have accepted this policy as part of the natural order of things. In any case, it would have been tactless, with his own record, to seek to defend the Muslims; and in the light of his own family's record he might well have reflected that a man who was ready to die rather than adopt the currently respectable religion richly deserved to.

Albania was now safe for the winter. For the first time in many years she was ruled by Albanians and had no foreign occupiers on her soil. If the Hungarians and their allies could defeat the Turks completely, and either evict them from Europe or at least pin them down to the extreme south-eastern corner of

Europe, this happy state of affairs might be expected to become permanent; unless, indeed, one of the Christian powers sought to fill the swept and garnished Balkans with an empire of its own. But though hopes ran high, it could not be taken for granted that the Turks had been beaten once and for all. They had so far merely suffered a reversal to one of their peripheral armies while their main forces were occupied in Asia Minor. They had yet to show their full strength. And while to the Sultan the King of Hungary was a sovereign to be treated with on equal terms, Gjergj Castrioti was no more than a treacherous vassal, to whom no quarter need be shown. Hence the need to spend the winter of 1443-4 in the attempt to consolidate Albania's military and political power.

The country around Kruja was quickly captured, and a short campaign in snow-bound country quickly reduced a number of nearby fortresses. Moving eastward, he met and formed an alliance with a leading chieftain of Dibra, Moses Golemi, a nephew of Gjergj Arianiti of Kanina, who was to become his friend and principal lieutenant in the years ahead. Together they tried to capture Svetigrad, a fortress strategically placed on the border between Albania and Macedonia. There are three roughly parallel routes into central and northern Albania from the east, and these are connected by the valley of the river Drin, running from south to north. Svetigrad commands the junction of this valley with the centre route. It was essential for the Turks to hold it if they were to mount any organised invasion of Albania, let alone keep a watch on marauding bands invading their territory. Held against them, it might make Albania invulnerable against attack from this side. But the fortress was inaccessible, being isolated on top of a hill; the Albanians had no siege artillery; and it was already winter. Scanderbeg, after finding that Svetigrad declined to yield, as the more isolated places had done, left Moses in charge there (the fortress fell to him soon afterwards) and returned home to Kruja for Christmas. Even in the moment of victory he had been living the rough life of a campaigner, we are told, eating and drinking vast quantities of food and wine, and sleeping as little as two hours a night in his anxiety to rid Albania of the Turks and replace them with his own men or others loyal to him.

It was impossible for him, high as his prestige now was, to hold the whole of northern Albania on his own. He had neither the authority nor the fighting men. He must therefore seek to build a coalition of all his allies; and he approached his fellow-countrymen with timely modesty. 'It is not that I have brought liberty hitherto unto you but that here I have found liberty ... it is not I have given you this city, it is you that hath given it to me': such, with the antithetical trimmings of a later writer, is what he is supposed to have told the people of Kruja. The value of his sisters' dynastic marriages now became clear, for soon there was an informal league of brothers-in-law which could put around 12,000 men into the field. They, and a number of neighbours, came together at the Cathedral of St. Nicholas in Lezhë on 2nd March 1444.

Lezhë was a Venetian possession, but that does not mean that the Venetians sponsored the conference. They merely permitted it to be held there, as the most convenient and sizeable centre, and they sent observers to make sure they knew what was going on. They were not permitted to undertake any obligations, however. Venice was not entirely happy about the way things were going. She wanted strong government in the Orient to ensure her trade, even if it happened to be Muslim. She did not want Hungarian dominance in the Balkans, for that would mean sooner or later a struggle for control of Dalmatia. She had no wish, either, to encourage Albanian unity, for she was quite happy to have a collection of weak, disunited and, she hoped, venal chieftains on the borders of her towns there. But since the conference would take place whether she wished it or not, there were obvious advantages in having it under her own jurisdiction. Use of the cathedral as a meeting place shows that it was the Church which played the leading part in forming an effective

Albanian coalition as part of its general plans for a resumption of war against the infidel. Nine main families were represented, in addition to the Castriotis, and five of these had already been linked by old Gjon's foresight—Musachi, Balsha, Arianiti, Thopia and the Montenegrin Crnojevic. The other four, with traditions of reserve or even hostility to the Castriotis—Dukagjini, Zaharia, Spani and Dushmani—had probably needed some priestly persuasion, or even intimidation, to abandon their animosities and join in the first national effort of military and political union.

To some of these men, even to some of those related to him, Gjergj Castrioti appeared not only as a national hero, but as the representative of a new and ambitious family whose expansion could only be at their own expense. Still, his leadership was not in question. His recent initiative had animated Albanian national feeling, which they could not neglect; he was master of the key point of Kruja and a military leader of evident talent. He was evidently the man preferred by the religious leaders, and though his family had wavered in matters of faith in the past, there never was much doubt in the fifteenth century at least that a northern Albanian would be Roman Catholic whenever he had freedom of choice. Islam was the religion of a conqueror, besides being new and relatively unfamiliar. Orthodoxy was the religion of the powerful and assimilative Slavs. And this time the Castriotis had really burned their boats by their defiance of the Sultan.

Accordingly, Scanderbeg was nominated Captain-General of what later became somewhat grandiosely known as The League of Albanian Princes. Its members were mountain chieftains and landed barons rather than princes; but it was a league in that each retained his identity and power to dispose of his own military contingent. Scanderbeg was less a commander-in-chief than the first among equals, who led their 18,000 or so soldiers, but had absolute control over only about 3,500 of his own, and had to convince his colleagues at every step that his policy and tactics were the right ones. With this instrument, backed by whatever finances could be raised locally or subscribed by well-wishers abroad, the Albanians prepared to await the Turkish revenge.

By next Spring the Turks began to think of taking it, and an army was sent out under a general called Ali Pasha to restore the situation. Scanderbeg moved east to meet them before they could cross the frontier, and the two forces met at Torviollo, a grassy upland slope flanked by woods. As the Turkish general approached at dawn on 29th June, he saw ahead of him a crescent of horsemen with Scanderbeg and his personal guard in the centre, and behind them archers on foot. They seemed so few in number, and looked as though they were drawn up to be reviewed rather than attacked, which caused him immense amusement. He ordered an attack, sententiously declaring that 'ever do the greater devour the lesser,' but as he advanced more Albanian cavalry emerged from the woods to his flank and rear, so that the innocent crescent waiting to receive him like lambs at the slaughter turned into a circle tightly drawn around his forces. By three in the afternoon the Turks had been defeated and lost their entire stores and baggage train. The proportion of cavalry in the Albanian army rose as infantrymen possessed themselves of enemy horses; and the victors rode home singing a popular but not obviously relevant song to the effect that 'the Turkish cow cannot escape from the bulls of Albania.'

By the time the story came to be written down, the Turks were credited with the loss of 8,000 dead and 2,000 prisoners. Perhaps one or even two noughts should be knocked off as having been put there by poetic licence. Much more important than the degree of carnage was the fact that a local chieftain, with only a few months preparation, had met and defeated a Turkish army in pitched battle. So far from accepting the Sultan's claim to overlordship of Albania, he had prevented him from setting his foot in Albania at all. It introduced a new military leader to the Christian powers; and congratulations began to flow in—from Venice, Hungary, Burgundy, and above all from Pope Eugenius IV. He gave thanks to God for raising up another defender for Christendom, and so began a series of papal commendations, including Nicholas V's often quoted description of him as the Athlete, or Champion, of Christendom—or, as the strict letter of the original Latin has it, 'that most redoubtable athlete and fearless warrior of the true faith.'[2]

The Turks had been beaten by the Hungarians the previous November. Now the Albanians too had repulsed them. It seemed that they were not invulnerable after all, and a mood of optimism was intensified in Europe at large. The practical effects of the victory of Nis had in fact evaporated with the approach of winter. The Christian army had pressed further south and east in the absence of serious resistance, and came to within a few days' march of the enemy capital at Adrianople. Had that been captured, the aim of destroying Turkish power in Europe might have been achieved. But armies were not then prepared, physically or morally, for warfare around the calendar. It remained, as in Roman days, an occupation for the better weather, and at the end of the campaigning season the warriors went into winter quarters to rest and recuperate.

Most victories were thus as impermanent as attempts to plough the sea: they recorded the changing fortunes of various kingdoms but did not permanently modify their character. Only when some powerful conqueror refused to recognise the rules of the game, like the Turks against the Serbs and Tamerlane in turn against the Turks, was the system of international stability shaken. Then the sovereign and his nobles were destroyed, and like a hive from which the queen bee has been taken, a society dissolved into an aimless mass of slaves. The King of Hungary and the ruler of Transylvania, true to their equally mediaeval strategy and code of conduct, returned unmolested to Budapest from their campaign, taking nine standards and four thousand prisoners as evidence of their triumphs. But they had changed nothing in the Balkan balance of power. Local Turkish forces had been engaged and worsted, but the main armies had not been brought into action, and there were in any case as many new conscripts available as might be needed.

However, Murad II was an easy-going man. He had never troubled to take Constantinople, that finest of diadems for any ambitious monarch, although it had lain within his grasp for years. He did not want expansion for its own sake: certainly not beyond his resources to administer, and as an administrator rather than a conqueror he was able to estimate these pretty shrewdly. He did not want to fan the crusading zeal among his enemies by a display of intransigence. And he also had serious difficulties in Asia Minor. Accordingly he proposed peace terms before the time came for the spring campaign of 1444. He offered to restore Serbian independence and to return to Hungary territory he had taken from her in the past. The crusade of the previous autumn had thus gained real, if limited, advantages for the countries who had contributed most. They accordingly signed a ten-year truce on these conditions.

This did not satisfy the Vatican at all. Pope Eugenius IV had wider objectives in view than a guarantee of sovereign rights here and a slight adjustment of boundary there. His strategy was to evict the Turks from Europe altogether, and the evidence suggested that this was entirely possible. The Hungarians and their allies were only one item, though the vital one, in his grand design. The Byzantine emperor had promised to set out from his capital to attack the Turks from behind. A flotilla commanded by the Pope's nephew had been sent to the Dardanelles to stop the Sultan from bringing over reinforcements from Asia Minor to Europe. On the western flank of the Turks was the new Albanian alliance under Scanderbeg.

The papal plan was certainly more comprehensive and forward-looking than any that the separate members of the alliance could produce. It recognised that the Turks, powerful and self-confident as they were, could hardly fail to expand against Christian Europe in the long run, whatever concessions they were prepared to make for the time being. Yet even Eugenius failed to appreciate the full measure of the problem. It was not enough to overcome the discords of the Christian states and put their forces under a common command, important as that was. Even when they had done this, they would not be able to rival the cohesion of the Turkish administration and the striking power of its centralised conscript army. The defeat of the Turks demanded changes in the social structure of the European states which none of them were prepared as yet to make.

To call for attack at all costs was thus to preach a policy of 'sauter pour mieux reculer.' But for the moment these consequences were hidden. What the papal legate, Cardinal Cesarini, saw was that a unique chance of final victory was in danger of being lost for ever because of an over-scrupulous respect for a word pledged to an infidel. 'I absolve your perjury and sanctify your arms' is Gibbon's celebrated version of the speech which overcame the royal niceties of conscience; 'follow my footsteps in the paths of glory and salvation; and if still ye have scruples, devolve on my head the punishment and the sin.' So strengthened, the Hungarians again marched south in September 1444 in the attempt to reach isolated Byzantium. But the papal flotilla had not managed to seal off the forces in Asia Minor, for the businesslike Genoese had ferried them across at a ducat a head, and at Varna on the Black Sea the advancing army was destroyed by Murad in person early in November. Among the dead was Cardinal Cesarini.

The Ottoman empire was now more powerful, intrinsically and comparatively, than ever before. It had destroyed the armies so carefully raised by the Christian powers and was under no obligation to keep the peace. The Despot of Serbia, content with the concessions granted to him in the spring, stayed neutral in the resumed campaign and had refused to allow Scanderbeg to send forces through Serbia to join the Hungarians. Scanderbeg had thus not been directly involved in the disastrous defeat, but he was now isolated; and the entire weight of the Turkish army was ready to fall on him whenever Murad might see fit.

Chapter Six

. . . .

WAR ON TWO FRONTS

WITH THE COLLAPSE of the Christian crusade there remained only four isolated obstacles between the Sultan Murad II and control of the entire Balkans: the city of Byzantium, enfeebled and awaiting its conqueror; a truncated Serbia, ruled by a Despot anxious not to offend the powerful Turks; the Despotate of Morea, in the far south of Greece; and the Albanian national rebellion based on Scanderbeg's possession of Kruja.

So far as Albania was concerned, the Sultan still regarded himself as the rightful sovereign of the country and liege lord of the Castrioti family. Without abating either of these claims, he sent an envoy with a private letter. As recast later for dramatic and didactic effect, this is said to have addressed Scanderbeg as a 'most ingrate foster son,' to whom Murad 'neither wisheth health nor sendeth greeting,'[1] but sent reproaches on his ingratitude for benefits heaped upon him since a child. Nonetheless, and here no doubt we have the true substance of the letter, the Sultan was prepared to forgive him and confirm him in the possession of Kruja and 'his father's kingdom' if he would return the other Albanian towns he had taken, recompense the Despot of Serbia for attacks on his territory and 'refrain from violence to the Sultan's friends and aid to his enemies.' These terms, which would in effect have recreated Kruja as a free city under the Ottoman empire, just as it had been under the Byzantine a couple of hundred years earlier, are not at all incompatible with a Turkish promise of Kruja in return for assistance or even neutrality the previous winter. Some of the Albanians were prepared to accept these terms. Scanderbeg was not. He was sure that Murad would merely await a favourable occasion to attack him, even if he did accept his offer; and, success stimulating his ambition, he pointed out that the Turks had after all been beaten. He appears to have suspected that Murad was trying to talk his way back into possession of towns he had not been able to keep by force; not, as was probably the case, that the Sultan did not want the danger and anxieties of a major campaign in the Albanian highlands in order to win back a few minor fortresses, if he could pacify the country and win its neutrality (as he had done that of Serbia) by a show of generosity with force in reserve.

We do not know what Scanderbeg replied: we have only the version as amended by the early biographers. The terms were refused, and the Sultan was told that his letter had been 'cause and matter for laughter rather than wrath or anger'. And upon receiving this insolent answer, we are shown Murad feigning detachment in order to cover a presentiment that the Albanians were going to cause him a great deal of trouble: 'in smiling wise (sometimes stroking of his beard with his hand),' he said to the absent foe 'Thou dost covet (most unhappy and unfortunate wretch) some memorable and famous kind of death, and thou shalt have it (believe me), thou shalt have it, we ourselves shall see thy obsequies performed.' With such an imperial tribute, Gjergj Castrioti would never be able to complain that his end had been ignoble.

For his part, the wretch was not aware of his unhappiness and had evidently been surprised that the vanquished should dare to try and impose terms on the victor. Had he not humbled the Ottoman empire at Torviollo, and thus given himself good cause to ask the Sultan to 'desist from objecting unto us so often the lamentable mishappe and misfortune of the Hungarians'? In fact this victory, morally important as it was for Albania, had not weakened Turkey at all. For every man lost she could put dozens more into the field straight away, a consolation not shared by her opponents. (A later Sultan was even to describe lost battles as being like shaving, after which the hair quickly grew again).

Murad decided to try a second army against the Albanians, and in 1445 a force of up to 15,000 men set out from Skopje, the Turkish administrative capital for Macedonia, under Firuz Pasha. Firuz did not intend to risk disaster at the frontier, as his predecessor had done a year earlier. He heard that the Albanian forces had been disbanded for the time being, so he planned to march quickly down the valley of the Black Drin beyond Prizren, and arrive unannounced outside Kruja itself. But his movements were quickly reported back to Kruja, and Scanderbeg collected a few thousand men and ambushed the invaders as they moved in crocodile files through one of the narrow passes near Prizren. Once again the praises of Christian Europe flowed in, for this new paladin clearly possessed generalship and not mere luck, and his triumph shone all the more brightly by comparison with the great disaster of the previous autumn.

Two successive punitive expeditions had now been ignominiously beaten before they ever left Turkish territory. The Sultan appears to have thought of leading a third one himself. Profiting by earlier mistakes, he was to have split his forces in two, outwitted Scanderbeg who would not have known which one to shadow, and eventually united both parts under the walls of Kruja. But he still feared the possibility of an attack by the Hungarians while so engaged. It would have been rash to commit himself and his main army to a risky—and what ought to have been a minor—enterprise in the mountains of Albania. So in 1446 the now annual invasion was once again led by one of his generals, this time Mustafa Pasha. Profiting again by experience, Mustafa was to avoid pitched battles and ambushes alike. Speed was to give place to safety: the army would destroy the crops as it went along, so that the local guerrillas would be unable to live off the land and so conduct harrying operations with impunity. Scanderbeg, having failed to bring Mustafa to battle, retired ostentatiously to the hills, followed by the civilians. This, it was assumed, could only mean that he had conceded victory and retired home to prepare his defence there. Vigilance was relaxed, and on the night of 27th September the Albanians entered the sleeping Turkish camp and killed those who did not manage to escape.

This third humiliation completed the first stage of Murad's education in Albanian affairs. He concluded, what he had suspected a year before, that he possessed an opponent who must be dealt with personally. Thus, until he was free to lead an army himself, and that would not be for three more years, the annual irruption of ill-fated generals was to cease. They were no match for the insolent genius of Kruja. It was not only Murad who found the need to adjust himself to the changed status of his former vassal. Gjergj Castrioti was well enough aware of his new authority, and symbolised it by the arms and the nickname he adopted. His banner was red, with a doubleheaded black eagle, 'these being the ancient arms of his family,' or more soberly, an adaptation of the Byzantine imperial eagle as probably granted to Kruja long before. His new name may have been first used in a mood of ironic bravado, but it had advantages of its own. Scanderbeg—Lord Alexander, or General Alexander—had certain overtones of grandeur not possessed by his own family name. It could be interpreted as a tribute from the enemy to his prowess; and its newness helped him in meeting a new situation inside Albania itself.

To the outside world he was already the outstanding figure among his compatriots. But to them, and especially to the older families among them, the very speed of his rise, the very success of his methods, represented a threat to the familiar pattern of life.[2] He had started on a course which, if successful, must lead him to become eventually the sovereign head of a separate nation. For the present, circumstances and the mediaeval cast of his mind led him no further than to seek a congenial overlord who would lend him support and protection. But his reputation, his talents, the strong position he had already won, combined with the needs of war to strengthen his personal position against that of the other leading families. They were prepared to accept him as first among equals; but a committee of equals could not keep the Turks at bay indefinitely, since the support he received, especially when things went badly, would always be limited by each chieftain's evaluation of his own private interests. Any attempts to centralise power, any accretion of territory to produce revenues for carrying on the war, seemed suspiciously like an attempt to increase the Castrioti possessions at the expense of rivals of equal status and more distinguished lineage.

An acute example of the stresses within the alliance arose in 1447, the first of the years in which Murad took no action against Albania. A couple of years earlier two members of the League of Lezhë—Lek Dukagjini and Lek Zaharia Altisferi—had started fighting when guests at the wedding of Scanderbeg's youngest sister, Mamitza Castrioti, who was rounding off the series of family alliances by marrying Musachi Thopia at his home between Kruja and Durazzo. Among the guests was Irene Dushmani, a woman whom both the Leks wanted to marry; and in the course of the festivities they started a quarrel over her. Two of Scanderbeg's lieutenants, Count Vrana Altisferi[3] and Vladen Yuritza, tried to separate them and were wounded, the first in the arm and the second in the head. The retainers of the two chieftains joined in, and several of them had been killed before peace was established.

Neither of the two antagonists had suffered any physical damage; but—which was much worse—one of them had been morally humiliated. Lek Dukagjini had at one point been forced to the ground in the course of the fight, and this he regarded as a stain that only blood could wipe out. Accordingly he managed, two years later, to ambush and kill his rival. Lek Zaharia had not married Irene and there was no one to inherit his fortress of Dagno. The Dukagjini hoped, therefore, to be able to take it over, as it adjoined their own lands; but Zaharia's mother decided, or was persuaded, to hand it to the Venetians in order to prevent this disgrace.

Nothing was more natural than that the Venetians should want Dagno for themselves. It was at the edge of their territory around Scutari, and one of the main trade routes to the interior of the Balkans passed immediately underneath it. A fresh claimant appeared, however. Scanderbeg demanded the fortress for the League: it was an Albanian possession, and it should remain in Albanian hands. After the Turk and the chieftains, it was now the turn of the Venetians to learn that they must adjust themselves to Gjergj Castrioti's changed status.

It would not be true to say that they were at this time opposed to Albanian national feeling. It had never entered their heads that such a thing existed. Venice wanted to be assured of her harbours and fortresses down the Adriatic, and she was content to see a number of weak, quarrelsome local chieftains whose jealousies, suitably nourished by parsimonious largesse, would preserve her from any combined attack. At the same time their ferocity, and the number of unemployed warriors each had to feed, made them amenable in case she wished to exert diplomatic pressure on Serbs or Turks. There was always the risk that they might try to blackmail her by threatening skirmishes in order to be bought off, and the Venetian government seems to have assumed this was happening over Dagno. For on 22nd February 1448 the Doge wrote to Pietro Mocenigo, Vice Captain of the Gulf ('the Gulf'—of Venice—being the patriotic term for the Adriatic), instructing him to go to Scutari as quickly as he could, and there discuss the state of Albania with the local governor, Count Paolo Loredan.

Loredan had been told two months earlier to try and reach some kind of settlement with Castrioti. If this had been done, well and good. If the negotiations were still going on, he should himself take part in them and try to smooth out any remaining difficulties with an offer of money. He was allowed to go up to one thousand ducats for Scanderbeg and the other 'lordlings' concerned: the word the Doge uses, 'signoreti', matches the brusque contempt of the offer.[4] In return the Albanian leaders must agree to defend the country and keep the roads free from violence, so that the trading caravans might pass unmolested to and from Scutari. It occurred to the Doge that perhaps the master of Kruja might not be prepared to bind himself in this way for a mere thousand ducats shared out among all his peers. In that case a truce was to be patched up and delegates sent to discuss terms in Venice itself.

Scanderbeg did not want either one or several thousand ducats. He wanted Dagno. No doubt the ducats also would follow in due course from the traders who used the road below it. So, having left a force under Vrana to watch for the approach of the Turks, he took a much larger one of infantry and cavalry and marched against Dagno. The garrison refused to surrender, so he left some of his men to start a siege, and with the remainder he turned south to threaten Durazzo.

This showed blithe self-confidence. Durazzo lay on a headland almost surrounded by the sea, and had withstood even Julius Caesar's attempts to conquer it. It was out of the question for the Albanian to take the great Byzantine walls by assault; but he could make life uncomfortable for the inhabitants by cutting them off from their local sources of food and trade. The local governor reported the danger and was reassured. Two galleys bound for Crete were redirected to Durazzo in May in order to keep watch on events there, and the Sultan was asked for help. In their anger at being unable to purchase Scanderbeg's friendship (or at least his inaction), the Venetians blinded themselves to all that had happened in the past five years, and were prepared to regard him still as a contumacious Turkish vassal who ought to be kept in order by his sovereign. And as they had a firm peace with the Sultan, they asked him to exert his authority and punish the offender and make good the damage he had caused. Durazzo had suggested making a separate peace with him, but this was sternly rejected, as it would leave him free to wage war against the other Venetian towns. Instead, attempts were to be made to wean the Dukagjini away from their alliance with him. They were neutral in the present conflict, and without them he would be 'very much weakened.'

Finally on 27th June Andrea Venier was sent from Venice with a series of instructions for all eventualities. He was first to approach the Turks and try to induce them to come to Albania as quickly as they could so that 'the said Scanderbeg may be expelled not only from Albania, but from the earth.' If it looked as though some time would elapse before the Turks could arrive to perform this service towards their allies, Venier was to go to Scanderbeg with his letters of credence and talk to him about 'the ancient and deep friendship' between Venice and old Gjon Castrioti, reminding him how many kindnesses and benefits the family had received from this friendship, and saying that Venice, who loved Scanderbeg like a son, was astonished to find him making war on her. He should persuade Scanderbeg to a truce by such arguments, seasoning them with the offer of an annual subvention, if that was what was wanted, or with the promise 'in general terms' of honours and rewards. In this way Venier was to draw out the negotiations 'from day to day, until the Turks approach and enter Albania.' At that point he should leave.

It might be that the Turks never would arrive. In that case he must 'come to the point' and offer money, though as little as possible: 'the smaller the sum, the more praiseworthy you will be.' And if a truce was found to be impossible after all, Venier must attempt to embroil Scanderbeg with the Serbian Despot, Gjergj Brancovic, and with the Dukagjini family. Although no instructions are given on how this latter intrigue was to be conducted, it may be assumed that the Serbs would be told that the Albanians wanted to strangle their trade, and the Dukagjini's that Scanderbeg wanted Dagno to add to his own private territories, putting a wedge of his own between them and Scutari as a preliminary to absorbing them at his leisure.

This obsessive cat's cradle of instructions dealt with every contingency except the only one that mattered. Scanderbeg wanted Dagno, not flattery or a subvention, and before negotiations could begin he had struck at the Venetian forces round Scutari. His temerity was extreme, for he had heard from Vrana that the Turks were intending to attack, and instead of rushing to meet them had decided he must settle accounts with the Venetians now or never. Perhaps he hoped that the hostile army would melt away at his approach, for about two thirds of them were Albanian mercenaries under one Daniele Iurich. He crossed the Drin and marched on Scutari, being opposed on 23rd July 1448 by an army reported as 15,000 strong, but almost certainly very much less than this in fact. He attacked and defeated it, and the prisoners were paraded outside the walls of the city to show the nature of the opponent that Venice had so lightly taken on.

This was a splendid gesture, worthy of a race that despises moral meanness and claims descent from Pyrrhus and Alexander, but more than that it could not be. Without artillery, there was no hope of capturing Scutari; and the annoyance of a siege was beyond his resources in view of the expected advance of the Turks. He withdrew, but left a fortified strong point of his own at Balsha, near Dagno, from which operations could be resumed in the future. Venice, for her part, prepared to await the news of Scanderbeg's destruction at the faithful hand of her Turkish ally. In the meantime she warned Venier not to give hospitality on Venetian territory to any Albanian refugees in case the Sultan should be annoyed, and as soon as the Albanian forces had left she attacked Balsha, forced the defender, Marino Spano, to evacuate it, and then burnt it to the ground.

Spano had had the misfortune to be given Scanderbeg's nephew Hamza (son of his eldest brother Stanisha) as a colleague in the defence of the new fortress. Hamza was young, popular and ardent for fame, and Albanian soldiers preferred attacking an enemy to the boredom of garrison duty. So, against Spano's advice, he took some of the meagre enough force to lead an attack on a nearby town of Drivasta. But the inhabitants there preferred offence to defence as well as he. They sallied out under their leader Ndreu Angeli; and Hamza, frustrated and furious, allowed himself to lay waste the fields around the town. He was too ashamed to encounter Spano, whose defeat he might be held to have caused, but went straight to his uncle, whose anger blazed out at the thought of innocent Albanian blood being shed by an Albanian commander. Hamza was silent, 'only turning himself a little to his companions, "Good God" (quoth he), "there is nothing more infamous than a man that is vanquished; for he must on the one side accept to endure the insolence and triumph of his enemies; and on the other the fearful countenance and wrathful visage of his friends."'

Friends interceded and Scanderbeg was pacified quickly, 'so familiar and courteous was his disposition.' He put Hamza in charge of the siege of Dagno, for he had not given up hopes of conquering it yet; but though this was a mark of confidence that the young man had yet done nothing to deserve, it was received with some reluctance. No doubt Hamza wanted to distinguish himself in the coming war with the Turks, where the opportunities would be greater and a hero's prestige higher. We do not know why the opportunity was not granted him. Had Scanderbeg reflected that this nephew of his, born a Muslim and baptised only after the battle of Nis, might be vulnerable to Turkish overtures? Or that as the son of an eldest son he might be held the true heir of Gjon Castrioti's lands, and thus prove too valuable a hostage if he fell into the enemy's hands?

The Turkish army, 15,000 strong we are told, began to move in from Ohrida under the leadership of Mustafa Pasha, and Count Vrana harassed and slowed it down until the commander could bring the bulk of his forces from Scutari. This force was more successful than the earlier ones, for it penetrated to within a few miles of Kruja before it was finally brought to battle. As the two armies met, a Turk called Karagöz shouted a challenge to his foes, and it was taken up by Pal Manasi on the Albanian side. The Turk suggested that the body of the vanquished should be handed over to the victor; the Albanian agreed, as he was sure that his leader would not want back that which had shown itself 'so faint and sluggish as to be vanquished.' The two men were well matched, and they rode towards each other with 'rich cassocks made of silk, shining very bright and glistering.' The Turk was pierced through the eye and then beheaded, and the champion was rewarded with 'a rich coat of arms of gold tissue and a great demesne and livelihood.' Scanderbeg seconded the personal victory in his speech to the troops, urging them, "Go you to, therefore, and Pass on hardly in this path of honour;" and the Turks, perhaps dispirited by the result of this personal combat, gave way almost as soon as the battle started. Standards, baggage train, even the Turkish general himself fell into the hands of the Albanians, and his sovereign had to pay 25,000 ducats to get him back.

Glorious as the victory was, the effect was spoiled by news of the loss of Balsha, which now reached the main army. Scanderbeg took it as a personal outrage that the people of Scutari, whose possessions he had tried to spare in the late fighting, should have attacked him in this way. So, he who had just defeated a Turkish army, reduced himself in his anger to a frontier marauder and did what damage he could to the Venetian possession nearest to hand. He had blamed 'the immoderate choler of his nephew but could not acknowledge the infirmities of his own passion.' It was quenched, however, by the cold and rain of winter, and he settled down into winter quarters under the besieged and disputed fortress of Dagno.

The methods of the Venetians might have been tortuous and their motives often petty, but they remained magnificently free from illusions. The Sultan had failed to eject Scanderbeg from Ottoman territory, let alone from Albania or the world of the living. If he could not be destroyed, he must be accepted. The wild beast must be forgotten and the dear son embraced again.

Accordingly, negotiations for peace were opened at Lezhë, with Paolo Loredan and Andrea Venier as the Venetian representatives; and Gjergj Pellini, Abbot of St. Mary of Rotezo, and Bishop Andrev of Kruja as representatives of Gjergj Castrioti, Nicholas Dukagjini and the other Albanian chiefs. Peace was signed between them on 4th October 1448.

The treaty contained formal preliminaries on the desire of the illustrious Venetian nobles on the one hand and the magnificent Scanderbeg and the worthy Dukagjini on the other (as representatives of the Albanian lords) to reach a true, sound and lasting peace. There was then a flourish of generosity from the Venetians, who were ready to pardon the offences and injuries committed by the Albanians and take them for 'good, true and dear friends and neighbours'. The heart of the agreement was that Scanderbeg and his male heirs were to receive 1,400 ducats a year, including 200 that were already being paid to him by the local authorities at Durazzo, and that he would relinquish Dagno and the surrounding lands to Venice, and would retire from the Venetian territory he still occupied around the river Drin. Both he and Dukagjini pledged themselves not to oppose any action Venice might take to deal with Pal Dukagjini, who had profited by the war to take a few villages for himself around Dagno. Scanderbeg was also to have a payment of a further 1,400 ducats when the time arose to take what forces he could and effect a junction with those of Gjon Hunyadi, now the ruler of Hungary. He was also given the right to buy two hundred loads of salt a year from Durazzo without payment of duty, as Gjergj Arianiti, the only other Albanian leader mentioned by name, was to be allowed to buy bread free of tax there. The subjects of either side who had rebelled and fought against their rulers were to be pardoned and allowed to return home, and Scanderbeg and his colleagues were to have the right to take refuge on Venetian territory in case of need. There was also to be an exchange of gifts each year 'in accordance with ancient custom': Venice was to give Scanderbeg two scarlet robes, and would receive from him two hares and two falcons, symbols presumably of speed and heroism.

On the essential point, the future of Dagno, Venice had her own way. This could have been foreseen once the Turks resumed their attacks, for it was impossible to think of conducting a war on two fronts against two such powerful opponents. Whatever rashness Scanderbeg's anger may have tempted him into, he could not act indefinitely without the support of the other chieftains, especially the Dukagjini, whom the Venetians managed to bring into the treaty discussions as principals on the Albanian side, thus pointing out to the world at large that he did not as yet possess the right to speak exclusively for all the Albanians. The treaty was thus in some ways a moral as well as a material victory for Venice. But so it was for Gjergj Castrioti. He was now 'the magnificent Scanderbeg'; he had been involved in negotiations as an equal and not as a penurious pensioner to be bought off in a hole-and-corner fashion. And though he was now receiving a subsidy by treaty, it was on a scale beyond anything that the Venetians had thought of offering hitherto. It was related to the political and military significance of the Albanian and not to his personal nuisance value. Both sides, that is to say, made a realistic appraisal of each other's real power, and bowed to the facts.

The treaty was ratified in Venice on 21st April 1449, and the envoy sent to sign it tried also to use the end of the war as the foundation for a new and closer relationship between Venetians and Albanians. For his own purposes, Scanderbeg asked for artillery-men. The Venetians, probably remembering how useful to them his lack of such people had been at the time of the siege of Scutari, said he could certainly have them if he was prepared to pay for them. His offer of cavalry and infantry for the Venetian forces, as a method of finding them employment, was declined with fulsome thanks, on the grounds that if he used them to defend his own realm, Venice would consider them as useful to her as though they served her directly. Quite such suavity of evasion was not possible in answering a further and more fundamental suggestion: that Venice should take over the protection of

Scanderbeg's territory, in return for which he offered to transfer to her the 6,000 ducats a year he paid—or at least was nominally bound to pay—to the Turks as tribute. He was offering, that is, to reject the sovereignty of the Sultan for that of the Doge, and by so doing threatened, and clearly hoped, to turn any local struggle between Turkey and Albania into a general one between Turkey and Venice. Venice excused herself on the grounds that her own treaty of peace with the Sultan prevented her from seeking to turn him from his undertakings.

This offer and its refusal marked the limits of any possible understanding between the two parties. In strict legality, Albania, apart from the towns held by Venice, was Ottoman territory, and the Albanian chiefs were merely rebellious feudatories of the Sultan. It might be unfortunate, perhaps, that Christians should be under Muslim rule; but at least, the Venetians could argue to their more zealous neighbours, they had a large degree of freedom so long as they did not provoke Ottoman reprisals. And Venice was well aware that both sides could make tempting offers to the Albanians: if she started an auction in favours, the Turks might well instigate attacks on her own towns.

When for her own reasons Venice was on bad terms with Turkey, she could with impunity encourage the Albanians to act independently, as in the case of Gjon Castrioti in 1430. But when by doing so they caused her any embarrassment, as at Dagno more recently, she quickly resumed her legalistic point of view and called on the Sultan to keep his subjects in order. Scanderbeg sought to deprive her of this resource by showing his willingness to throw off even nominal Turkish overlordship if she would take the responsibility of assuming it for herself. Neither his own strength nor the political ideas of fifteenth-century Christendom justified him in claiming personal sovereignty over Albania. He had a master, the Sultan, whose religion and rule he had rejected, and he was now looking for a Christian under whose protection he could conserve and expand his power and prepare to fight the Turks with a chance of success. Venice made clear that whoever else might volunteer for this heavy and compromising role, it would not be she.

Chapter Seven

. . . .

SCANDERBEG AGAINST THE SULTAN

IF THE VENETIANS would not pay his troops of their own free will, then the Turks must be forced to; so, in the intervals of making war on the one and repelling attacks by the other, Scanderbeg led his men in raids on Ottoman Macedonia, taking with them the offer of conversion or death, and returning with all the spoil they could find. 'Hereof it grew that the Princes (his neighbours) were wont (in way of mirth and jest) to call the territorie of the enemie, Scanderbeg his treasurie.' Peace with Venice, now sealed with 'diverse very rich and princely presents,' and the offer of citizenship to the Albanian leader and his posterity for ever, freed him for this stimulating and profitable occupation. When sated of it, he and his guard retired to Kruja to enjoy their rest, guarded by a screen of three thousand men along the frontier.

The Sultan Murad was an easy going man under great provocation, but he had a strong sense of the respect owed to him, and of the protection which his own subjects had a right to demand from him. He must therefore make an end, if not of the rebel himself, at least of these incessant raids. So far all the forces sent against Kruja had been defeated and repelled, but they had served his broader purposes. They had at least kept Castrioti tied down in his own country and prevented him from either joining Hunyadi and the Hungarians or, in association with them, from intimidating the Sultan's weak-kneed father-in-law, the Despot of Serbia, into joining them on a campaign to avenge the defeat of Varna. For Hunyadi, having assumed the regency of Hungary after the death of the young king, had prepared a new army; and between August 1448, when Scanderbeg repelled Mustafa Pasha's army, and October of the same year, when he finally came to terms with the Venetians, Murad was able without distraction to meet the long-awaited Hungarian army and defeat it on the now (for the Turks) doubly well-omened plain of Kosova. Hunyadi himself fell into the hands of the Serbs, who feared his aggressiveness almost as greatly as they feared the Turks; and before they let him go he was made to sign a peace treaty returning territory he had previously taken from them, including their strongest fortress of Belgrade on the Danube.

There was now no immediate threat of a combined Christian attack on the Turks, and Murad was able to turn his personal attention, and as great a military force as he needed, to the task of subduing Gjergj Castrioti. The strategic position of the Albanians depended on a triangle of fortresses: Svetigrad, which covered the passes from Macedonia in the east; Berat, which covered the passes from Greece; and Kruja, the heart and head of the resistance. Svetigrad was the natural first choice. It was a Turkish possession, lost in a moment of weakness. It was an Albanian bridgehead in Turkish territory, making possible these frequent marauding raids; and it could be a grave danger if another anti-Ottoman coalition were to be built up in the future. So long as Svetigrad was in Albanian hands, Scanderbeg could hope to fight his battles on the Sultan' s territory rather than his own. Murad therefore decided to take Svetigrad, thus showing the patient common sense that marked all his actions.

While the Sultan took his decisions like a tireless, dispassionate administrator, it was immediately assumed in Kruja (such is the endemic vanity of the Balkan mountaineer) that he was raising his new army to settle his personal quarrel with Scanderbeg. Honour, not public policy, was seen as the mainspring of his actions. 'No house, street, nor corner of the town was exempted from grief and sorrow' as the people lamented the fate that was coming upon them. The churches were full of men and women interceding for help; and the women tore their faces and beat their breasts to call up the aid of older and forgotten gods. The priests played their part in improving the morale of both army and people, telling of the celestial visions they had had, all of which proved that the national hero would destroy the infidel invader. Scanderbeg himself vouchsafed a vision that had come to him: St. George, the Christian warrior and the patron saint of Albania, had personally presented him with a flaming sword to destroy the enemies of the true religion.

Not content to depend merely on supernatural help, he pressed forward more material preparations for meeting the forthcoming invasion. All able-bodied men were conscripted for the armies, and those who could not actively help in the fighting, the old men, the women and the children, were assembled inside the towns or sent down to the sea coast. The garrison at Kruja, 'the key of all his realm', was strengthened. Count Vrana was appointed governor and left in charge. Scanderbeg addressed the defenders and then consulted his allies, Moses Golemi and the other fighting chieftains, on the conduct of the campaign. Passing through the threatened countryside, he did 'enflame the faithful hearts of his subjects, sometimes by commending them, sometimes by presents and gifts, and sometimes by the shewes and representations of the danger imminent'. So he came to Svetigrad, which was defended by men of Dibra under Peter Perlat.

On 14th May 1449 Murad also appeared there, just as the corn which was to feed his armies had begun to sprout, and the snows had vanished, showing the fresh green of the grass in the clear upland valley. He brought with him an enormous force. Later estimates went as high as 150,000 men; and exaggerated as such a figure may be, it indicated that he intended leaving nothing to chance. Certainly the Albanians now appreciated for the first time the vast power deployed against them; and they may well have felt, as did the Serbian storyteller on a similar occasion, that 'the Sultan had so many men that a horseman could not ride from one wing of his army to the other in a fortnight; the plain. . . was a mass of steel; horse stood against horse, man against man; the spears formed a thick forest; the banners obscured the sun, and there was no space for a drop of water to fall between them.' They pressed forward, the cavalry with lance and plate of mail and great swinging mace, like a spiked chestnut of iron; the infantry with sword and shield, among them Murad's newly organised corps of Janissaries, and even, we are told, three thousand debtors and bankrupts taking to war as a means of buying their freedom again.

The first act of war was to parade this host around the walls, in order to leave the garrison in no doubt about the size of the force that had been brought against them. Then Murad began to consider how he might subdue the fortress. It was not easy to assault, being on the crown of a hill, so his first thought was naturally to win the population over by flattery and the governor by money. He offered to respect all the old privileges and liberties of Svetigrad if it gave itself up to him, and he promised Perlat 300,000 aspers for the formality of opening the gates and letting him in. The heralds bearing these offers thought it wiser to approach the city walls under cover of night. They were mocked for not daring to expose their dark suggestions to the light of day, but their suggestion of a delegation to discuss the terms was accepted, and next day an Albanian-speaking pasha arrived with three soldiers and two servants. They were interviewed in the church of Svetigrad, but only the elders and principle men of the town were allowed to attend; the younger element were excluded, possibly because the courtesies incidental to such a meeting might have seemed treachery to them, provoking some rash action on their part. Perlat congratulated the pasha on his speech, but said that as they were all 'vowed to the maintenance of their liberty,' Murad would have to try and defeat them by force of arms. Before letting the embassy depart he gave it a splendid dinner so that they should return with the impression that Svetigrad was well equipped for a lengthy siege.

The unprecedented size of the Sultan's army seems to have troubled Scanderbeg because of its possible effect on the morale of the Albanians. He moved from village to village, sometimes travelling disguised as a simple soldier, and encouraging the fighting spirit by occasional judicious oratory. He even thought it worthwhile to go back to Kruja and harangue the garrison there. Vrana was inclined to see in this a lack of trust, and reacted accordingly: 'It shall be more pleasing, and farre more acceptable unto us beyond comparison, to see the face and countenance of the enemy, than to have thy presence and company, because thou bringest us nothing but secret plaintes and doubtfull feares, as though we were inclining to revolt and were likely to prove disloyal.' The unwelcome visitor could only protest that he came not to exhort but to give news of the campaign. Taking the rebuke to heart, he returned to Svetigrad to give what help he could to the garrison.

What were the 'secret plaintes and doubtfull feares' that Scanderbeg brought back with him from the front, and Vrana did not want to be troubled with? For the moment, the leader's self-confidence had been disturbed, evidently. To some extent, no doubt, the sight for the first time of Turkey's main fighting force had revealed to him the true nature of the enemy he had light-heartedly conjured up by his defection at Nis. But its main effect was felt by him indirectly, through the change he found in the chieftains of the Dibra region among whom the imperial forces were now encamped. Scanderbeg's own lands were miles away to the west, and protected by a high mountain range; and if the worst should happen, he could always retire into Kruja and hope to tire out an invader. But they were completely exposed to the finest army in the world, and while their patriotism may not have diminished, their prudence quickly grew to balance it. These local leaders sought to persuade Scanderbeg not to attack the enemy single-handed, but to draw up his plans in concert with them. In other words, they would give no help to schemes that did not have their approval. Whatever their hopes for Svetigrad, they would not rashly invite disaster for themselves by provoking the besiegers.

Left thus largely to his own resources, and constantly fearing that Murad's patrols might discover where he was hiding, Scanderbeg moved around the Dibra hills a prey to restlessness and almost animal suspicion. This was so far removed from his usual coolness in action that people around him could not make out whether it was genuine, or assumed to prevent his followers from becoming complacent. 'For this expert chieftain either was continually in fear and doubt, or else he did purposely fain and dissemble a kind of fear by a singular dexterity of his spirit, to the intent that he might make his soldiers more wary, circumspect and advised, and the more attentive to all accidents whatsoever.' By way of warning, he was constantly telling his men that more commanders had been beaten by surprise attacks than by set battles, and that he would rather fight ten men openly and prepared than two by surprise. There seems no doubt that the worry and fear were genuine for to the usual uncertainties of guerrilla warfare—the possibility of unexpected attack present to the minds of both hunter and hunted—were added this special one that he was operating on the territory of allies on whose loyalty he could not count for certain. At the same time he could not withdraw; both honour and his military sense told him he must do what he could, by harassing the Turks, to ease the burden of the Svetigrad garrison.

He aimed to evade the Turkish patrols and close in to attack the main encampment. On 22nd June he reached a hill overlooking it, and saw his quarry below. It was two o'clock on a hot afternoon and the men were asleep, 'wallowing all along under their tents pell mell amongst their horses.' There came to him the idea, novel for the time, of a night attack. He approached to within about half a mile and sent on a couple of men to reconnoitre. One of them was Moses of Dibra who, dressed as a peasant but with a sword for use in case of danger, managed to get right inside the camp and look around. Scanderbeg then spoke to his troops and, bashful perhaps since his reception by Vrana at Kruja, excused himself for thinking a speech necessary. It was not that he did not think them brave, but he ought perhaps to give them some advice in view of 'the novelty of the course which we now take, and this unaccustomed fashion of fight which we are now to begin.' What he had to tell them was to keep their minds off booty, the hardest of all lessons for an impoverished Albanian mountaineer to learn. He wanted them to preserve discipline until the end of the operation, and not to burden themselves with private loot in case the Turks rallied and counter-attacked. He was not looking for pillage, but was trying to destroy the Turkish sense of security, to make the besiegers feel that they were themselves besieged by an invisible enemy who might strike anywhere, at any time. Thus, perhaps, they might eventually be induced to raise the siege and go home.

It was a brilliant idea but it had not been quite thoroughly enough rehearsed. The noise of the Albanian armour and the neighing of the horses prevented the surprise from being complete; while the periphery of the camp was thrown into confusion at the point of attack, the bulk of the troops in the centre had time to organise themselves and march out in close formation, a phalanx too solid for the invading cavalry to penetrate. The victory was real but limited, and the Albanians retired about a mile away to their own camp, carrying the heads of slaughtered Turks, which 'did singularly grace and beautify the sight of this triumph.'

To prevent further such disasters the Sultan detached a contingent to hunt down Scanderbeg's forces and so leave the main army unmolested. Firuz Pasha was chosen for this task, and seems to have been given some of the worst troops available, either Asians or Balkan nationals pressed into Turkish service. There was a high rate of desertion. Such a force was no match for a commander familiar with the wild Dibra country and, as might have been expected, it was destroyed and its baggage train captured.

There was in fact so much booty that merchants came over from Italy to buy or to barter goods of which the Albanians stood in need.

In his main purpose Murad, so far, had no better fortune. At one point, after a three day assault by artillery, a breach was made in the walls, but an infantry attack to profit by this failed to reach the top of the hill on which the fortress stood. The feeling gained ground that the Sultan must sooner or later acknowledge defeat and return to Adrianople, at least until the next spring. But there was no means of compelling him to go, and apart from occasional guerrilla attacks, the Albanians could only wait and hope.

Both leaders worried about what they should do next. Scanderbeg was disturbed that inactivity might give the defenders time to think of the peril in which they stood, and have their resolution weakened thereby. 'He was not ignorant that the walls of many towns and the bodies of many men who had contemned all danger of sword and armour, who were unconquerable by force, and against whom iron could not prevail, had yet been tempted and overcome by gold and silver.' The Sultan was advised to despoil the countryside so that his enemies would have nothing to live on; but he replied that his opponent had done that already. He also refused to think of wasting more men in chasing the Albanians through their thick native forests. In a burst of contempt born of frustration he suggested that such a country was best left alone as 'a covert for wild and savage beasts,' being no fit place for 'men imbued with reason and discretion.' Another policy suggested to him was to leave Svetigrad and strike at Kruja, the heart of Albanian resistance. This the Sultan refused to think of; he had already consumed three months of the campaigning season, Kruja would be even better defended than Svetigrad, and he was not prepared to risk having to retreat through the passes on the eve of winter, with an unsubdued fortress between him and his capital.

Nothing remained then but to continue the attempts at assault and bribery. What exactly happened next is obscure. The official account is that the Turks finally discovered someone who was willing to throw a dead dog in the Svetigrad well, and that the Dibrian garrison, who belonged to the Orthodox Church, refused to drink of it and, 'intoxicated with foolish scrupulosity,' insisted on surrender, though their commander and some of the inhabitants had drunk the water and come to no harm. It is most unlikely that there was only one well in such a large and important town.[1]

Equally there seems no reason why Orthodox Christians should be less willing than Roman Catholics to drink water that contained a dead dog: this part of the story seems merely to point to a resentment felt against the Orthodox Dibrians on religious and cultural grounds by the more westerly Roman Catholics to whom we owe the story. It has been suggested as more likely that the Turks managed to cut off much, if not all, of the town's supplies of water; but even if they did not, the increased population caused by the presence of refugees and garrison would place a heavier strain than usual on the wells, and if the summer happened to be unduly hot they may well have dried up. The story of the dead dog seems to suggest that the wells, their levels lowered, began to yield the detritus of years and showed the soldiers they must either give up the fortress or die of thirst.

The most that Perlat could now hope for was that his men would be allowed to pass unhindered through the Turkish lines. Murad gave his word, and the town was handed over. The Sultan had been joined on this campaign by his son Mehmet, later to be known as the Conqueror of Constantinople. Mehmet is now said to have urged that the garrison should be massacred in order that the Turks might show themselves 'by all possible means mortal enemies to the Christians.' His father replied with a simple maxim of statecraft: society endures only if pledged faith is observed. He was probably conscious of the moral (and material) victory he had won when his Christian opponents rejected the ten year treaty of peace they had signed with him, and had no intention of putting himself in the wrong at the moment of triumph. He rebuilt the damaged walls, provisioned the place for a year, left a garrison of Janissaries and returned to Adrianople, content with his season's campaigning.

Safe though they were from enemy reprisals, the garrison of Dibrians still had to meet their own commander-in-chief. They placed their girdles round their necks as halters, and threw themselves on the ground at his feet. There was no suggestion of deliberate treachery, and little therefore that he could do but formally forgive them for the surrender, thank them for fighting so long and so well, and offer presents of money and horses to the reluctant Perlat, who now abandoned war and retired to become an abbot in a monastery in Mirdita. Scanderbeg shadowed the Turkish forces as they moved eastwards in the hope of doing them some serious damage before they reached home, but he had too few men to risk provoking them. He said now, as he so often did when discretion held him back, 'I would rather this place were noted as the scene of my flight than of my grave.'

The loss of Svetigrad was a terrible one, however, and not to be alleviated by pleasantries. It meant that the Turks could march well into Albania before meeting serious opposition. The Turks were now able to launch as many as three separate but co-ordinated attacks, dissipating the Albanian forces and keeping them in the dark as to where the main blow would fall. It was now to be expected that Murad would follow up his advantage with an expedition against Kruja, and Scanderbeg decided he must make some attempt to retake the lost fortress. From late September, therefore, the new Turkish garrison was itself being besieged. Scanderbeg's horsemen had to keep out of range of the Turkish arquebusiers, but the foot soldiers went nearer under cover of wooden palisades. There was nothing they could do, however, to make an impression on the rebuilt walls. Neither the Albanian archers, the Serbian swordsmen or other foreigners who had been attracted by hatred of Islam or the lure of booty could hope to storm such a fortress; and the only artillery was a few small field pieces in the charge of about fifty French mercenaries.

The Albanians rode up and down before the walls to try to induce the garrison to come out and fight; but the torrential autumn rains had now begun, and the sight of these dripping zealots ploughing through the mud provoked mirth rather than anger. Three frustrated attempts were made to enter Svetigrad by ladders placed against the walls, but the spirit of the men was affected by the weather and the rumour that Murad was on his way back to relieve the garrison. On 23rd October, Scanderbeg acknowledged defeat by returning to Kruja to make preparations for the inevitable testing time to come.

In Kruja, after so long in the field, he found 'a new kind of exercise wherewith he was unacquainted, namely to the administration of justice, and to matters of state.' One of these was the proposal by his neighbours and allies that he should marry and beget an heir for Albania. He was now in his late thirties, but he was also the centre of an alliance of chieftains, and whoever he chose as a father-in-law, he must disappoint the remainder and run the risk of straining the League of Lezhë by personal jealousies, just at the moment when it must be prepared to meet its first great test.

Equally, he could not as yet choose a bride from outside this narrow circle, and so appear to set himself apart from it, although Barletius suspects that he already had somewhat grander notions of what his bride should be like: 'the haughtinesse of his conceiptes did aim at greater matters.' So he answered the suggestion with banter. There was nothing, he told them, 'so burdensome and insupportable to a free mind as the dominion of a wife.' Marriage would curtail his liberty. It would probably be tempting fortune, too. However, he agreed on a compromise. 'Notwithstanding at the last because he would not seem one that was given to over much austerity, nor to neglect the good zeal and sincere affection of his friends,' he was finally persuaded 'to submit himself to that yoake.' His only condition was that he should not be expected to marry until Svetigrad had been recovered, as it would be a disgrace to enjoy all the junketings of a marriage ceremony while his friends were still under the Turkish tyranny. His friends, 'yielding him a thousand thanks as if he had done them some special grace and favour,' spread the news of his decision.

Their request, and his promise, had been made before the short and abortive campaign at Svetigrad, but as the town was still held by the Turks he was still under no obligation to marry, and could concentrate on preparing for the coming Turkish attack. Count Vrana was confirmed as governor of Kruja; a popular choice, for he was a man of courage and had the reputation of never trying to take for himself the credit due to others. As if this were not commendable and unusual enough, 'the ancient nobility of his race did greatly beautify and (as it were) season all these good parts in him.' He was given a garrison of 2,000 men, mostly arquebusiers and crossbow men, including Albanians, Italians and Germans; and as at Svetigrad the artillery was in the hands of Frenchmen, who received five crowns a day in both peace and war. New turrets and platforms were built, and the walls were strengthened on the Tirana side, where age had weakened them. The place was victualled for a year. This would have been impossible from the country's own resources, because of the devastation and neglect of recent years; but the needs of Kruja and the other smaller garrisons such as Stellusa and Petrela were met by the Venetians. They, despite their peace treaty with the Turks, furnished the Albanians 'of victuals secretly and under hand.' Scanderbeg was personally well aware of the value of Venetian help, limited though it was in this fashion. More than heroism was needed to resist the Turks, and he was to acknowledge how Venice had made it possible for him to win some of his most memorable triumphs. But some of his supporters, particularly in the papal camp, were less inclined to see the wisdom of such limited engagement.

Barletius, who acknowledges Scanderbeg's own attitude, feels impelled to qualify it immediately: '...but many will marvel, no less than I myself, that the Venetians should make this peace with the Infidel not comprising Scanderbeg in the same ... For my part I will not wrong that Senat which hath ever been reputed both sage and religious, to suspect that they did it in any other respect and consideration, but only for the good and preservation of Greece.' He refrains from pointing out that they did not even preserve Greece, but lost the greater part of their possessions there some years later. However, had they challenged Murad, they would probably have lost them sooner, and they might equally have lost the Albanian towns from which Kruja was able to draw food and supplies.

Once the towns were supplied and garrisoned, there was little to do but wait until Murad was ready to attack. Impatient for action, Scanderbeg released his physical and nervous energy in a series of tours of the threatened land, pounding through the winter snow, sometimes disguised as a shepherd and sometimes on horseback. Accompanied by no more than ten followers or so, he moved as far as the very hills of Svetigrad, discussing prospects with his troops on the Macedonian frontier, where about two thousand men were living in hastily built cabins, guarding against a surprise attack. But no surprise attack came. The Sultan was wintering more peaceably in his capital, and his troops had been disbanded to their homes, waiting for the good weather when they could march out and destroy the Albanian rebel.

The print is a copy after an etching by Johannes van Vliet made in 1631 to Rembrandt's design. By courtesy of Patricia Nugee

Scanderbeg by an unknow artist from the collection of Galleria degli Uffizi, Firenze

Scanderbeg, a wall painting in a house where Scanderbeg stayed in Rome

Scanderbeg and Huniad. An 18th century engraving.

Scanderberg by an anonymous artist at the end of XVIIth century, from the private collection in Öl auf Leinwand, Germany

Armamentarium Heroicum 1593. From "Albanien, Schätze aus dem Land der Skipetaren", Verlag Philipp von Zabern, 1988

Donika, Scanderbeg's wife, an Italian engraving of the XVIth *century*

Scanderbeg (1483 - 15552), from Paulus Jovius, Scanderbeg, Rome 1968

Chapter Eight

. . . .

'That Furious and Untamed Lion'

When spring arrived, the Sultan Murad II and his vast army moved westwards to destroy the 'inexpugnable walls' of Kruja. With it went the new weapons, the marks of Turkish technical superiority, the small artillery on the backs of the lunging camels and the supplies of brass and other metals from which the great guns were to be cast on the spot. And with these again a mass of crowbars, mattocks and pickaxes for undermining the walls. Each fighting man, and there may have been as many as 160,000 of them, brought with him provisions for several days so that he could feed himself on the march through the forests and mountains between Macedonia and the Adriatic plains.

The march began on 5th April 1450. As he heard the vanguard was due to arrive, Scanderbeg with a few days in hand destroyed the crops in its path and withdrew his garrisons from the frontier, leaving only a few scouts to keep him informed of what was happening. For ease of movement, to make sure that a single defeat would not end the campaign, and to have a reserve of recruits to draw on in emergency, he kept only 8,000 men under arms, a quarter of them infantry. With these he moved back to Mount Tumenishta, four miles to the north east of Kruja, and there waited until he could be sure what the Turks proposed to do.

Their lightly-armed vanguard, perhaps a quarter of the entire force, thus met no resistance and was able to pitch camp unmolested in the coastal plain to the west of Tirana. There was now nearly a month to wait before the Sultan himself arrived, due to the delays in bringing his huge baggage train through the wild country. When he finally arrived and pitched his tents before Kruja, 'you may imagine you see his companies disposed all over the fields, with tents and Pavilions like a fleet at anchor on the dark green sea of Plain, stretching white and formidable for six miles or so.' All this took place within sight of the garrison, who tried to show their enemy how little concerned they were by appearing in full view, singing around their camp fires. At other times 'you might have seen the soldiers, standing upon the walls, as gallant and resolute as was possible, every man with a kind of jealousy inquiring and entermedling with the charge and duty of others.' And Vrana would encourage them by walking round, talking to the Albanians and Italians himself, and to the French and other nationalities through an interpreter. The city did not exist to protect them, he pointed out, but they to protect the city. And he casually took hold of a soldier to illustrate his point: 'These are the bulwarks of cities and towns; these are the firm and substantial ramparts of wall; these be the stones that are not batterable; this is the strongest and surest kind of lime and mortar.' Thus encouraged, the soldiers threatened to shoot the envoys that came with offers from Murad. They were not admitted to the town but merely allowed to approach the gate, and there they made their offer of safe conduct for the garrison if it surrendered, with a payment of 200,000 aspers and the offer of religious freedom for the townspeople. His proposals rejected, the Sultan had no alternative but to begin the siege.

Nothing now remains of Kruja but the vestige of a single watch tower; like the canvas of the Turkish tents, its cliffs of stone exist only in the imagination. Enough examples of mediaeval fortresses still exist in the Balkans and elsewhere, however, to show what it must have looked like, with its vertical walls broken every so often by towers. On a magnificent scale it presented the simple, toy castle appearance still familiar in a world where gunpowder was a novelty, and the main threat came from scaling ladders, fire, arrows and battering rams. To batter these walls down, it was proposed to cast ten pieces of artillery on the spot, six to take 200-pounder cannon-balls and four to take the then tremendous 600-pounders.

Against this formidable armament, which could tear holes in any existing walls, the defenders could rely on two factors apart from their own bravery. Though intimidating, these guns were not yet reliable, either with regard to accuracy, speed or safety. They might equally well overshoot their mark as hit it. If they did succeed, they were too hot and cumbersome to use again immediately to widen the breach. And as like as not they would blow up and kill attackers rather than the attacked. Turkish artillery was to become a decisive weapon in later campaigns, but for the moment its effect was as much moral as material. In the case of Kruja, too, the Turks were at a further disadvantage. The fortress did not stand up isolated in the middle of the countryside, or even as at Svetigrad on the crown of a hill. Like an eagle's nest, it was almost part of the mountain against which it had been built. It was one thing to use a bombard against an isolated town, and quite another to fight the works of nature; and as the biggest guns could be fired only two or three times a day—even on the days they did not disintegrate and require recasting—the men of Kruja had reasonable cause for their optimism.

The first fortnight or so was spent in casting the artillery. Two large and four small guns were placed on the Tirana side, where weaknesses had been noted earlier by both defenders and attackers, and the remainder were aimed at the main gateway. When a large breach had finally been made, the Turks prepared to go in by the use of scaling ladders, and the crown prince Mehmet promised 100,000 aspers to the man who first planted the Ottoman colours on the ramparts.

Both the prince and his father addressed the troops, who then ate a meal. By the time they were all drawn up ready to advance it was high noon in the heat of summer. Though it might have been better, and certainly more congenial, to postpone the attack until a cooler part of the day, Murad wanted the action to be over before dark. He was rightly afraid that Scanderbeg might come down from Tumenishta under cover of dusk and attack his men from behind. He thus also sent a company of men to keep the Albanian mobile force in sight, for 'he was wont ever to say nothing was sufficient to make resistance against the fierceness and fury of this beast,' his opponent; and so it proved. Scanderbeg did manage, at the height of the attack, to make a quick raid on the Turkish encampment, killing a few hundred men (and almost losing his own life) and doing a certain amount of damage, but above all showing that the Sultan's great army was not immune from reprisals. The news of the diversion caused the prince to swear that 'he would get this savage wild beast to fall into his snares' and he was almost successful.

Scanderbeg was lost in the counter-attack for some time, and when he did rejoin the bulk of his men, his shield was 'so battered that its shape was scarce to be discerned.' He himself was unwounded, and he lost only ten dead and a handful of men wounded; but the assault on Kruja continued despite his diversion, the guns thundering from time to time above the rallying blasts of the trumpets and the echoes of the drums.

The defenders, however, were looking after themselves well enough. Sixty of them even sallied out to do whatever damage they could, and those who remained on the walls repelled all attempts to enter. The main weight of the attack had come from the Tirana side, and here the Turkish losses were correspondingly heavy, for 'the arrows did fly so thick in the air, as if it had been a cloud darkening the brightness and clearness of the sun.' When after two hours the first wave had clearly failed, the Sultan doubted whether he would be justified in ordering another. The staff persuaded him that he should; their arguments were his own honour, his desire for revenge and the need to exhaust the already hard-pressed garrison.

During the second phase the Turks, as enthusiastic as when

the first charge began, even tried to break through the gate with their lances. But the walls still held. Murad saw that he was losing men pointlessly, for there was no hope of victory that day. He ordered the retreat to be sounded, and for the next two days held a council of his generals to decide what should be done next.

One immediate precaution was to guard the camp against a further surprise attack. A force was placed at the point where the original attack had taken place that afternoon, in the hope that Scanderbeg would repeat his exploit and so be captured. Prince Mehmed stayed with them the whole of one night, but his 'wild beast' was equal to so unsubtle a ruse. He went one stage further and ambushed the ambushers. Moses of Dibra, with about 500 horsemen, feigned an attack one night; the alarm was duly given and the Turks prepared their reception for him. Meanwhile Scanderbeg and his force moved round the camp and broke into it where least expected. He retired before the defenders could rally, and withdrew under cover of a cavalry force stationed in the woods outside the camp to fall on any would-be pursuers.

There was no loss on the part of the Albanians; they did not leave behind 'anything save wounds, tears and lamentations,' except for an uneasy feeling among the Turks that they were never safe from the sudden irruption of an invisible enemy. While they were besieging Kruja, they were themselves in a state of siege and acknowledged the fact by removing some of their artillery to the perimeter of their camp, pointing outwards towards the guerrillas and not inwards at the fortress.

In addition, a further ruse was devised. A large force of cavalry was sent out with no apparent purpose; Scanderbeg, who had moved to the coast near the mouth of the river Ishmi, cautiously followed them at a distance to see where they were going and what they intended to do. Having thus taken him for a tour of the countryside, they turned and went back to Kruja. In their absence, and that of the Albanians, a frenzied attack had been mounted on the town. Mattocks had been used to try and hammer down the gateway, and a wild fire of cannon balls on the

Tirana side had hit the unlucky front line Turkish troops as often as the Albanians. Once again the assault was called off, and an attempt was made to mine the fortress, but this proved impossible as it was built on rock.

These successive delays forced the Turks to look to their food supplies. Whilst the garrison within the town had food for a year, they did not. Furthermore, their convoy routes home lay through dangerous country. So the Turks turned to their commercially minded ally for help, and the Venetian merchants of the coastal towns sold them oil, wine, corn and whatever else they needed. The occasional trader may have been killed by an indignant Albanian patriot, but Scanderbeg did not protest. He was already receiving help from the same source; and the Turkish convoys to and from Lis were a tempting target and a means of provisioning his army at no cost.

The Turks had made no headway and they were losing many dead and wounded; but they had very many more to lose than the Albanians. Of their original 8,000 men, about a thousand had been killed, wounded or demobilised for one reason or another. Scanderbeg's main lieutenants, Moses of Dibra and Tanush Thopia, raised a couple of thousand more, and the augmented force was divided into three equal parts, each led by one of the three men. This form of organisation made attacks on the Turkish camp easier, for as soon as a defence had been organised against one group, another could come into action elsewhere. In the first of these operations, Scanderbeg moved fairly ostentatiously towards the Turks and was discovered a couple of miles off. A force of 8,000 was hastily assembled and moved against him; he retired slowly before it, giving Moses and Tanush the opportunity to break into the camp. Scanderbeg then lured the Turks towards the foothills and next morning, gauging from the dust in the distance that the other two leaders were on their way back, he showed signs of preparing to give battle, in order to persuade his enemies to stay and be massacred. Almost too late, the Turks realised that their retreat had been cut off, but they forced their way back with heavy losses and many prisoners. Next day, with the same leisurely insolence, Scanderbeg was observed on the rocks above Kruja, in conference with Count Vrana, who had slipped out from the fortress. Murad is supposed to have been rendered speechless by the misfortunes of his punitive force the previous day; this time he found words of a kind. 'With a dog's laugh (as the saying is) he told them that the best way was to let alone that furious and untamed lion.'

This may have been an oblique criticism of his eldest son, for whom the capture of the Albanian leader rightly seemed the one sure means of conquering the country; but it was easier to say Scanderbeg should be caught than to follow successfully the complexities both of his tactics and of the hills and valleys that made them possible. Murad saw the difficulties more clearly, and he evidently argued that without Kruja, Scanderbeg would not be able to cause him trouble for long. So he continued with more traditional methods of warfare, and before launching a third assault decided to see whether Vrana was yet ripe for subversion.

A pasha was chosen to go up to the town, accompanied by servants carrying rich presents. The meeting took place in full view of the garrison, and the envoy began by saying that acceptance of the gifts need not compromise Vrana in any way, but that he should reflect how much better a master Murad would be than a man who was 'scarce able to sustain his miserable body.' There was nothing to be expected from the Venetians either, he pointed out; they were at peace with the Sultan and, as he possibly did not mention, engaged in that moment in victualling his army and so helping him to maintain the siege. He finally asked for a few words in private with Vrana, and the garrison had confidence enough in him to permit this without a murmur. Whatever offer was made was turned down, and the Turks knew the failure of the mission when they saw the presents still in the hands of the returning deputation.

The third assault was now launched, but it proved as costly

and fruitless as the others. Murad had to decide whether to try and starve the town into submission; turn his back on it and try to hunt Scanderbeg in the mountains; or else negotiate. He decided to negotiate, and was prepared to accept Scanderbeg as his tributary in return for an annual payment of 10,000 crowns—which might be halved in the event of hard bargaining. Scanderbeg would of course retain his possessions undisturbed.

An envoy called Joseph was appointed, and a group of Dibrian prisoners were offered their liberty if they would take him to the Albanian leader. They found Scanderbeg on the plain beyond the river Ishmi, and Joseph spent the night in his camp, where the guards were doubled and Moses of Dibra spent the entire night on patrol, in case the embassy were a trick. Next day the audience took place, again in the presence of the troops, who interrupted the proceedings whenever Joseph said something they did not care for. He tried to convince them that Murad was immensely powerful and their own position hopeless. They remained unconvinced, even though Scanderbeg almost certainly did not say in reply: "Nay if Murad did divide with me and make me co-partner with all his empire, I would never suffer the name of Albania to be stained and blemished with this blot of disgrace and infamy." Whatever variations on a plain negative may have been used, however, Joseph was sent back without success.

Though the overture had been turned down, the Albanian position was growing desperate; if Murad continued his policy of cannonades and assaults much longer, Kruja must fall. In order to awaken the Venetians to the seriousness of the position, Scanderbeg, using the Abbot of Rotezo as his intermediary, once again offered the city to them; according to the governor of Dagno, who transmitted his message on 14th October 1450, he threatened to give it up to the Turks if they refused. This dramatic bluff was unnecessary. On 26th October Murad raised the siege and returned defeated to Adrianople, having decided not to add the Albanian winter to his other handicaps. When they heard the news, the Venetians replied to the letter from Dagno. They had heard with satisfaction, they wrote on 23rd November, that the siege had been lifted. They would very much like to see a reconciliation between Scanderbeg and the Sultan, and they begged him to keep Kruja for himself.[1]

The men of Kruja came out of their confinement and began 'wandering up and down the fields yet moist with the blood of the Turks.' Scanderbeg entered the city and people jostled each other to touch their leader and icon. Bells rang, bonfires blazed; songs were composed to honour the recent heroes; and after the short commons came the celebrations with all the pageantry of a tournament beneath the walls. The garrison received extra pay and new clothes, and Vrana was given gold and silver, 'two coat armours of purple and one richly wrought in gold, and four goodly manors.' Soon came greetings, money and other help from abroad: from the Pope, the King of Hungary, the Duke of Burgundy; and from Alfonso of Aragon, who sent money, wheat and barley, together with workmen to repair the city walls. The Albanian victory had removed a great shadow from Europe: the fear that the Turks might use Albania as the launching-pad for an attack on Italy. So long as Kruja held out, this was hardly feasible.

Barletius, weaving his national epic, makes Sultan Murad die under the walls he has been unable to subdue, delivering himself of a final piece of sententious advice to his heir: 'Let my example be a warning unto thee, my son, never to contemn and despise any enemy, be he never so weak and feeble.' Murad, however, left Albania alive; he died the following January, of apoplexy. And his son Mehmed was the last man who needed to be advised not to leave anything to chance.

With the departure of the Turkish army, and the collapse of the siege of Kruja, the pressure was now renewed on Scanderbeg to choose a wife. His original condition, that Svetigrad should first be freed, was now forgotten. He had an even greater achievement to his credit: that of having frustrated the greatest army of the day. He had less need to fear the jealousies of his fellow-chiefs, and could choose a bride more fitted to 'the haughtiness of his conceits' about the creation of an Albanian principality under his rule. So 'this formidable captain, who never fought without Victory, killed near two thousand Turks with his own hand, without receiving the least wound; but Love did what all his enemies could not do and wounded the heart of this Invulnerable Conqueror'—as the author of *The Great Scanderbeg* put it, an anonymous novel 'done out of the French,' which appeared in London in 1690.[2]

The author cannot allow that public policy had any hand in choosing the bride; for such a hero it must be love only. And since the bridegroom, according to the old story, was a Turkish hostage until the age of nearly forty, then the bride must clearly have shared his exile. So we have the story of Arianissa, daughter of Aranit, an Albanian slave at the court of Adrianople, who is loved by both Gjergj Castrioti and Sultan Murad. Gjergj saves Arianissa from drowning; they fall in love; and she bids him return home and assert his insulted royal rights. In fury the Sultan orders her death, and his rival collects Albanian warriors to avenge her. She has been taken away by the executioner, and is only found and saved at the last moment, just as his dagger is descending to stab her. Scanderbeg and Arianissa ride away as fast as they can to Kruja (although she was 'not used to any hard exercise'), and within a few days they have married and the Sultan is dead from shame. ''Tis enough for us to have tyed him here for ever with his Charming Arianissa comments the novelist 'The great Atchievements of his Reign are so commonly known that it would be to no purpose to relate them here.'

This is fiction frankly dressed as such and not as history, like so much of the remainder of the Scanderbeg canon; and fiction is perhaps the only way in which the theme of romantic love can be made to play that part in Scanderbeg's life which modern ideas demand. Stern fact has already shown us a picture with no room for dalliance at an oriental court: the guerrilla expeditions, the journeys through the snow, the rough living, the short snatches of sleep. Yet Arianassa is not wholly a myth. She existed, and she became his wife. But they met in Albania, not Adrianople, and their encounter had more of political calculation than affection about it.

The Aranit of the novel is, of course, Gjergj Arianiti of Kanina castle, overlooking Vlora Bay, the first Albanian leader to inflict defeats on the Turks when they invaded the country from Greece in the thirties. Scanderbeg was predominant in Albania north of the Shkumbi river; and in so far as there was an equivalent figure in the south, it was Arianiti. He was a rich man, and the greatest of the landed proprietors, and though his fame was now dimmed by comparison with the northerner's more recent and more brilliant exploits, his pedigree was incomparably more desirable, being even linked in the not too distant past with some junior branch of one of the Byzantine imperial families. Fortunately, too, he had a daughter Andronica, or Donitsa to her intimates, who was 'the true image and perfection of beauty.' Thus when Tanush Thopia, together with two or three friends, was given the task of choosing a wife for his uncle, there could have been little doubt whom they were expected to suggest.

Neither Andronica's beauty, nor her traces of purple blood, were allowed to lessen the importance of the dowry, however. This was left to her father's discretion, but with the stipulation that it should correspond to the dignity of both giver and receiver. Perhaps there was something of a dutch auction of pride between the two, for there is a story that the three sons of Arianiti sulked throughout the wedding celebrations because they felt their father had been induced to part with too much of his wealth, and hence their inheritance, to this new son-in-law. Other families had reluctantly admired the ability of the Castrioti family to expand its influence by arms and the marriage bed alike; these young men possibly felt that their brother-in-law, backed by his victories and the prestige of this marriage, might one day become the effective ruler of the whole country, taking in their lands as well as his own.

The wedding took place in May 1451, at Kanina, attended by most of the chieftains and honoured by 'sumptuous presents.' Those from Alfonso of Aragon, King of Naples, were indeed so magnificent that the bridegroom hesitated to accept them and was induced to do so only when he found himself able to send back others 'of no less value and estimation' that he had taken among his spoils of war. After the triumphs and tournaments of the wedding celebrations, the couple made a journey around Albania, attended by a troop of horse and visiting 'every particular place.' People flocked to see them and devised 'shows and spectacles and presents' for their entertainment.

Yet even on his honeymoon, as they travelled receiving congratulations and good wishes, the guerrilla leader within Scanderbeg remained active. In Lower Dibra he noticed for the first time an unguarded pass through which the Turks could enter unopposed. So he had workmen and ordnance sent in from Kruja, and within six months a new fortress had been built on the top of a hill called Modrici. At Kruja also there was reconstruction work to be done. Here, the Neapolitan engineers sent by Alfonso learned the lesson of the recent bombardments, and made adjustments in design that were shortly adopted for castles everywhere to gain some protection from the terrible new weapon of artillery: vertical walls were modified to sloping ones in order to minimise the damage done by the canon balls.

It was thus only comparatively true when Scanderbeg complained that an entire year had now been spent in recreation during a conference of his allies at Kruja, called within a month or two of his marriage. They must not fall victims to sloth while Svetigrad and Berat(an even more recent conquest) remained in Turkish hands. He had no comfortable assurances for them: 'For my part I can promise you nothing without expense and loss of blood, without vehement and earnest labour.' There was little enthusiasm for a resumption of war in the short time that remained for campaigning before the bad weather set in. Vrana tactfully explained this by assuring his leader that 'in thy company the snow shall be pleasant, the showers shall seem sweet, the winter be thought mild.' Scanderbeg bowed to the polite irony and went off to join his wife at the castle of Petrela which was to be her summer home.

Chapter Nine

. . . .

Byzantium to Berat

The city, as it was simply known to the rest of Christendom—the vast, emptying, doomed and golden city of Byzantium—had lingered on under the ghost of an imperial family, its conquest seemingly inevitable yet indefinitely delayed. But the succession of Mehmet II to the Ottoman throne early in 1451 decided its fate; for whereas his father had been content with the realities of power, knowing that possession of the ancient capital would add little or nothing to these, the son desired both the power and the glory.

In this he was a Renaissance man of his century, for whom true virtue consisted in imposing, and in being seen to impose his will both upon events and his fellow human beings. The quest for personal glory was strong in him; but he had no need—unlike so many of the princes of his day, blessed as they were with only a modicum of power and talent—to spend his energies in killing, plotting, fawning, persuading, and strutting like a peacock in imitation of the imagined heroes of classical days. He was free to kill only when he wished to strike terror into his opponents. He was too strong to plot and too astute to be worth plotting against. Men fawned on him, not he on them. He persuaded them by the fact or the threat of his vast army.

During the military decline of the eastern empire, a spirit of renewal in art, science and political thought spread from the enfeebled centres of Byzantine civilisation and quickened the imaginations of Turks, Serbs and Italians alike. The wars in the Balkans meant that the process had the chance of developing furthest in Italy, culminating in a Michaelangelo, a Leonardo and a Machiavelli. But the fighting isolated Italy from the perennial sources of her inspiration in Greek art and thought, and the warm spring–like spirit of the early Renaissance congealed into the glacial arrogance of the later. The humane naturalism of a Giotto, echoed in its day by a corresponding spontaneity in the frescoes of Serbia, gave place to a didactic search for scientific rules in art and to a national obsession, not with a living tradition of antiquity such as remained in Byzantium, but with that fragmentary glimpse of the classical world that was to be found in the ancient stones of Italy herself, models now half destroyed and often debased copies of greater originals even when new.

The infatuation of Italy's rulers with imperial grandeur beneath their own soil led, in its combination of weakness and pretentiousness, to a parody of the very thing they admired. Alfonso of Aragon, King of Sicily and Naples—tactfully christened the Magnanimous by the scholars he hired for his court—would halt his army in pious tribute at the birth place of one Latin author, and profess to have been cured of an illness by reading a few pages of another. On his campaigns he took the books, but not the genius, of Caesar.

Mehmet II did not need to perform such charades to show his respect for the cult of antiquity. He did not need to fill his palaces with statues to show his reverence for an unattainable past; when he wanted to visit the Acropolis, he conquered Greece. Nor for him was the classical world some almost forgotten memory to be reconstructed only from decaying ruins and excavated busts. The empire of Rome still lived on in the traditions of Byzantium, moulding the political ambitions and artistic aspirations of the Ottoman Turks. Thus Mehmet could see himself as the true heir of Rome, first in its eastern and then in its original western form. And the poets (introduced to the court by his father) had invented flattering legends of Osmanli Turkish origins and destinies, just as Virgil had for the thrusting imperialists of his day. Thus Mehmet's will to power was as much a rebirth of the original mood of imperial Rome as a revival of its outward forms.

In character, as well as opportunity and circumstance, the man who later threatened to conquer Italy seemed fitted by nature to fill the role of the Prince whom Machiavelli would have chosen to liberate and unite her. Insatiably curious, generous or cruel to excess at need, ruthless and tireless in action, he resembled the Renaissance thinkers who welcomed all accomplishments, whether in war or intellect or sensibility, as a means of exploring the possibilities of one's own personality within and of subduing the world without. There was the same love of watching the well-tuned mind in action, as in his discussions on the ancient Greek philosophers. The same ironic lack of fanaticism in matters of belief: he appointed and admired the Orthodox Patriarch and enjoyed listening to him expounding the intricacies of Christian theology. The same eagerness to master scientific method: the great cannons with which he blew the Middle Ages to oblivion were built to his own specifications. The same patronage of art and scholarship that led him to ask the Ragusans to pay money they owed him in the form of Italian humanist manuscripts; and though as a Muslim he could not decorate his buildings with the human form, he could invite the Venetian painter Gentile Bellini to his court and be painted by him. This portrait shows the physical traits that might have been expected from his character: the combination of cunning and discrimination; the refinement that could preserve and emulate the architecture of Byzantium, but the barbarism that ordered prisoners to be sawn in half when he wished to teach the survivors a lesson; and, above all, the inflexibility of will with which he pursued power.

In that pursuit he had two decisive and related advantages. His army was the finest in the world, and had become so because it belonged to the Sultan directly and not to barons with wills of their own. His social system was the most modern, since the ruler could choose and attach to himself the individual most fitted for the job he wished to have done; and he did not have to contend with the feudal conflict of interests that destroyed one Balkan power after another. The Christian states in the Balkans were to be overwhelmed not because the Turk was inherently braver, more brutal or more clever, but because their forms of organisation, military and civilian, were out of date, and they were unaware of the fact. They had been warned when the English, in one of their early innovations, introduced the new weapon of cannon at the battle of Crécy in 1346. The fact of the cannon conflicted with the idea of war as a chivalrous exercise waged between knights for honour as much as gain, thus the countries of Europe (England once more typically to the fore) failed to think through the practical consequences of their own discovery. When the Turks came along and saw a weapon which, improved and developed, would batter down the existing fortresses of Europe, they promptly adopted it.

In contrast, their opponents continued to rely on the cavalry for operations in the field; and to resist sieges they began to increase the thickness of their castle walls, rather as the primitive saurians grew ever more formidable defensive armour in their steady march to oblivion. In the very last month of her existence, Serbia was preparing to repel Mehmet by building at her capital of Smederevo a gigantic system of fortifications, with walls at one point 15 feet thick.[1] It was never put to the test for, as the Turkish guns approached, the defending garrison realised that rather than providing protection, the walls turned the city into a death trap. Today the fortifications still stand on the bank of the Danube, beautiful, huge and useless, the perfect memorial to the dangers of social conservatism in a time of technical progress.

Scanderbeg alone survived in the path of the Turks—despite the very disadvantages that overwhelmed leaders with greater resources because his cavalry was light and quick and deployed in small bodies in and near the hills, as opposed to large formations of heavy and cumbersome troops deployed in the plains. And because in Kruja the defences were made by nature and man in combination, and artillery had not yet reached the point where it could destroy half a mountainside in order to overwhelm a fortress perched on its slope.

The very scope of Turkish military power also meant that the character of Mehmet's rule had to be different from that of his predecessors. Even in his father's day it had been the practice to leave the government of conquered countries to their native rulers, so long as they acknowledged the Sultan's overlordship. Serbia for some time preserved a shadowy independence in this way, and Scanderbeg had a chance of keeping Kruja on similar terms. But the new weapons destroyed the basis of the old states, which now called for a new class of administrators; and here tried and traditional Byzantine models were infused with the fresh blood of the most promising Christian boys. Mehmet thus deserves the title of 'Fatih', or Conqueror, not simply for taking Constantinople, but because for the first time since Roman days he was able to incorporate his conquests into a vast centralised empire.

Such were the qualities and circumstances of the man who became Scanderbeg's opponent on 5th February 1451. His first concern was to possess Byzantium, and how he went about it is common knowledge. He built a castle on the European side of the Bosphorus and this, combined with the existing castle on the Asiatic side, controlled the only remaining access to the city, that by water. Byzantium was now a depopulated triangle, protected by water on two sides (the Bosphorus and the inner harbour, or Golden Horn) and on the landward side by the strongest walls in Europe. Mehmet's plan was to cast the largest cannon yet known and batter the walls with 1,500 pound cannon balls, while at the same time distracting the meagre defences by naval bombardment from the harbour. Despite repeated attempts, his ships could not fight their way into the harbour, so he built a tramway of logs across the peninsula and towed them across several miles of land to a point higher up, and then sailed them down into the city. On 29th May 1453 he entered the city through a breach made by his great gun Basilik, and the last emperor of Byzantium was found dead among his own soldiers.

In the prestige of triumph, Mehmet turned to four immediate tasks that awaited him. The first was to restore and embellish the city itself, bringing back the artisans, merchants and professional men to replace those who had drifted away in recent decades or had been killed during the war. The second was to subdue Serbia once for all, so that he could control the dangerous northern frontier over which successive crusading armies had emerged from Hungary. The third, to secure effective control of the Byzantine despotates in southern Greece. The fourth was to deal with the contumacious Albanians.

Mehmet's routine in the early years of his reign was to direct building operations at Constantinople during the winter months and set out in spring with his army, 50,000 cavalrymen and a still larger number of infantry, returning at the end of each campaigning season with the prisoners he had captured. Such of these 'as seemed to be better than the rest in their knowledge of trades' were settled inside the all but lifeless city, and the remainder were given land, grain and oxen outside it in order to produce food. Repopulation was 'almost his very first care,' and he did not mind whether the citizens were Muslim, Christian or Jewish so long as they had the skills which could recreate the old prosperity. At the same time he began to equip the new capital for defence—or, more truly, to prepare it to serve as a capital, for Adrianople remained the centre of administration for some years to come. He began a fortress on the site of an old imperial castle and decided to build a royal palace.

In the spring of 1455 he set out for Serbia and captured a number of fortresses by what had now become a routine procedure for him—devastation of the countryside to cut off food supplies for any foragers; as complete a siege as possible; and use of his heavy cannon. Gjergj Brankovic, the Serbian Despot, asked for terms and peace was made whereby both sides kept what they held, and the Serbs went on paying an annual tribute to the Sultan and once more agreed to let him have soldiers for his future expeditions.

Mehmet returned to find his palace finished, and he spent the winter there. The walls had been repaired and the fortress built, and now he turned his attention from defence to trade, ordering roads to be made to the capital, with inns along the way at intervals; and, for the traders who made use of them, a 'very fine marketplace, in the centre of the city ... protected by very strong walls on the outside, and divided on the inside into very beautiful and spacious colonnades.'

In the spring he returned to Serbia to try to capture Belgrade which, being on the south side of the Danube and in an immensely strong natural position on high ground at the confluence of two rivers, protected the crossing of any army coming from Hungary to attack him. Under cover of cannon fire, which both made breaches in the walls and prevented the defenders from repairing them, his own soldiers filled in the moat on the landward side. This made the position somewhat similar to the siege of Byzantium, for there too the defenders were confined to a city on a promontory and subjected to concentrated attack from a neck of land. But Byzantium had been isolated from the rest of the world, whereas at Belgrade Gjon Hunyadi and his Hungarians were able to cross the Danube and so repel the attackers. The Sultan was forced to return home without his prize, taking consolation during the winter in building aqueducts and 'splendid and costly baths.'

During the next year, 1457, he did not leave, but built 'splendid residences, inns, and markets all over the City, and caravanserais, and he planted public gardens. He brought in plenty of water, and did all he knew how to give the City ornamentation and beauty as well as what was necessary for practical life.'

His first clash with Albanians since becoming Sultan did not happen in Albania itself, but in Greece. There, the large number who went the century before as soldiers and settlers in depopulated areas had taken their national turbulence along with them. Early in Mehmet's reign those in the Peloponnese had revolted against the two reigning Despots, both of the former Byzantine imperial family of Palaeologus. The Despots appealed to the Sultan. He, in return for a promise of an annual tribute and the recognition of his sovereignty which went with it, lent them an army which defeated the Albanians.

The Despots were thus in a position to make the Albanians pay the tribute to them; but they overlooked the second stage of passing it on to their new master. When it was three years overdue, Mehmet sent to ask for it; he was offered a derisory sum on account and asked to sign a treaty with them. He answered that he was sending an army to the Peloponnese to discuss a treaty. He was no doubt pleased to have this excuse to intervene; the two weak Byzantine states, though able to agree to keep the Sultan waiting for his money, could not live at peace with each other, and were thus a temptation to a stronger Christian power to take over their territory.

Such an event would create a new foothold for any future crusade launched against him from the west. He had already watched the activities of the 'High Priest of Rome as his chronicler Kritovoulos calls the Pope, sending an expedition of thirty triremes to the Aegean, where they conquered the islands of Lemnos and Thacos. Such an expedition drew attention to a major shortcoming in his own strategic system.

With typical thoroughness he began to study the theory and practice of sea power. He 'learned by diligent search and consideration of the history of kings who had the greatest power, that operations by sea had the greatest chance of success and brought the most fame, and that it was on the sea that those kings had accomplished the greatest things. For this reason he decided to secure control of the sea for himself, because when land and sea are both under one control, they quickly bring that control to its highest pitch.' Accordingly, 'he gave orders that triremes should be built everywhere along his shores, knowing that the domination of the sea was essential to him and his rule, especially for expeditions to far countries. For he knew that in his approaching undertakings naval operations would be of the first importance.' His ambitions were naturally turning to Italy, which was both the birthplace of that Roman Empire whose heir he felt himself to be and the centre of all the military forces ranged against him. In such a campaign to restore the empire of the world under a single ruler, the Peloponnese would be of great value, since it was 'well situated on the voyage to Italy and had safe harbours that could be bases for large armies and navies during the war.'

So in 1458 he set out for the south of Greece, capturing Patras and Corinth, and quickly bringing about a third of the Peloponnese under his direct rule. In the course of this campaign he came to Athens, and here the man who had destroyed the empire of the Byzantine Greeks paid his tribute to the classical empire of Athens. For he was not only a great king, says Kritovoulos, the Greek historian who served him, but also a wise one (and a Philhellene, he adds in the margin of his manuscript) who was duly astonished with the relics he now saw, 'especially the Acropolis as he went up in to it;' the Venetians had not yet turned the Acropolis into a ruin with their cannon, and it stood as complete and, in that clear air, almost as fresh as in the days of Pericles, the great frieze still intact against the azure sky.

Though Mehmet was a conqueror with active plans for still further aggressions in his mind, and as a future master of the Mediterranean took care to learn 'the facts about the sea near by (Athens), its harbours, its arsenals, and, in short, everything,' he was still the friend of the philosophers come to visit the first home of philosophy. 'He was greatly enamoured of that city and of the wonders in it, for he had heard many fine things about the wisdom and prudence of its ancient inhabitants, and also of their valour and virtues and of the many wonderful deeds they had done in their times when they fought against both Greeks and barbarians. So he was eager to see the city and learn the story of it and of all its buildings, especially the Acropolis itself, and of the places where those heroes had carried on the government and accomplished those things.'

The writer is admittedly a Greek, justifying his own collaboration to his fellow-countrymen and presenting his master to them in the best light; but the picture is essentially a fair one. The Muslim Mehmet, like his western counterparts, had been touched with the same general spirit of renaissance, and impressed like them with the achievements of Greek and Roman antiquity. The Ottoman empire at this stage regarded itself in no sense as a destroyer of classical culture, but rather as the purifier and successor chosen by Providence and the fortunes of war; and in some ways, through its recent association with Byzantium, it was more closely linked with the continuing tradition of the classical world than were, for example, the artists and architects of Italy. On his return from Athens, and perhaps under the inspiration of the magnificence he had seen there, Mehmet selected a new site in the heart of his capital for a mosque, the original and now vanished Fatih Cami, or Mosque of the Conqueror, which was later damaged in an earthquake and then dismantled.

There was nothing unusual about the architecture. It owed no debt to Athens, nor even, as later Ottoman mosques in Istanbul, to that sublime creation of human ingenuity, the church of Santa Sofia. It was a large, simple, domed room which carried on in conservative fashion the style of building to which the Ottomans had become accustomed when Bursa was their capital and they did not dream of their present grandeur. But it marked a stage forward in splendour. Mehmet's buildings so far—the first of the two palaces erected in his reign, the great market and the other new landmarks of the city—were all of wood. They have long since vanished in one or other of the many fires that swept through the narrow streets, and they could not begin to compare with the vast, sombre monuments of their predecessors.

Now, however, the Conqueror resolved on a mosque which 'in height, beauty and size should vie with the largest and finest of the temples already existing there and he ordered for it 'the very best marbles and other costly polished stones as well as an abundance of columns of suitable size and beauty.' He instructed his rich subjects to build great houses, baths, inns and market-places, workshops and mosques, and food kitchens for the poor, and he 'planted gardens with trees bearing all sorts of fruit for the delectation and happiness and use of many.' He also chose a site for a new palace 'on the point of old Byzantium which stretches out into the sea—a palace that should outshine all and be more marvellous than the preceding palaces in looks, size, cost and gracefulness.' This was the palace which, with later and larger accretions, came to be known abroad as the Seraglio, and at home as the Topkapi Serai, or Cannongate Palace, in reference to the spot where the great bombard had been set up during the assault.[2]

It was with the hostility of such a talented, energetic and powerful enemy that the Albanians had now to reckon. But though his accession eventually proved a disaster for them, at first it gave the Albanians a welcome respite by changing the direction of Turkish aggressiveness. Materially, the Albanians were exhausted when the siege of Kruja was raised in October 1450, some three months before Murad II died. Their fields were laid waste and their main fortresses badly battered, and the League of Lezhë had also suffered political damage; The Spanis, Dushmanis and Altisferis left in protest when war broke out with the Venetians over Dagno. Those subject to Turkish pressure either became neutral or, like Gjergj Arianiti, put themselves under direct Venetian protection. He had the good fortune to possess a castle overlooking the wide and protected Bay of Vlora, which the Republic had long coveted for herself, and so she was prepared to risk more in his case than in that of Kruja, for she still hoped to persuade the Turks to agree that Vlora should belong to her.

Scanderbeg had now two tasks: he must recreate the League despite Venetian indifference or hostility, and he must win back Arianiti, as the only leader with an influence comparable with his own, to an active nationalist policy. The wedding with Andronica, the eldest of Gjergj and Mary Arianiti's eight daughters—a woman 'elegant, beautiful, most virtuous' and 'not unworthy of her father'—took care of the personal problem. The political problem demanded a sponsor for a revived League, and the only man who could fill this role was King Alfonso V, the Aragonese king of Naples.

There were certain drawbacks in such an alliance. It would rouse the suspicion of the Venetians and make them still more ready to settle Albanian affairs in collusion with the Turks, because Venice did not want to see Neapolitan influence on both sides of the Adriatic, since it might be used to hamper her trade and strategic routes to the Levant. Moreover, though Venice had never been more than lukewarm towards Albanian ambitions, her own claims were limited; she did not want the responsibility of annexing any more Albanian territory, coastal towns apart. But the Aragonese had ambitious territorial policies in the Balkans. Alfonso sought to carry out two policies, either one of which would have beggared and frustrated him. He sought to give Italy unity and stability under his leadership, and he dreamed of an empire across the Adriatic that might one day stretch as far as Constantinople. In him the Albanians found not just an ally, friend and supporter, but a sovereign, although in practice his sovereignty was never exercised and the military and financial gain was all on the Albanian side.

The treaty between Scanderbeg and Alfonso was signed at Gaeta in March 1451, a month before the wedding at Kanina.[3] By its terms he became a vassal of the Aragonese king, whose viceroy, Ramon d'Ortofa, soon afterwards took formal possession of Kruja with about a hundred Catalan soldiers. The Albanian promised to pay to the King the tribute at present claimed by the Sultan, once his lands had been won back from the Turk with Aragonese help. When they were all in his possession again, he would go in person to render homage to Alfonso, who would then grant such lands as he might choose to Scanderbeg and his relations. They would buy salt only from Naples, and the ancient privileges of Kruja and the Albanian chieftains would be confirmed. Alfonso subsequently signed similar treaties with the other main chieftains, among them Arianiti, Musachi, Balsha, Spani, Dukagjini and Thopia.

So in effect the original League of Lezhë was recreated; but in place of the former ambiguous detachment of the Venetians, it had the new stiffening of direct Neapolitan direction. Alfonso had direct links with the various chieftains, and clear obligations towards them, and Scanderbeg became Captain General of the Crown of Aragon, which gave him a status he had not possessed in the former alliance. He appeared to have all the advantages of powerful outside support with none of its drawbacks, both politically and financially. The Neapolitan contribution in armed men and weapons was too small, because of commitments in Italy, to take the direction of operations out of Albanian hands; and far from being called on to pay tribute, except in such token form as captured trophies of war, Scanderbeg received 1,500 ducats a year from Alfonso, apart from the help in arms and soldiers.

Consciously or not, the Gaeta alliance was a strengthening of Albanian military power to meet the growing aggressiveness of Turkey in the reign that had just begun. Its first test came with the fall of Constantinople in 1453. Inevitable as this had long seemed in theory, the survival of the city had gradually accustomed men to feel that its twilight might continue indefinitely; and the long-deferred disaster, when the regular miracle of coincidence failed to happen to save it, seemed like the subversion of a law of nature. It now appeared, quite irrationally, as though the Turks were truly irresistible. Perhaps if the city had been starved out, or had been induced to surrender by means of cunning, the sadness of Europe might have been as great but its anxiety less. What had happened, however, was that Constantinople had been destroyed at the very point where it was thought to be indestructible. The strongest walls in the world had not been taken by guile or treachery, but had been blasted through by cannon. It had been a triumph of new technology; and the physical overthrow of the city was a symbol of the social and technical backwardness of Christendom in the face of this new and modern power.

Under the effect of this shock, the Venetians even forgot their suspicions of the Neapolitans for a time, and their governor in Lezhë was ordered to accompany Scanderbeg when he went to Rome and Naples to discuss what gesture could be made in Albania to make up in some way for the disaster at Constantinople, and to restore a measure of initiative to the enemies of the Sultan. The obvious choice was the fortress town of Berat. Berat stands right in the heart of southern Albania, at the point where the road from Durazzo to Janina leaves the central plain and enters the mountain valleys. It had therefore a dual purpose: to guard military communications from north-western Greece, and to overawe the people of central and western Albania. It was essential to the Turks if they wanted to bring in and deploy armies to conquer the whole country. It was equally essential to the Albanians if they wanted to create a national state, making use of the fertile plains for providing the population and revenues they needed; and forcing the Turks to dissipate their military effort by fighting all the way round the inaccessible perimeter of Albania instead of concentrating their forces, as Murad had done in 1450, inside Albania itself. Victory or defeat depended still, as Gjergj Castrioti had seen after the battle of Nis, on possession of the triangle of strong points—Kruja, Berat and Svetigrad. With those three in his hands, there can be little doubt as to the course Albanian history would have taken.

There would have been a principality able to sustain itself indefinitely against attack, like its neighbour Montenegro, and probably entering the modern world as an independent unit still under a dynasty boasting of Scanderbeg's exploits and Andronica Arianiti's imperial blood. Unlike Montenegro, however, where the land never subdued by the Turks stood remote and indigestible, like the kernel of a fruit that cannot be cracked but guards the vital principle of the tree, Albania crouched against the Adriatic like some great turtle, its succulence shielded from the enemy by its solid carapace of mountains. Such a country could have opened itself to all the discoveries of the Italian Renaissance, and in the court of the Duke of Illyria Shakespeare has pictured life as it would have been lived by Gjergj Castrioti's great grandson.

Even with Kruja and Berat in their own hands, the Albanians could have hoped to compel the Turks sooner or later to accept the fact of their independence. It would have been a hard struggle, above all now that Mehmet had awakened to the importance of naval warfare, and saw so near at hand the Adriatic coastline with its fine, well protected harbour ofVlora. If he lost Berat he would have no strong point on the seaward side of the mountains, and the Albanians could hope to fight the war in future on his territory rather than their own. Berat was important to both sides; and in July 1455, when Mehmet himself was engaged in Serbia, the siege began.

Scanderbeg and his local allies raised about 12,000 men, and the Neapolitans added another 2,000, equipped with the siege artillery the Albanians had always lacked. A breach was soon made in the wall and the garrison, on being asked to surrender, replied that they would do so in eleven days time if no help came. Presumably to prevent bloodshed, the allies agreed to accept these terms and fighting stopped. Scanderbeg then left the town with the intent, presumably, to look out for any relieving force from the direction of Janina. During his absence, the mass of the army began to celebrate their forthcoming victory. It was premature. It is surprising that the Turkish terms should ever have been accepted, and from what we know of Scanderbeg's methods it can be assumed that he, once the first breach had been made in the walls, would have followed up the initial advantage and made sure of the town there and then.

But the Captain General of the Crown of Aragon was not in command; that role was filled by Musachi Thopia. Berat was traditionally the possession of the Musachi family, and we know that they had suspicions about Scanderbeg's personal ambitions in this part of the world. The Thopias had once held Durazzo as representatives of the Neapolitan kings of the House of Anjou, which preceded that of Aragon. We can only suppose, therefore, that local family considerations rather than national strategic ones determined the choice of commander and policy. Why should the Albanians pound away at the buildings of the town that was so soon to be theirs, and waste the lives of soldiers who in a few days would be enjoying a bloodless victory inside the walls? There is no sign that Scanderbeg withdrew from the campaign, like Achilles to his tent, but rather that, knowing Turkish methods from personal experience, he kept his men from the general demoralisation of the camp and used them to look out for a surprise attack. If so, he was unsuccessful.

During the celebrations in the besiegers' camp, Izak Bey arrived unannounced with a large force of cavalry—the figure has been given as 40,000—and proceeded to massacre those besiegers who were not able to escape. It was a repetition of Scanderbeg's technique at the siege of Kruja, the main difference being that in this case the relieving force was larger than the besieging.

Scanderbeg received warning too late to affect the issue, but returned over the mountains to see the carnage in the plain below. He 'gnashed his teeth, and with his mouth all bludie, he was clean out of patience...For this one thing which is reported of him, is not to be omitted, that whenever he was upon the point readie to charge the enemie and likewise in the heat and furie of the fight besides other strange signes of change and alteration in his countenance, his neather lippe would commonly cleave asunder, and yeeld forth great abundance of bloud: a thing oftentimes marked and observed in him, not only in his martiall actions and exploites, but even in his civill affaires, whensoever his choller did abound, and that his anger did exceede more than ordinary.' Choler was not useless. The allied commander, Musachi Thopia, was killed, and the Neapolitans annihilated.

Scanderbeg returned with his own men to Kruja, where rumours of the disaster brought the women out to meet them, calling out to know what had happened to their husbands and sons. He had yet to learn the full extent of the reverse. He was met by one of the army leaders called Demetrius, or Dhimitri, who began by consoling with him about the fickleness of fortune and then 'came at length to the fact of Moses.' Moses of Dibra had deserted the Albanian cause and gone over to the Turks.

After his earlier failure to take Kruja, the Sultan had decided to try to win Scanderbeg's allies away from him, and the first person with whom he began was Moses. His lands bordered those of Turkey in the neighbourhood of Svetigrad; his friendship would reduce the threat to that fortress and also open the door into Albania for any future army of invasion. Acting on the Sultan's instructions, the governor of Svetigrad sent a trusted household servant, an Albanian by birth, to see Moses and suggest that he went for negotiations in the fortress itself. The impudence of such a proposal amused him, but soon 'he swallowed up the cunning and close bait of his own praises: namely, when the messenger told him that the great Turk did so highly honour and esteem of him, that he thought him only of all the flower of Epire, worthy to be solicited both by letters and by speeches.'

Moses' reply was so tactful that the messenger did not know whether to take it as encouraging or discouraging, but he took his leave and promised to return. Moses told his intimates that a spy had come to see him with news of conditions inside Svetigrad, and naturally enough this story was believed. There was a second visit, this time with valuable gifts. Moses did not accept the gifts, but sent back some sybilline message to the effect that the Sultan should not find him an enemy hereafter.

Moses had made no pledge, nor compromised himself by accepting money or gifts, and the governor was encouraged to continue negotiations. At this stage he probably wished to do no more than lie low, to evade Turkish reprisals for the defeat at Kruja (to which he was more exposed than any one) in the hope that Scanderbeg and the Sultan would eventually come to some agreement to live and let live.

At the same time that these overtures were being made, Scanderbeg was thinking of the necessity of turning the Turks out of the towns they still held in Albania, believing that the time had now come, with the death of Murad, 'to plucke this thorne out of my foote.' It was then that he first approached Alfonso of Aragon, sending him two shiploads of presents and a letter asking for the soldiers that he needed most, both artillery-men and arquebusiers and crossbow-men 'such as are skillful to fight aloofe and trouble the enemy a farre off.' Of these latter he thought he needed only a few (his envoys were satisfied when Alfonso offered 500 arquebusiers and 500 crossbow-men) because he had plenty of good archers and the towns to be surrounded were not large. What he needed above all was artillery and other assault weapons, and bombardiers to look after the ordnance.[4] (Along with the soldiers, Alfonso is credited with sending letters urging the Albanians to take some care in their attitude towards them, for these Italians 'were expert and skillful not onely in combatting with men upon the wals of strongholds and defenced towns, but with ladies and gentlewomen in their privat chambers.')

Scanderbeg's first thought had been to use any help Alfonso sent him against Svetigrad, in order to avenge his only serious defeat and to protect his own area of northern Albania. Accordingly he went to see Moses, from whose Dibra lands any such attack would have to be launched. Moses said that the spy from the garrison had brought him news which made quite clear that the town too strong to attack. It is also probable that the Neapolitans dissuaded Scanderbeg from an expedition into the

Dibra mountains while Berat in Turkish hands was still a menace to the plains. Certainly from their point of view, and in the Albanian national interest, Berat should come first. When the attack was switched to Berat, Moses loyally joined in. Not to have done so would have given countenance to ugly rumours after the recent approach by the 'spy,' and the Sultan could have no reasonable complaint against a man who merely took part in an expedition arranged without his initiative, and to the result of which he could hardly make the least difference.

On the morning after the Berat disaster, however, Moses was nowhere to be found. It was assumed at first that he had gone off to reconnoitre the enemy's movements; but the more cynical thought he had gone over to the Turks. Lest he should carry the frontier garrisons with him, two brothers, Dhimitri and Nicola, themselves rushed to the frontier, where they found that Moses had gone to Svetigrad and obtained a safe conduct into Turkey. They raised new levies, assured that the garrisons were loyal to the Albanian cause. Then, while Nicola remained in command, Dhimitri hurried back to report to his leader. The news astonished Scanderbeg and hurt him bitterly; but, taking a longer view than might have been expected, 'with a princely voice said openly and aloud' that he pardoned Moses. The calamity of Berat might have caused the most constant man's faith to waver, he said; and, leaving a bridge open by which the renegade might perhaps one day make the return journey, he refused to allow anyone to suggest that the defection had been planned before Berat. Having thus forgiven Moses, however, he went straight into Dibra, assumed the governorship personally, confiscated Moses' goods and estates, and looked in vain for any similar evidence of conspiracy. That done, he returned and paid his respects to his widowed sister Mamitza, whom Musachi Thopia had married; and there they not only mourned her loss but talked of the future of their unhappy country, and what should be done next, for he 'was much and usually advised and counselled by her.'

Chapter Ten

. . . .

A Highland Hamlet

THOUGH SCANDERBEG is often spoken of by his early biographers as King of Albania, this is a title and an office that he never came near to possessing. He was the commander of a group of equals who acknowledged his leadership but not his rule, and these were men normally suspicious of each other's motives, and unable to see far beyond their own estates or mountain valleys. A leader was doubly suspect, for in planning the defence of a whole nation, choosing the best strongpoints, ensuring garrisons in the right places, demanding men and money for the war, it inevitably seemed that he was trying to increase his personal authority and extend his direct rule. And so, in the long run, he inevitably was. In Albania as elsewhere, facts would have impelled him to curb feudal anarchy by strong centralised rule. The same process had happened with the Nemanjas in Serbia, and it was the only way in which a subject people could assert and maintain their independence.

But in the early stages the actions of such a leader were restricted by the traditional rights of his colleagues, and the general assumptions of the society in which he lived. Defections like those of Moses of Dibra were not treason to Albania, because Albania did not yet exist as a political unit. He, like other chieftains, was open to persuasion by Scanderbeg or anyone else; those who were Roman Catholics could be intimidated from time to time by threat of excommunication if they did not join in the fight against Islam; but there was no means of coercing them. The decision about whom they would support was theirs alone, and the assumptions on which they made it were a mixture of ancient tribalism and more modern feudalism. That is to say, their roots-and this applies more especially to the men of the northern mountains-lay in that tradition-sanctioned anarchy we have already seen at work, where the doings of the various tribes were regulated in the most complicated detail by custom, and law in its formal sense did not exist at all. Justice between men, as between tribes, was dispensed in the course of the blood feud, whose protocol had been fixed since time out of mind. When, therefore, Scanderbeg said he forgave Moses and refused to believe he had planned his desertion before Berat, he may well have been influenced by feelings of personal affection for his old ally and of a desire to smooth his return if that should prove possible; but equally he knew the limits of action open to him. Moses had his own tribal followers, as Gjergj Castrioti had. Vengeance against him by an outsider would have been in their eyes the murder of one Albanian by another; it would have created the demand for answering blood, not out of emotional desire for revenge, but because that was the next step in the highly formal dance of the vendetta. The full extent of Scanderbeg's achievement as both statesman and military leader can be appreciated only if this handicap, and the way he accepted and transformed it to a bond of national unity, is borne in mind.

If their roots were tribal, the chieftains had to live in a feudal world, whose assumptions they accepted in the main. They were quite content to fit into a scheme of things where they acknowledged some sovereign Lord in return for protection, assurance that they would go on possessing their lands, and if possible financial and economic help. To this end they were prepared to negotiate with Venice, Naples, Serbia, and even Turkey, for though they naturally preferred an overlord with the same religion and culture as their own, they were concerned first and foremost to preserve their lands and status intact. If Scanderbeg, by skill in the field and in diplomacy, could preserve both their authority and freedom of action, well and good. Success was the finest cement for the Albanian national cause, and after the disaster of Berat the building came tumbling down. Moses was not alone in making his peace with the Turks. Encouraged by Venice, Nicola and Pal Dukagjini made a bow in the same direction. Leaders near the coast, such as Gjergj Arianiti in the south, and Stefan Crnojevic in Montenegro, turned back from Naples to Venice in search of a protector.

Albania was weakened, too, by the loss of the prisoners sent back to Adrianople by Izak Bey's victorious army at Berat. Of these, the younger Italians had their lives spared, and were sold as slaves; but the Albanians, together with a number of Bulgarians who had been fighting alongside them, were regarded as 'men unmeet for service, as being proud, lofty and imperious, and such as will never come to be good Turks and Muslims.' So they were impaled; and later their heads, stuffed with straw, were used as footballs by the street urchins. Such, at least was the story spread in Albania; and whether true or not, had probably the double result of flattering native vanity and encouraging future warriors not to allow themselves to be taken prisoner. While these atrocities were supposed to be happening, Moses was being held on probation by the Turks, the better to judge his true reasons for defection. He was given a pension, but his request for an army to lead into Albania was turned down on the valid ground that winter was approaching and it was too late to start campaigning that year. As spring came, he asked again, promising that once he appeared in his own part of the world several of the local leaders would declare for him. He was allowed to choose and organise a force of about 15,000 men, and with this he left Adrianople late in February.

When he heard the news, Scanderbeg 'could not yet let it sink into his mind' that Moses was really his enemy. He was half willing to believe that this was some cunning stratagem in which his one-time friend had coaxed an army out of the Turks merely for the satisfaction of leading it to destruction. At the same time he made all his dispositions for defence. Moses necessarily deserved respect for his personal ability, his knowledge of the terrain and his understanding of the way the Albanian leader's mind worked. Like his former commander, he was 'an old and expert arts master in sleights and subtleties such as ambushes.' From fear of the worst and hope of the best, then, Scanderbeg held his army in good order and took no immediate steps against the invader, who was allowed to march without interruption to the plain of Oronichea. Even when he had arrived there, Scanderbeg was ready to treat with him, but could not bring himself to take the initiative of sending envoys to him. That would lower his prestige and perhaps even cast some doubts on his resolution, and in any case feeling among his own men was running too high. Against all appearances, he still hoped for some way out of war between them, 'even as a kind and natural father when he seeth his own son standing and behaving insolently before him . . . is laden and surcharged with care and grief (and) doth temporise and seek delays . . . seeking first by sweet words and persuasions to convert and dissuade him.'

The two armies met, and as so often in these encounters, the battle began with single combat between two champions. A Turk called Ahimaz stepped out and issued a challenge, which was taken up by an Albanian, Zaharia Gropa. Both men were mounted and wore richly ornamented armour. They wheeled about, giving themselves enough distance for their horses to fly full career, then turned, applied spurs, and with lances couched galloped towards each other. Each hit the other's shield, and both men fell to the ground. They seized swords to continue the fight on foot, but were too heavy to do more than stagger. Then they took to wrestling. The Turk was forced on his back, and Zaharia stabbed him in the throat and then cut off his head. The two horses had dashed off together towards the Albanian ranks, which was taken as a good omen.

Upon this, Moses himself stepped out and challenged his old

leader to personal combat, a gesture which astonished all the Albanians and caused Scanderbeg to 'stand for a time in doubt and mammering with himself, as he did not wish to have the blood of a former friend on his hands. When the challenge continued, accompanied by insults, Scanderbeg began to move out towards him. As he did so, Moses turned about and sped back to his own army. Perhaps he had hoped to stifle some remaining feeling of obligation by this public display of hostility, and a remaining sentiment of loyalty had asserted itself when he realised that he might be responsible for causing the death of the one man who had trusted him above everyone else. He did not wait to explain his action, however, or make a speech to the troops, but gave the order for battle to begin.

The Turkish forces were in two lines, the second being of picked soldiers who were to support the first and prevent it from flying in case of trouble. Behind these two lines was Moses himself with his reserve of Albanians, presumably his own tribal supporters. Scanderbeg's forces, about two thirds the size of the enemy's, and said to have been made up of 6,000 horse and 4,000 foot, were divided into three as usual, with the commander in charge of the midmost group. Both Turkish lines quickly broke under the shock of the Albanian cavalry attack, and the battle became one of hand-to-hand fighting, with both the leaders dangerously involved. Moses, said Scanderbeg later, could not have fought more eagerly in defence of his own country or his own children. And Scanderbeg was at one point thrown back on the crupper of his horse by an enemy lance. But the initial impetus gave the Albanians an advantage they never lost, and Moses escaped with perhaps a third of his army. With memories of Berat and its aftermath, no Turkish prisoners were taken.

Moses wandered around the frontier area for some time and then returned to Adrianople, where he was regarded with contempt. Some kind of prosecution may have been started, but if so, it was dropped, possibly because he was now felt to be below the reach of revenge. His allowance fell into arrears, and he lived in an atmosphere of fear and foreboding. Suddenly he decided, like the Prodigal Son, to go home and throw himself on Scanderbeg's mercy. He left at night and rode as fast as he could to his own country of Dibra, where he was well received, and his own supporters offered him 'infinite salutations and embracements.' Scanderbeg was at a nearby garrison, and one evening Moses went there, girdle around his neck in the form of a halter, fell on his knees and wept, asking for forgiveness. Scanderbeg took him by the hand and 'without any difficulty or delay did freely pardon him' and asked for his views on Turkish policy. Moses had his lands restored to him; bonfires were lit to celebrate his return; and people were warned that his offence should never be publicly referred to.

However, the full tale of desertions had yet to be told, and defections also took place in the Castrioti family itself. Scanderbeg's nephew Gjergj Stresi Balsha, son of his sister Helena, handed over the frontier fortress of Modrica to the Turks. This was a valuable position, especially as Svetigrad had never been recaptured, for it was near the frontier, on the Albanian side of the river Drin, and formed an obstacle to any invading army almost from the moment it entered the country. Balsha claimed that he had lost it by a ruse, an argument that might perhaps have been expected to impress a man who was supposed to have taken Kruja the same way. Scanderbeg's critics believed him, or affected to; and said the young man was only being suspected in order to give his uncle an excuse for annexing what remained of the once extensive Balsha lands. The ugly fact, however, was that Modrica was lost, whether it had or had not been sold for 30,000 ducats as alleged. Balsha was sent off to life imprisonment in Naples, himself knowing best whether this was the reward of treachery or of inefficiency.

More serious was the desertion in 1457 of another nephew, Hamza Castrioti, son of Scanderbeg's eldest brother Stanisha, who married a Turkish, or at least Muslim woman, and brought up his son in the mother's faith. Hamza became a Christian during the general revolt after the battle of Nish. His uncle Gjergj's rise to fame, though it increased the influence of the Castriotis as a family, undermined his own position as an individual. He was, in fact, the Hamlet of the Albanian highlands; but not, thanks to the existence of the Turkish Sultan, a Hamlet who need conjure up ghostly admonitions. It is true that Hamza was not the first to be passed over in this way, for in lands like Albania primogeniture is not an absolute law: the ability to rule is of more importance than the date of a man's birth. And the problem was not at first acute. Like Hamlet, Hamza could console himself that he was his uncle's heir, and in his case there was not a too greatly loved mother to complicate the story. This uncle was a confirmed bachelor who said he would never fall into the trap of matrimony. In such conditions, Hamza had room to develop his ambitions. He was ambitious and talented, and eager to make good the very modest showing he had given in the battle against the Venetians at Scutari. He was small and far from good looking, but he had character and intellect and was a persuasive speaker. He could hide his own true feelings, and yet never give the impression of being sly or chilling. He was 'officious and serviceable to all men;' that is, easily accessible. And his men were fond of him because he was liberal in disposing of his own share of the booty. He was also impatient and could not bear to be idle; for him, any action was better than none and this trait perhaps finally weighed the balance in favour of joining the Turks.

He was a long time in making up his mind to desert his uncle, whose marriage had taken place six years earlier. For some years he had ceased to be heir without taking action. Even after the defeat at Berat he did not move, although the lands he now held in his own right were near the eastern frontier. He acted in 1457, almost on the eve of Mehmet II's first attack on Albania since his accession to the throne. Perhaps he now argued to himself that Scanderbeg was doomed, and all members of the Castrioti family would be involved in the ruin unless they disassociated themselves from him. He, as a renegade Muslim, would be in an especially awkward position if he remained loyal to Christianity in its moment of peril. He wrote to the Sultan offering his help, protesting that he had been robbed of his rightful succession and had been given only a meagre estate in return, one which would hardly produce enough for him to live on.

Hamza was a splendid gift to Mehmet, for if Scanderbeg's own nephew were to desert, who was likely to stay with him at the next test of arms? Here, too, was a man with the glamour of the Castrioti name, with a semblance of legal right to the possessions of his grandfather, old Gjon Castrioti. Hamza was therefore declared the rightful ruler of northern Albania in the place of his uncle; and in the course of the summer he prepared to invade his native country along with the general Izak Bey Ivranoz, their combined force numbering perhaps 40,000.

Scanderbeg thought at first that Mehmet would not allow himself a major diversion in Albania as yet, particularly as Belgrade still stood out against him and gave the Hungarians an open door into Serbia and the Ottoman territories. But it may well have been decided that Hamza was a wasting asset, to be used at the earliest possible moment if full effect were to be gained from him; and soon intelligence reports reaching Albania left no doubt that he had collected a sizeable army around him. In Albania the soldiers were ordered to help in getting in the harvest; the corn, some of it still in the sheaf, was taken into the villages and fortresses as quickly as possible. Moses was put in charge of the frontier defence, and Andronica Castrioti was sent from Petrela to the greater security of Kruja. Scanderbeg warned his men to evade open battle, and reminded them that this time they had an opponent who was familiar with their strategic ideas from the inside.

Hamza, marching only by day in case of ambush, reached the frontier by way of Ohrida. Once he could see their dust, Scanderbeg struck camp and began retiring inland, moving by the rougher and higher mountain tracks, so that the enemy in the valley roads could see but not reach him, except for a few horsemen sent for purposes of reconnaissance. He was trying to produce the impression that he was afraid of meeting so large an army with so few troops available to him, and he set out in the direction of Lezhë. This suggested to Hamza that he was probably going to get help from the Venetians. If so, there was no danger of immediate attack, and Izak prepared to press on for Kruja with all speed. Hamza suggested a day or two's delay, to make sure his uncle had really gone out of the area, and was not still shadowing them, but Izak moved as fast and as far as he could in the great heat of the summer days. At night the army camped in the valley, surrounded by a ring of guards in the hills. Scanderbeg had disappeared from view, but was now advancing by roughly parallel mountain valleys. Bursts of fire from his own fortresses along the route, and a series of prearranged signals from individual scouts on the peaks who waved small pennants to say what was happening, kept him informed of what the Turks were doing almost at the moment they were doing it. He took no action against them, however, and allowed them to reach the coastal plain. Here Hamza was chaired around the camp as the new ruler of Albania, and Scanderbeg took up his position on Mount Tumenishta, above Kruja, waiting to see what the invaders intended to do.

The Turkish army camped close to the sea, south of the Mati river, and began plundering the neighbourhood, no doubt to secure victuals, intimidate the population and furbish morale with a few easy victories over the civilians and their livestock. The idea that Scanderbeg had run away to Lezhë to seek refuge or help seems to have been quite accepted, and a heavy guard was put only on the northern side of the camp in order to deal with him if and when he felt able to return thence. The eastern side, facing the mountain where he actually was, remained lightly defended. These dispositions were such as he might have advised his nephew to make in order to ensure the destruction of the Turkish army. He was elated at seeing what had happened, and planned the coming attack with an attention to detail noteworthy even in him. 'If you had seen how Scanderbeg was busied and did bestir himself, you might aptly have compared him to one who expecting at his house some great company of guests, and being to make them some magnificent and sumptuous banquet, with most exquisite dainties and viands prepared more than ordinary, dareth not trust his servants nor yet refer the care thereof to his friends, or to his wife, but will see it done with his own hands: ordaining, fitting and disposing all things most carefully.' The exquisite dainties ranged from the positions Moses and Tanush Thopia were to occupy to the number of trumpets and drums which he proposed to use as offensive weapons.

The scene in the Turkish camp that July afternoon could not have been more tranquil. The horses were feeding, unsaddled and unbridled. The men were sleeping, gambling, lounging or arranging their booty. The high command had been persuaded by Hamza that they should attack Kruja, and preparations had been made to strike camp that day when the main heat of the early afternoon was over. Before this could happen, however, Scanderbeg crept down with eight of his men and they began to cut the throats of the few sleeping guards, 'leaving them there to keep everlasting watch.' One of them escaped and ran back into the camp to give the alarm.

At first the Turks doubted his evidence; but Hamza knew his uncle of old, and guessed that the reassuring effrontery of a foray of nine men against the periphery of an army of many thousands was quite in character. So he began to get his men into some kind of shape for battle; and Scanderbeg, realising that the ruse had been discovered, ordered his infantry to attack immediately, shouting as loudly as they could, and banging drums and sounding trumpets in order to let Moses and Tanush know the attack was beginning and also to give the Turks the impression that an enormous force had broken into the camp. Hamza was aware of this ruse, and tried to get his men to realise that this was the sort of trick only a weak and small force need adopt. Izak

Bey rallied his forces to help Hamza's, but the arrival of the new Albanian contingents under Moses and Tanush forced him to turn his attention to them. Cavalry charges and counter-charges kept the battle moving to and fro for some time, but a rain of missiles from Albanian archers and arquebusiers gradually forced the Turks back into the heart of their camp, and when they had been herded into a mass in this fashion the attackers slung their bows over their backs, seized their swords and marched into the slaughter. Hamza shouted incessantly to the beleaguered Turks to hold on. The Albanians were few in numbers; they could be quickly tired, and then the Turks could go over to the offensive and scatter their foes. But not enough of the Turks ever 'presented themselves to the encounter of a full and just battle,' for too many were surprised and captured, fled from the battlefield or were 'murdered and like a many of hogs had their throats cut by the Albanians.' So the Turkish force melted away. Izak escaped, but Hamza was captured. His hands were bound behind him, and he had to watch his captors looting and carousing in the abandoned tents and pavilions, where 'in many places they found cloth and napkins ready laid, and the victuals set upon the table.'

Next morning the triumphal march back to Kruja began. The start was delayed, we are told, by a quarrel between two tipsy soldiers over booty which came to the commander's notice. He told them to make friends again over another drink, an order which his early biographer clothes in the toga of classical phraseology: 'Bacchus hath made you enemies, and I will that Bacchus, and not Mars nor any other of the gods, shall make you friends.' As the procession moved forward, it was joined by peasants who had taken to the woods in fear and had now come out of hiding. Behind them came the army in battle array, and even the infantrymen had at least one horse and some spoils each. The prisoners came behind, two deep, and carrying some of the captured standards and the purple tents of Izak Bey. Hamza and the enemy commander's standard bearer, were sent separately. At the city gates the companies were dismissed. The standards and

Scanderbeg's personal booty were carried inside, and the soldiery went home to enjoy their new possessions and to sing ballads about the victory. Mehmet is said to have heard the news of the defeat in silence. He sent a messenger to ransom the standard bearer for 15,000 crowns and about forty of the more distinguished prisoners for a thousand crowns each. Half of the money for the latter ransoms came, as was customary, from the royal treasury and half from the families concerned. Many of the other prisoners were allowed to go free. Some chose to be baptised as Christians, and settled in Albania. Others were 'dispersed abroad for presents in a manner to all the Kings of Christendom and with these slaves went horses and trophies of various kinds to Naples, France, Spain, Rome and elsewhere, as Scanderbeg had determined 'to the uttermost of his power to bind unto him by his courtesy almost the whole world.' Hamza, whom the Sultan had not troubled about (not that 'all the gold in the world' would have ransomed him) was sent for safe keeping in one of Alfonso's dungeons.

The envoy, an official called Mezhet, sent to ransom the Turkish prisoners, also took with him a message from the Sultan offering Scanderbeg a truce. Mezhet was 'glad and cheerful for this his commission,' and started to discuss it even before he had finished counting out the ransom money. But, he was asked, since the Albanians had refused peace when things were going badly for them, was it likely they would bind themselves now that things were going so well? Mezhet said he was talking of a ten-year truce, at which Scanderbeg began to show more interest. His reply shows that he had clearly defined to his own satisfaction the minimum terms on which he could hope to secure an independent Albania under his own leadership. He said he was prepared to consider negotiations only if Svetigrad and Berat were first handed over to him, and would maintain an informal truce until he received Mehmet's answer to this offer.

It is just conceivable that Scanderbeg, having once shown that he was not to be dislodged from Kruja, might have secured some such terms from Murad II in return for acknowledgement of his own sovereignty and a payment of tribute. But it was impossible for the conqueror of Constantinople to exile himself permanently from Albania and the Adriatic coast. He therefore ignored the terms suggested to him, and strengthened the frontier garrisons in the neighbourhood of Svetigrad and Modrici, to prevent any raids on Turkish territory and probably to deal with any moves against the disputed garrisons. Moses and Scanderbeg mounted a number of small provocative attacks against the newcomers in order to try and test their intentions; but though the Sultan had no intention of giving up any fortresses, he instructed two new commanders on the frontier, Hamur and Sinan, to get on friendly terms with their enemy. Accordingly, after a letter saying that their intentions were purely defensive, they paid a courtesy visit to his camp. When gifts had been exchanged-of equal value, so that neither side might compromise the other-Hamur remarked 'how goodly and pleasant a thing it would be if these two great and puissant princes could be conjoined and united in amity.' By this time the other puissant prince had allowed a year to elapse without saying what he thought about Scanderbeg's conditions for peace. He had neither agreed to hand over Svetigrad and Berat, nor given any sign of sending another army to win Kruja for himself. Scanderbeg said he could promise nothing, but he commended Hamur's own 'honest and good carriage,' and touched upon 'this our private friendship.' The Turk in return kissed the hand of 'him that was both his friend and his enemy.' The Turkish armies remained where they were, and the populace and soldiers both 'inclining to peace,' the summer of 1458 was spent 'in great sloth and idleness.' No truce had been declared, but there was peace in fact, if not in name, and the outlook better better than it had been for some years. The Albanians were able to start rebuilding after the destructions of the recent wars, especially in the plains, 'where many goodly marks of antiquity lay defaced and overthrown.'

Suddenly three grave blows fell. Count Vrana Altisferi died, the lieutenant who had served Scanderbeg for sixteen years. He had learned the art of warfare in Italy, hence his courtesy title, and his integrity had been proven by the severest test-his indifference to Murad II's bribes during the great siege of Kruja in 1450. He was wise, loved by his men, and unaffected by the jealousies and recriminations of the chieftains in general. There was not another such man in Albania. The second blow was the death of Callixtus III, the Spanish Pope whose enthusiasm for war against the Turks helped to focus the attention of Europe on Gjergj Castrioti. Callixtus called him the soldier and champion of Christendom, and appointed him Captain General of the Holy See after the rout of Hamza's and Izak Bey's army the previous year.

Third, King Alfonso of Naples died. No other monarch had contributed to Albanian resistance on such a scale as he. He had not merely doled out a pension calculated to keep Scanderbeg on the shortest possible lead, but had given money, food, prestige and the much-needed artillery. His Balkan policy, imperialist as it was in theory, tended in practice to create of Albania a large and coherent national unit. Berat, it was true, had been lost at the last moment by a foolish lack of judgment and relapse of discipline, with consequences that might have proved fatal. But Berat could just as easily have been won back from the Turks, thus undermining their whole position in Albania; and this could never have been seriously contemplated without Alfonso's interest and support. So both personal grief and political apprehension were involved in the public mourning that followed the news. Messengers were sent to offer condolences to his natural son and successor, Ferrante, to congratulate him on his succession and to ask for a renewal of the alliance. Behind this gesture of loyalty, however, were two unspoken questions. How far would the new king wish to be implicated in Balkan problems in addition to a complicated Italian heritage that had taxed even his long- experienced and highly self-confident father? And, even worse, how long would it be before the Anjou family (who used to rule Naples) claimed the throne for themselves and took up arms against him?

Scanderbeg took advantage of the change of rulers in Naples, and the general amnesty which followed, to have his luckless nephew Hamza sent back home. Hamza had made several attempts at reconciliation with his uncle, who probably now thought to gain any goodwill there might be in such a gesture, while at the same time having the young man more directly under his control. On his return, he was at first kept under close arrest; but little by little restrictions were relaxed, and eventually he was offered his liberty, and his former estates were restored to him.

But the old father-and-son relationship could not be restored. Scanderbeg had a son of his own, and Hamza's wife and children were still in Adrianople. He wanted to be with them, either there or in Albania, so he asked to be allowed to appear to escape from detention in order to join them. He intended, he said, to ingratiate himself into the confidence of the Sultan and await an opportunity to bring his family home for good, together with any information he could secure on Turkish plans towards Albania.

It is doubtful whether he was sincere in this, since to him home clearly implied the Muslim religion and Turkish culture. His uncle does not seem to have troubled about whether Hamza was sincere in his request. He had granted him his life, he said, and Hamza could do with it what he wished. If he deliberately put his faith in the Sultan a second time, he was the only one who would be injured thereby. An escape from prison was arranged; the jailers were soundly and publicly berated for the sake of appearances; and Hamza crossed the frontier.

He was well enough received in the Turkish capital, and no doubts were expressed about his story, though they may have been implied in the fact that 'he was not wholly and fully restored to his former estate, honours and pensions.' Within a short time he disappeared, and is thought to have died within a few months of his return, before he could demonstrate where his future loyalties lay. Not unnaturally, the Sultan has been accused of having him poisoned on suspicion of espionage. Though there is not a jot of evidence for this, it would provide a dramatically fitting nemesis for a man who, unable to endure 'the smoke and shadow of servitude' in his own country, deserted it and so 'fell into the very flame and raging fire of bondage.'

Chapter Eleven

. . . .

THE FRIEND OF VIRTUE

THE ARAGONESE AMBITION to create a Mediterranean empire had for some time proven to be beyond their capacities. King Alfonso had found that even to have his rule accepted in Italy was almost more than he could manage: he certainly could not play the part of arbiter of the whole peninsula, about which he had dreamed. This passive policy even at home meant that he had no chance of undertaking a successful crusade against the Turks; and it left Scanderbeg master of as much of his own house as he could win by tact and arms, making him in effect independent of his overlord.[1]

It had taken Alfonso many years to realise that he had not the strength to grasp the position he had marked out for himself. He had built up an efficient state administration in Naples, one of the best in contemporary Europe; but this too was a source of weakness by tempting the king into attractive paper schemes which he could not afford or had not the strength of arms to carry out. Social and economic power in the kingdom lay with the barons, who had lately turned vast stretches of the Apulian tablelands over to sheep grazing in order to bring in quick money, thus distorting the economy and weakening the free cities. Alfonso needed money and could get it only from the barons; as an inducement he offered them further concessions, with the result that they grew in real power and he only in apparent glory. The greatest of these lords was Giovannantonio

Orsini del Balzo, Duke of Taranto. Alfonso owed much to him in the days when he had been fighting for the throne of Naples; but he forgot that a king must act in the public interest and not merely indulge his own personal feelings. To this old colleague he had handed over the city of Bari, a former provincial capital of the Byzantine empire and a great port, with the right to export whatever he would, and a grant of 100,000 ducats with which to maintain his armed followers. While on the surface a centralising Renaissance monarch, surrounded as he was with artists and scholars of a kind, Alfonso was in fact thrusting his country further back into feudal anarchy.

As might have been expected, his concessions did not win the loyalty of the barons, who rightly attributed them to weakness. So long as Alfonso was himself able to control and willing to placate them, they were prepared to tolerate him. But as and when they were ready to revolt, they could always rely on help from outside. The Papacy, though it encouraged the Aragonese kings to support its crusading policy in the Balkans, feared their ambitions in Italy and was prepared on occasion to encourage civil war against them. Equally, the French house of Anjou, the former rulers of Naples, were willing to help anyone who would fight for their right to the throne.

The barons' opportunity came on the death of Alfonso. Ferdinand, or Ferrante, who succeeded him, was his 27-year-old natural son, whose mother had been a married woman from Barcelona. He was taken to Italy at the age of eight, was there during the dramatic years during which his father conquered Naples from the Anjou, and was proclaimed Duke of Calabria and heir to the throne at the age of twelve. To strengthen the links between the throne and its greatest subjects, Alfonso chose as wife for his son Isabella di Chiaramonte, sister-in-law of the Duke of Andria and niece of Giovannantonio Orsini del Balzo. Ferrante's handicaps were many. Not the least was the general reference to him as the *Bastardo*; in triumph it might have become almost an affectionate nickname, but it soon became a contemptuous epithet for a man who was likely to lose a throne he was only doubtfully entitled to. He had a bankrupt treasury. It was so dramatically and literally devoid of money that when revolt had begun against him, Queen Isabella had to stand at the entrance to the church of San Pietro Martire in Naples and beg contributions from passers-by. The new king was involved in the odium attaching to all things Spanish, for Naples had provided wealth and influence for many fellow-nationals of the new dynasty, especially the shrewd Catalans who built up banking and trading interests there.

Ferrante wisely began his uncertain reign by sending a number of Spaniards home, reducing taxes, including those on salt, and telling the barons that he intended to govern 'with their affection.' This they declined to show him. Instead, encouraged by Pope Callixtus III, they started a revolt and invited John of Anjou to come and take the throne. However, Ferrante received a partial reprieve by the timely death of the Pope. The new one, Pius II, was amenable to persuasion by the Sforza family of Milan, who did not want to see the French in southern Italy as well as on her north western frontier. In return for the gift of Benevento to the States of the Church, the Pope recognised Ferrante as king and he was accordingly crowned in Bari in February 1459.

Although this gave him improved status abroad, his problems only increased at home. The barons did not disarm in spite of the Pope's refusal to go on supporting them. And when John of Anjou landed near the mouth of the Volturno river in the autumn of 1459 to win back his family's throne, Orsini del Balzo and his friends called in the soldier of fortune Jacob Piccinino to organise their armies. Piccinino followed a family calling: his father and elder brother had been *condottieri* before him. He had served many different masters, including Venice and the Sforzas, as well as acting on his own behalf. He had good personal reasons as well as the usual mercenary ones for accepting the new appointment, for in the adjustment of frontiers leading to Pius

II's recognition, Ferrante had acknowledged the Pope's right to some lands in Umbria which Piccinino had made his own. It was not long before he had the revenge he sought. Though the Pope did not himself send soldiers to help Ferrante (he was engaged in a war against Sigismondo Malatesta of Rimini), he permitted Alessandro Sforza to send a detachment from northern Italy across his territory. Piccinino made a quick dash across country to intercept these reinforcements, and caught and defeated them at San Fabbiano near Giulianova in July 1460. After this triumph he was given command of all the Anjou forces in the Kingdom of Naples.

Ferrante himself had already been disastrously beaten a few days earlier, and had hardly managed to get back to his capital. There he had to remain for the time being, waiting for more troops from Sforza, hoping for quarrels in the rebel command, and looking around for other allies. One name immediately came to mind, that of his Albanian feudatory, Gjergj Castrioti. Castrioti had no more obligation to the king than the rebel lords. He was, as they were not, menaced by a mighty and aggressive empire on his frontier, and could have pleaded that his place was in Albania, in the interests of Naples as well as his own. Yet, to support the apparently hopeless cause to which he felt himself in honour bound, he made a local truce with the Turks and prepared in the second half of 1460 to send forces across the Adriatic.

Two worlds—the fastidious sense of obligation of the Albanian mountaineer on the one hand, and on the other the overweening pride of the Italian baron—were now to meet. The contrast between their values is brought out in the letters between the leader of the rebels, who sought to persuade Scanderbeg to stay at home, and the loyal feudatory, who explained why he must come to Italy. The version that has reached us has been edited and displayed to best advantage by a classical humanist, but behind all the trappings of pseudo-antiquity the characters of the two men emerge clearly.

On the one side, the correspondent was Giovannantonio Orsini. The Orsinis—who in the best Romulan traditions took their name from a progenitor said to have been reared on the milk of a she bear (*orsa*)—had married into imperial and royal families, and had provided popes and cardinals and statesmen in considerable numbers. The family tree had spread its stock in all parts of the Italian peninsula. One branch, linked with the del Balzo family of Soleto, had taken possession of Taranto in 1399, and set up there a princely court with the usual fashionable ration of writers and lawyers. When the reigning Orsini died, however, King Ladislav of Hungary married his widow and promptly declared himself successor to the late Prince of Taranto. Giovannantonio was the disinherited heir. Despairing of ever seeing his claims to the succession recognised under the Anjou kings of Naples, he revolted against them and took Part in the risks and later the triumph of Alfonso of Aragon's campaign. He had nothing to complain of while Alfonso lived, but he suspected that Ferrante, a shrewd observer of his father's difficulties, intended to reduce his great lords to submission and create a centralised monarchy. So he slipped away from court, fortified Taranto, and put himself at the head of the rebels.

It now seemed that the Aragonese monarchy, which had once looked like becoming so powerful, would soon be the mere tool of the Orsinis, Andrias and their like, or even be driven off the mainland and back to Sicily. What was the point of Scanderbeg prolonging the agony and postponing the inevitable end? And why should the Aragonese have the advantage of his name, which was known and respected by everyone in Italy? Orsini decided to induce the Albanian leader to abandon his project.[2]

'Respected, magnificent and valorous hero, our dearest friend' he began, and went on to say he had heard tell that Scanderbeg had promised Don Ferrando—an insulting suggestion that Ferdinand had already ceased to be king—to send men if ships were sailed across to Albania to collect them, and that they would be used to wreak havoc at Brindisi and lay waste the country around. He had been unable to believe this, as he had always regarded Scanderbeg as a wise and prudent man; but he now learned that both foot soldiers and cavalry had in fact been sent to Apulia, where they were causing much damage in the lands of His Majesty King Rainier (father of John of Anjou) and of the writer. He was surprised at this, for what injury or insult had Scanderbeg ever received from his aforesaid majesty or, again, from the writer? Scanderbeg had been reported as saying that he was acting out of respect for the memory of King Alfonso; but he could be assured of greater assistance and favours than ever he had received from that quarter, for he could be certain that the Kings of France were better Catholics and Christians than any other princes in the world. Moreover, since practically everyone, princes and people, had changed their allegiance to the new monarch, it would be quite impracticable for Scanderbeg and his Albanians to give Don Ferrando the help he needed. At the same time, he could make powerful enemies for himself, and was most earnestly counselled and entreated therefore to take back his men the way they had come. If, having done so, he wanted peace and friendship with the illustrious Duke of Calabria, son of his aforesaid majesty King Rainier (i.e. with John of Anjou), he should let Orsini know, and it would be possible for him to get better terms for him than he would be able to gain for himself. If he had it in mind to make war on someone, then near at hand he had the Turk, who could bestow on him more glory and honour than he would derive from a venture—and most assuredly, a lost venture—in a cause which did not concern him, but in which he stood to lose all the men he had sent or proposed to send in future.

It was a letter to send to a fellow Italian princeling, making as it did all the right appeals, in the deftest manner, to the fears and cupidities they shared with each other. It was not in any way adapted to touch the springs of Scanderbeg's conduct, for if he had been the type of character open to such persuasion he would never have embarked on his resistance to the Turk, or at least would have abandoned it when the Sultan was prepared to come to terms with him. There was an exchange of letters, but not of ideas. Machiavelli began the correspondence; Don Quixote replied:

'Serene Prince and highly honoured lord,' began Scanderbeg, writing from Kruja on 31st October 1460. As to the story that he had sent forces to help His Most Serene Majesty King Ferrando, he would like to say it was true that having heard of Orsini's rebellion he had certainly offered the king help. If there had been no rebellion in the first place, no damage would have been done by him around Brindisi. Orsini's concern should have been to defend his own possessions, and not rouse the state against the king to whom he had sworn an oath of fealty. As for the attempt, by promises of favours to come from 'this King you have made,' to wean him from loyalty to the family of 'that blessed and immortal King of Aragon, on whose memory neither I nor any of my vassals can dwell without tears, we make answer to you that if you were to regard us as faithful, in the same way that you say you regard us as wise and prudent, you would not be at all surprised at this, because you would remember that the advice, subsidies and favours and blessed work of that angelic King were what guarded and preserved myself and my vassals from oppression at the cruel hands of our enemies the Turks, and the Catholic faith along with us. If I had been overwhelmed, Italy would certainly have known about it, and that realm you speak of as yours might well have been theirs. So, having received benefits on that scale from his Majesty, neither I nor my vassals could fail in our duty to his son without humiliating ourselves and branding ourselves with infamy and the guilt of the grossest ingratitude.'

As for the Christianity of the Kings of France, and the benefits to be expected from them, he neither knew nor wished to know this new King. He did not regard him as an enemy. All who had been baptised were Christians equally one with another, but what the Turks respected and feared were the flags of the House of Aragon, 'for which I am willing to die.' The argument that King Ferrante was beyond help because everyone had deserted him was repulsed on two counts. If the King had suffered so far, the responsibility belonged above all to Orsini, who had led barons and people like sheep to the slaughter. That, however, did not mean that the cause was lost, for God would defend his own justice, and friends and helpers would not be lacking.

'Do not forget that the power of the Grand Turk was greater than either yours or that of the sovereign you are supporting, and that when there remained to me only the city of Kruja—which now belongs to His Majesty and the House of Aragon—and I found myself besieged there, I defended and preserved it against those great forces to such effect that the Turks were hurt and shamed into raising the siege; and I, in a short time and with a very small body of men, won back what so many enemies had taken so long to win for themselves.' The fact that the King might hold only Naples, then, gave ample reason for thinking that he might yet recover the whole realm. As to the suggestion that Albanians might not suffice to put down his potent enemies, 'if our historians do not lie to us, we are named Epirots,[3] and you ought to be aware that on several occasions in the past our ancestors crossed into the land that you hold today and had some great battles with the Romans, which for the most part ended in honour rather than shame for them.' (This argument was a double-edged weapon, for had Orsini continued the correspondence, and taken up this allusion he could have pointed out that the greatest Epirot of the past, Pyrrhus, had indeed fought in Apulia and given his name to a type of victory more costly than defeat could have been).

For his part, the Albanian continued, he would do everything he could to help his sovereign, and he was not prepared to accept advice and exhortations about fighting the Turks. 'We have not sent our people in order to call them back straight away, but so that they can serve King Ferrando until he has united his kingdom again; and they are the kind of people who feel the necessity of facing any threat of death in his service.'

Scanderbeg now unmasked his heaviest batteries against his opponent. The forces which had crossed already into Italy were nothing compared with those he had promised. He was coming in person, with men enough, he thought, not only to reconquer Apulia with the help of God but to repopulate it. There was no point in denying that the Turks were close at hand, because everyone knew how long he had been fighting them, and with what results; but he had in fact made a truce with them for three years in order to be able to discharge his obligations to King Ferdinand. Orsini's advice to fight the Turks instead of him 'would have had more to commend it, as well as being more conducive to both your bodily and spiritual health, if you had taken it yourself. You are an extremely old man (he was in fact 65; Scanderbeg himself was not far short of 60) and the nearest of all the Italian princes to the Turk, so that there is no more glorious enterprise in which you could have consummated your days and employed your wealth.'

The same day, Scanderbeg wrote to the beleaguered King Ferdinand. 'My Lord,' he began, 'the worst kind of people in my opinion are those who see their lords or allies or friends over-taken by some kind of trouble and wait to be called upon or asked for help. I am sure Your Majesty will remember that as soon as disturbances and rebellion broke out in your kingdom, I sent word to you in accordance with my duty, offering you my person, my goods and all I have in the world. Your Majesty, thinking either that you would not have need of them, or that I would not put my promises into effect, never asked me for anything. But on receiving news that Your Majesty's affairs were daily going from bad to worse, I did not consult you further but sent some infantry and cavalry into Apulia to help Your Majesty, using such few ships as were available. I do not know what effect they have had yet, only that the Prince of Taranto wrote me a letter, a copy of which, and of the reply I made him, I am sending to Your Majesty. I am very surprised that His Lordship should think to turn me from my intention by his brusque words, and I should like to say one thing: May God guard Your Majesty from ill and harm and danger, but however things may turn out I am the friend of virtue and not of fortune. I would inform Your Majesty, if my men have done you service or are likely to do so, and if others should be sent, and how many, that a few days ago I equipped two hundred good horses, which await Your Majesty's orders. I most earnestly ask that you would be pleased to advise me if there should be any doubt at all about the outcome of your affairs; because, my Lord, I will myself come over with so many men that even if you have no other helpers, my followers and I have spirit enough to make good the lack and faith one and all to die in the service of Your majesty.'[4]

In some ways, notably the mention of a three year truce with the Turks and the threat to bring over enough men to settle the issue whatever the conditions in Italy itself, the form of this letter is no doubt an exercise in wartime propaganda. At the same time here is the essential Scanderbeg, frank, warm-hearted, and in no doubt about his own abilities, for all that he signs the letter as the king's 'servant and vassal,' and writes it 'humbly at the feet of Your Majesty.' Its sincerity is in no doubt, as his conduct immediately afterwards shows; but equally he could not have been unaware that interest as well as sentiment bound him to the Aragonese dynasty. If they fell, there would be nowhere to turn for support. Naples would be reduced to baronial anarchy and cease to have any serious ambitions in the Balkans, and there would be no one to take her place. Ferrante's crisis was Scanderbeg's own, and he was quick to see that the struggle against the Turks could well be decided against him in southern Italy, where alone he could find the diplomatic and financial support, and perhaps the eventual refuge, that he needed.

His wife Donica was appointed to act on his behalf at home, and a council of local notables was set up to help her. He sent about 500 horsemen ahead under his nephew, Gjon Stresi Balsha, as the vanguard of his own forces. These were taken straight to Apulia in Neapolitan galleys, and were presumably the soldiers who caused such annoyance to Prince Orsini. The main force did not sail directly to Italy, but went by way of Ragusa. Some of the galleys set out from the Venetian ports of Durazzo, Lezhë and Shëngjin, and the leader sailed from 'Ascriunia' which is presumably a garbled reference to the Acroceraunian range whose rocky claw guards Vlora Bay from the south and west.

There were a number of reasons for calling first at Ragusa. For one thing, the Pope had given permission for some of the money collected there for a crusade against the Turks to be paid to the Albanians to cover their expenses in their present Italian expedition. For another, the Ragusans wanted to see and honour a man of whom such stories had been told. His situation, on the seaward side of the hills from which a Turkish army might appear at any time, was similar to their own, and all his successes were an encouragement to them. And Gjergj Castrioti's high standing in the eyes of the Vatican reflected glory on Ragusa, where so many of the clergy were of Albanian origin and thus felt more than the general pride in his achievements. So he was received as an honoured guest. 'Divers sorts of shows and pleasant triumphs' were prepared for him, such as tournaments and jousts. He was shown the harbour, the arsenal and the ramparts. The Senate received him in their chamber, gifts were exchanged and orations made, the Chancellor speaking for the hosts and Pal Angeli, Archbishop of Durazzo, for the guests. The army, consisting perhaps of 3,000 cavalry and somewhat fewer infantry, with victuals for a fortnight in case of delays in reaching Italy, was embarked; and the galleys were prepared in battle order in case an attempt at interception was made, with Scanderbeg in charge of the right wing and Moses, Gjin Musachi and two others in charge of the left. A prayer was said to St. Michael, whose legendary home on Mount Gargano, the spur on the Italian foot, would be their landfall. Mass was sung and anchors raised. They sailed with a favouring wind but were delayed first by mist and then by a heavy storm, and they rode at anchor for eight days under shelter of one of the islands near the eastern coast. Once they could move, they reached the huge green hummock of Gargano in a day and a night and from here they sailed across the Gulf of Manfredonia. Their goal was the town of Barletta, where King Ferrante was a prisoner, being besieged by the main body of the French army under John of Anjou and Piccinino. On seeing his fleet approach, they withdrew for some distance outside the range of gunfire, and the King welcomed his new ally with tears and embraces.

The military situation could hardly have been more simple or more desperate. John of Anjou held the entire kingdom except for the city of Naples and the two fortresses of Barletta and nearby Trani. Barletta would have fallen if help had not arrived, and the governor of Trani, Antonio Josciano Infusado, was thought to be on the point of yielding up his trust to the French. Now, however, the arrival of the Albanians allowed Ferrante to take the initiative. Under cover of this diversion and the local retreat it had forced on the besiegers, Ferrante was able to leave Barletta in Scanderbeg's care and break out of the town, leading his men northwards through the Appenines to join the second contingent that Alexander Sforza was sending down from Milan. The juncture was made at San Bartolomeo in Campania, just over the Apulian border, so that Ferrante once again possessed an army with which he could hope to meet the Anjou.

Scanderbeg conducted a number of forays from Barletta-the booty from which was shared with the townspeople-both to announce his presence and to acclimatise himself and his men with the countryside and the unfamiliar type of war they were now to engage in. They could no longer rely on the familiar cover of their forests and mountain hideouts. This was open and for the most part flat or gently rolling country where the heavily-armed cavalry of the twilight age of chivalry, which formed the backbone of both Ferrante's and Piccinino's strategy, would have a moral and physical advantage over their lean light mounts. So from the first, Scanderbeg sought to convince his light cavalry that they had nothing to fear from the weight of their opponents. Instead of being unnerved by it, as well they might when they could no longer rely on ambush and surprise, they must look on it as a piece of good fortune. The weight of the French would be their undoing, he said, since 'their well-shielded horses (were) neither so ready to pursue nor yet so nimble to fly from us . . . we being lightly armed and mounted.' Even more than at home, then, they must rely on speed to produce their victory.

Having prepared them in this fashion, he mounted an attack on the French camp, adopting the tactics familiar to many of them since the destruction of Hamza's army a few years earlier. Three separate contingents were to take part, the defenders never being allowed to know which was intended as the most serious one. There were to be simulated panic-stricken retreats, followed by a sudden rally and a turn when the enemy had been coaxed out of his defended positions. This was war as it had been learned and perfected by a general fighting for existence against an enemy who might offer him a principality one day or flay him alive the next. But this was not war as understood in fifteenth century Italy. There it was played as formally as a game of chess, of which the pieces, the mercenaries and the professional *condottieri* such as Piccinino, were returned to the box when the encounter was over, to be taken out again when prestige, honour, boredom or a quarrel over a village or a castle provoked two other players to pit themselves against each other.

Machiavelli[5] may have exaggerated when he ridiculed some great Italian battle in which only three men lost their lives, and that by suffocation in a muddy ditch; but he has shrewdly described the methods of the *condottieri* who 'used every art to lessen fatigue and danger to themselves and their soldiers, not killing in the fray, but taking prisoners without exchange of blows. They did not attack towns at night, nor did the garrisons of the towns attack encampments at night; they did not stockade or entrench a camp, nor did they conduct campaigns in winter. All these things were sanctioned by their rules of war, and devised by them, as I have said, to avoid fatigue and peril; and thereby they have brought Italy to slavery and shame.'

The professional soldiers supposed that Scanderbeg would be King Ferrante's 'condottiere' as Piccinino was Duke John's. They never expected to find a man for whom war was a matter of life and death. His tactics, such as taking advantage of a camp's defencelessness to attack it, would destroy the common asset of professional soldiers on both sides: the men they led, who were to be hired out at so much a head and set upon each other in a series of formalised encounters whose number and duration would be stretched out to the extreme limits of the Paymaster's patience. The Anjou had the less reason for changing their tactics as they now wished to withdraw from Barletta to prevent Sforza and Ferranto from joining their forces. They had no desire to waste their strength on unorthodox diversions imposed on them by a man who obviously wanted to win the war, and as quickly as possible. To make him see reason, to recall him to his duties as a condottiere, Piccinino arranged a personal meeting in the no man's land between the two armies. The count, a diminutive figure, was so astonished and impressed with the sight of his opponent-with his tall figure, his white beard and helmet he must have seemed to belong to some primeval race of heroes-that he could say nothing, but stood looking him up and down. Thereupon Scanderbeg lifted him up, gave him a kiss of greeting and gently replaced him on the ground.

A great condottiere had to be a shrewd judge of the human heart. He needed to know one kind of generalship to outmanoeuvre the enemy and quite another to do the same with his own employer, who was today's friend but would possibly be tomorrow's enemy. To such a man Scanderbeg was easy work. Though far ahead of Renaissance Italy in his methods of warfare, since these had been forced on him by bitter experience, he was far behind it in methods of diplomacy. He might retain something of his father's craft and cunning; but this did not go very deep, it had more of the peasant than the courtier in it, and a skilled negotiator could usually assess its significance without much difficulty. He remained a mediaeval man, with an innocent and quixotic sense of personal honour, and it was this gift, or failing, that Piccinnino now decided to turn to his own uses.

The Italian saw the kind of man with whom he was dealing when, in the course of their meeting, Scanderbeg without a second thought let free a hundred prisoners whom his lieutenants had taken that same day. Piccinnino had only to protest, rightly or wrongly, that they had been taken after the bugles had sounded a cease-fire. So he made himself amiable and spun out the talks so that they had to be adjourned to the next day. A time and a place were fixed, and on the following morning Scanderbeg set out with seven horsemen to resume the parley. On the way he was met by a Frenchman who warned him that he should go no further, as there was a plot to ambush and capture him. Presumably the Frenchman explained his action as the due owed by one man of honour to another. A short reconnaissance was made, and it seemed that the Frenchman had been speaking the truth. Outraged by such perfidy, a formal defiance was sent to Piccinnino,[6] challenging him to battle the next morning. Soon after sunrise he advanced 'with his army in good order and full resolution.' He found no enemy. The Anjou army had decamped without hindrance. True, it did not carry the prize of Scanderbeg's person away with it, so the main part of the *condottiere's* plan failed, but it bought time in which to pack up and move unobserved.

Scanderbeg remained in defence of Barletta, and his next immediate task was to secure the fortress of Trani, which seemed in danger from Infusado's dubious loyalty. He arranged an interview to sound out the governor's loyalty, and suggested that there should be no question of betraying the king who put the town into his hands. Infusado replied that Ferrante owed him some thousands of ducats in payment, and that if he did not receive them he knew what he would do. This showed an obtuseness in face of Scanderbeg's old-fashioned standards of honour quite as remarkable in its way as Piccinino's shrewdness. He was immediately bound and made prisoner, and only gained his freedom by surrendering the castle, which Gjon Stresi Balsha occupied for King Ferrante early in December.

The Albanians had no major encounter with the Anjou forces, but conducted a series of skirmishes against any enemy detachments operating near the Adriatic coast. Pius II later gave his impression of them as 'lightly armed cavalry, swift horsemen, good for looting and plundering, but useless for warfare according to the Italian style, and helpless against our swords and spears.'[7] Out of context this sounds more patronising and less just than the author, an ally of Ferrante, probably intended. The Italian style, as we have seen, was not the be-all and end-all of warfare, and the Albanian light cavalry could no doubt have been as effective here as they were at home in a war of no quarter. Scanderbeg, however, had not gone to Italy to fight pitched battles, but to release his liege lord from an impasse, to defend the Aragonese positions on the Adriatic coast, and to do what incidental damage he could. This limited programme was carried out to perfection; and even the looting and plundering, though somewhat beneath the dignity of a classicising Pope, were of considerable value in this campaign. Rounding up the sheep from which the barons gained so much of their revenue and devastating the crops their soldiers would have used for food were forms of economic warfare far more useful to Ferrante than conducting an elegant cavalry chess match with the enemy across the grassy uplands of Apulia.

Scanderbeg stayed five months in Italy harassing Anjou's supporters and robbing them of supplies. In February 1462 he returned home, again by way of Ragusa. He was summoned by his wife, it has been said, with news of a Turkish threat; but it is quite as likely that he left because the purpose of his expedition had been achieved and he wanted to be back in Albania for the new campaigning season. The war was to drag on for two more years, but his arrival had allowed Ferrante to take the initiative again, and after a decisive victory over the Anjou at Troia in August 1462 there was no longer any doubt about the result. Most of the barons surrendered. John of Anjou tried to rally his supporters again when he returned to Italy in 1464, but he was beaten at sea before landing and took refuge on Ischia until he could find a means of getting back to France. Piccinino held out for some time in the mountains of the Abruzzo, but in 1463 he too made his peace. He kept Sulmona, which he had conquered for himself, and was acknowledged as its captain general by Ferrante, whose vassal he became. He had always been able to rely on the protection of his former employer Sforza, whose natural daughter he had been allowed to marry. But John of Anjou's attempt to start the rebellion again made both Sforza and Ferrante decide that it would be a good thing to have him out of the way. The difficulty was to persuade him to leave the safety of his own fortress and go to pay his respects to the King at Naples. This task was successfully undertaken by his father-in-law. He went and was made most welcome. Not until the farewell banquet on the eve of his return home was he arrested, accused of incitement to revolt, and strangled in the fortress of Castel Nuovo. The Prince of Taranto, that other pillar of the Anjou cause, showed a more wary spirit and died in his bed (though not without the suspicion of poison) in 1465, at the age of seventy. Only then could King Ferdinand complete his victory by entering Taranto and taking possession both of the city and of the million ducats in gold which it had been the delight of his old enemy to accumulate.

Chapter Twelve

. . . .

THE LAST CRUSADE

WHEN SCANDERBEG SAILED to Italy to protect his protector, it will be remembered that the Ragusans let him have some of the money that was being accumulated for a Crusade against the Turks. There had been few enough contributions, measured against the military problem; but perhaps the wonder is that anyone should have sought to rouse enthusiasm for an essentially mediaeval and spiritual idea amid the secular classicism of the fifteenth century.

The meaning of the word had changed, it is true, since the days when a few saints and many more soldiers set out at the call of the Pope to win Palestine back from the Saracens for him, seeking for themselves salvation or a prosperous little principality, or even both. For one thing, the Infidel was no longer a chivalrous and exotic marauder on the far fringe of Christendom. He was now entrenched just the other side of the narrow sea from Italy, and was moving steadily into the heart of Europe with the finest army in the world. The first task was to remove the danger that Rome and Budapest might become Muslim cities rather than restore Jerusalem and Byzantium to Christianity.

The Pope, too, though the only ruler able to rise above frustrating local jealousies in order to point out their danger to the other princes of Europe, had lost most of his old compelling authority. It is true that he had not always been obeyed, even in the days of those towering mediaeval Popes who could lay whole nations under an interdict or force emperors to wait in the snow for them like lackeys. The Venetians had cold-bloodedly forced a Crusade to turn aside from the route to the Holy Land and sack Byzantium in the interests of their own trade and vanity. But the assumption behind the earlier Crusades had been that Europe was, or ought to behave as though it were, a united Christendom in which political and military power existed to serve certain divine purposes as interpreted by the Papacy.

By the time of the Renaissance all this had changed. Nation states were growing up, their interests often visibly opposed to each other. Trade had revived after the long slumber of parochialism that followed the collapse of the western Roman empire. With it had come private wealth, and new and unfamiliar ideas in the minds of a new and educated class of laymen. As ideals in rulers, piety and self-abnegation were giving way-even in the rulers of the Church-to the cult of glory and self-expression. And when there was no longer room for a Pope towering above the kings and princes of Europe in secular affairs, there developed within the Church itself a strong reforming movement which sought to limit his powers in religious matters, robbing him of his absolute kingship and making him rather the constitutional spokesman of a General Council. Under these circumstances, the chances of a Pope rallying the warring sovereigns of Europe to a successful Crusade might well have seemed hopeless; and the latest attempt had indeed led directly to disaster to the Christian cause at Varna in 1444.

Yet the Pope did act, and if he had not done so it is hard to see who would. Italy, where he was a temporal ruler, was in grave danger, but she was split into dozens of quarrelling states and was a victim of both French and Spanish ambitions. He felt both the threat and the humiliation; and he alone could speak as a European figure and not just as a local princeling. He knew better than anyone the true nature of Muslim ambitions, for the main Turkish attacks were being made on the frontier of the

Roman Catholic world, in Hungary, Croatia and Albania. And he, with more detachment and sense of historical perspective than any other ruler now that Byzantium had fallen, could see the long-term threat to nations who were not worrying unduly because the Turks were not yet on their own doorstep. So it became an aim of Papal policy to create an alliance that would expel the Turks from Europe, or at least prevent them from advancing any further, all in the name of religious solidarity.

Whilst everyone in western Europe—and almost everyone in the Balkans—would like to have seen the Turks driven out, this policy raised difficulties which threatened to destroy the alliance even before it had been completed. If the Sultan was attacked in one place, he might well take reprisals elsewhere, and the people who could expect to suffer were the Venetians. Their merchants were established in Muslim cities under treaties of peace, and they might find the valuable Oriental trade routes closed to them or handed over to an other Italian city that had stayed neutral. They might from time to time be driven to war against the Turks over some specific dispute, like an island or a fortress that the Sultan wanted from them; but they could not contemplate a permanent, impoverishing hostility merely from a general dislike of the other side's religion. As a serious Crusade could not be contemplated without the ships and financial support of Venice, such thoughts had to be adjusted in timing, scope and aims to suit Venetian foreign policy.

Again, if the Turks were to be driven out of the Balkans, who was to rule in their place? Many people might be prepared to help the King of Hungary so long as he ruled only north of the Danube and even there seemed hard pressed. But if his armies advanced as conquerors into Serbia and Bosnia, would they ever leave? Serbia and Hungary were old enemies before the Turks came, and would presumably be so again when they left; but this time the Serbs might find themselves with no army and no guarantees. And, from an entirely opposite point of view, the German Emperor claimed the crown of Hungary for himself, and did not see why he should be expected to contribute men and money towards propping up his rival and so perhaps making his own claim impossible to achieve.

There was another serious obstacle to the success of any Crusade: the feeling among the Orthodox Christian majority in the Balkans that its success would be followed by forcible conversion to Rome. There was a strong belief, with much evidence to support it, that for the Papacy the expulsion of Islam from Europe was only the first stage of the programme; and that in the second stage, the schism with Constantinople would be ended on Rome's terms. If Orthodox kingdoms like Serbia, or the old Greek empire of Byzantium, could not be revived, then most of the people under Turkish rule found themselves faced with a choice between two evils: Remain under the Sultan, who (out of contempt and arrogance though it might be) tolerated their religion and gave it a measure of self-government, or fight in support of the Pope, whose zeal for Christian unity might well destroy their religion, and with it probably their hopes of national revival.

All this is not to deny that the Turks could have been defeated; but it does mean that no one was able and willing to observe the conditions which would have made a victorious coalition possible. It must be presented to those whose help was needed in terms of their own national self-interest. It must accept dynastic jealousies for the powerful motives they were and provide safeguards in advance, rather than try to sermonise them out of existence. It must assure the Balkan Christians that an alien liturgy and an alien political rule would not be forced upon them. And it involved the creation of a modern, well-trained army with a clear strategic plan and a centralised command.

Most of these needs were hardly appreciated, let alone solved, and so the preparations for the last Crusade moved forward in an atmosphere of complete unreality. The main responsibility for this must rest with the man who, despite the advice of his counsellors and the evidence of his own eyes, revived, fostered and died of the idea: Aeneas Silvius Piccolomini, Pope Pius II.[1]

His name is the first clue to his character. He belonged to a Sienese family that pretended a descent from Roman days; but after the local aristocracy had been exiled from the city to the countryside they came down in the world, and his father was forced to work as a labourer on what had been his own land. He was one of eighteen children, which made his worldly prospects even more dismal; but Italy's rediscovery of her classical past had begun and the indigent Patrician named his son Aeneas after the founder of Roman greatness. With such a name, and with such incitements to grandeur in the family story and the Renaissance around him, he could not help coveting power and fame, and there was only one way to attain it—by putting his talents at the disposal of those who possessed it already. Those talents, a robust and subtle intelligence combined with a desire to please, were fortunately of a kind newly in demand. Social and political life was becoming immensely more complex, and there was a call for what in deference to the popular classical jargon was called Rhetoric: the capacity as secretary, adviser, diplomat, confidential agent, power behind the throne, orator and writer, to persuade others of what the current patron wished them to believe, and so to increase his power and influence. Aeneas quickly found that he could fill this protean role with ease and distinction.

For a time, however, his career was threatened when, under the influence of an itinerant preacher, he decided to become a monk. He needed advice on whether he had a vocation, and characteristically did not seek it at home, but walked all the way to Rome. Had he then decided to enter the Church he would almost certainly never have been Pope. What preserved him for this highest of spiritual offices was his frank awareness of his addiction to venery. In this, as in his dealings with cardinals and kings, he had mastered the art of Persuasion and enjoyed its advantages, and in the course of his various missions he presented his parents with one half-English and one half-Scottish grandchild, both born out of wedlock.

Persuasion through speech was the key with which he believed he could move men to do anything. 'Hold fast and enlarge the eloquence which you possess,' he wrote to an English friend; 'think it most honourable to yourself to excel mankind in that, in which men themselves excel the rest of animate creation. A mighty thing is power of speech, and, to confess the truth, there is nothing that rules the world like eloquence. For whatever we do in politics, we do under the persuasion of language, and popular opinion cleaves to him who knows best how to persuade.'[2]

For all his ambition, Pius retained a saving innocence throughout his life. He not only appeared to believe in his brief of the moment; he really did believe in it: He was the first victim of his own powers of eloquence. So he never came to realise that he was convincing the great ones of the earth because by some intuition he managed to say exactly what they wanted to hear, only expressed more wittily and pungently—in a word more persuasively—than they could have managed on their own account. Some of his critics have wrestled with the apparent contradiction between his pliability towards his patrons, which far surpassed that of the calculating cynic, and his single-minded devotion to such an old-fashioned and highly emotional idea as a Crusade against the Infidel. But the contradiction is more apparent than real. It was only in their own eyes that the men of the Renaissance were rational and scientific, free of illusions and of old superstitions. In fact, they were deeply rooted in the past. There was even a strong element of nostalgia in their craze for antiquity: an attempt to fly from the facts of Italy's present weakness into imagined memories of her old Roman grandeur.

A peninsula waiting to be conquered by France or Spain or Turkey conjured up visible reminders of the days when it had itself conquered all three. The new colonnaded palaces were thus romantic follies, for all the classicism of their outward form. The petty dukes and brigand lords who would normally have passed an uneventful and relatively harmless lifetime in their dark stubborn castles, blossomed out into a career compounded of pride and nastiness when some architect with an ancient text book built for them houses befitting a reborn Caesar. Only the very greatest artists followed the true classical spirit-the distillation of an ideal from the flux of appearances-and sought to recreate it in the context of a whole new world of knowledge. For the majority then, as always, the classical disciplines were admired only for the sense of grandeur and fulfilment they could add to the most pedestrian ambitions. Aeneas shared the mood of the majority. He was an impressionable, uncalculating character, and so he wished to get on in the world while at the same time observing the simpler standards of honour he had learned at home. It never occurred to him, for example, to enter the priesthood until he was sure he could observe his vow of chastity, but alongside that innocence was a burning ambition, fanned by the fashionable cult of glory. To such a man the idea of a Crusade could hardly fail to be attractive, for it combined the possibility of private piety and worldly success. It was an unselfish ambition that might persuade kings and princes to do his bidding.

His first real opportunity to make a name for himself came when one of Pope Eugenius IV's cardinals changed allegiance and took the clever young Piccolomini with him to Basle, where the anti-Papal Council had its headquarters, and where it was considering the reform of the Church. For some time he travelled on various of its embassies. He was involved at one time in an abortive plot to kidnap the Pope at Florence; at another, in a journey to Scotland. Having vowed during a storm at sea that he would walk barefoot to the nearest shrine of the Virgin if ever he reached land again, he found himself involved in ten miles of snow and ice. The consequence epitomises his character as surely as the carefully qualified vow: his piety, and not his dissipations, caused him to be plagued with lifelong gout. It was during this tour, too, that he left his famous description of life in Scotland: the turf-roofed houses, the unshod horses, the coal that was prized above cash. And the raids across the border, where the English men and children trooped off to a nearby tower after the evening meal, leaving the women in the houses, since they had nothing to fear but rape. Aeneas knew this, not by hearsay, but from being left behind with the village dogs and geese and a hundred women.

Back at Basle in his early thirties, Aeneas spent about six years on the secretariat of the Council at the height of its conflict with the Pope; and when it deposed the irascible and irreconcilable Pope Eugenius IV and elected a hermit duke to succeed him as Felix V, he found himself the secretary of this new schismatic pontiff. The moderates in the conciliar party felt that they had gone too far. This new challenge risked undermining the authority of the Church entirely, for if people found that the Pope could be changed at will, they might decide to forego one entirely. This view was strongly held by the Germans around the Emperor; for if the Pope's position were to be challenged today, it might be the Emperor's turn tomorrow.

Already a neutral party had grown up in the Church around the German princes, whose aim was to secure control of ecclesiastical authority on their own territories, thus making them more independent of the Emperor as well as of the Pope. These two traditional foes thus found themselves with a common interest; and when Aeneas was sent to persuade the German neutrals that the Council had done right in deposing the Pope, he allowed himself to be persuaded by the imperialists that it had gone too far. He visited Frankfurt and met the Emperor Frederick III, who for no explicable reason crowned him Poet at a public ceremony. 'Had he given a diploma for the best grown cabbage,' says one historian, 'the compliment would have been appreciable, for on this subject Frederick was an expert.' There followed the offer and acceptance of a job in the Imperial Chancery, and Aeneas thus stepped from the waterlogged craft at

Basle on to the firm ground of an imperial-papal alliance. Who more natural than he to negotiate it? So the man who had tried to kidnap Eugenius IV went to Rome and made his peace, arranging at the same time a reconciliation with the Emperor.

Now at last Aeneas entered the Church himself. He negotiated a wedding and a coronation in Rome for Frederick. He became bishop first of Trieste, then of his native Siena. He wrote voluminously, but abandoned his former stories in the style of Boccaccio about light[3] Sienese wives and their cuckolded husbands. He also encouraged the new Spanish Pope Callixtus III in his firm intention to fit out a military and naval expedition against the Turks. Aeneas was now in his fifties: small, sparsely white haired, stooping, with the jowl of good-natured self indulgence, and eyes alert to catch fire with enthusiasm or offence.

Callixtus was an old man who died soon, and the question which now arose would be whether, as seemed probable, his successor would be a Frenchman, thus condemning Italy to still more French influence and control; or whether the Italians would now be able to secure a Pope of their own. Their favourite candidate was Cardinal Capranica, the first important patron Aeneas had ever had; and he now showed his continuing goodwill by dying two days before the election. Aeneas, as Cardinal Archbishop of Siena, thus found himself involved in persuading the Italian members of the College to stand together, and the Spaniards to support them against the French. So it happened that he found himself Pope at the age of fifty-two. He showed that he had not lost the confirmed Latinist's bleak sense of fun: having been christened, if that is the right word, with the Virgilian name of Aeneas he now added to it the appropriate prefix of Pius.

Warned by recent history, the cardinals had insisted that whoever became Pope should solemnly bind himself to consult them before embarking on a Crusade or committing himself on the subject of Church reform. Pius had bowed before these demands of a would-be oligarchy; but, confident that he would be able to persuade the cardinals he was right, he proceeded to do exactly the opposite. As a man deeply involved in the conciliar attempt to circumscribe Papal power, he now became its most fervent advocate. The former secretary to an anti-Pope elected by a Council shortly issued a Bull whose mood is intimated by its opening word *Execrabilis*: it condemned anyone who appealed from Pope to Council to all the penalties of heresy and treason, and has since been used by all who wish to maintain the extreme pretensions of the Papacy within the Church. He was also free to put into action his plan for a Crusade, an ambition which had remained with him throughout his public career. The urge to private piety, stimulated by the wandering preacher in his youth, but deflected by the hedonism of his sexual life and the classical paganism of his ideas, seems to have found here its expression.

As a young man he had met and been impressed by Cardinal Cesarini, a fellow-humanist who had the cause of a holy war very much at heart. They met again after Pius had entered the Emperor's service, only a few months before Cesarini was killed by Murad II's army in the disastrous battle of Varna. From this point he took up the martyr's burden as well as his own, and as his enthusiasm mounted, so did his intemperance of speech. All Christians who did not support a Crusade were Turks by proxy. When the Pope and the Emperor did not immediately act on a sermon he preached urging them to war, he thought that the Pope must be too old for his job and the Emperor too small-souled to rise to the level of his. When Constantinople fell, he had been outraged as both a Christian and a classicist. 'One of the two lights of Christendom has been extinguished; the fount of the Muses is dried up,' he wrote to Pope Nicholas V, and suggested that only a Crusade could restore both the illumination and the inspiration.

The Pope had shrewdly employed him to try to persuade the monarchs of Europe to take the cross themselves and lead their armies towards the east. Now he was Pope himself, Pius assumed the task in which Aeneas had failed. Two months after his election, he issued an invitation to the same unwilling monarchs to assemble under his presidency at a diet in Mantua. He had hoped to hold it at Udine, in Venetian territory; but the Venetians did not wish the Turks to think that they were willing hosts for, or perhaps even the instigators of such a project. So the Gonzaga family were reluctantly induced to lend their city, influenced no doubt by the thought that they had nothing to fear from Turkish reprisals and that this gesture of goodwill would discharge them of any further obligation. The delegates were invited to assemble at the beginning of June 1459 (the invitations had gone out the previous November) but they showed no hurry to arrive, and the proceedings could not begin until the end of September. The Pope's retinue spent the interval laughing at his idea and arranging riverside picnics.

The Emperor did not bother to come at all, saying that affairs in Austria were so pressing that he could not bear to leave them. This was a delicate way of hinting that he could bear with fortitude the idea of the Turks defeating his rival for the Hungarian throne. France, the strongest European power, was far from friendly to the Pope. He had so recently blocked the candidature of their own choice by his own election, and he had reversed Papal policy in southern Italy, switching support from the Anjou to the Aragonese in Naples. The threat of a Turkish invasion of southern Italy, though regarded with horror in Rome, appeared quite differently in Paris. There it seemed to have its uses in unseating the upstart Spanish dynasty. Florence thought that if the Turks would only trounce the Venetians, her own trading opportunities in the Levant would look much brighter. And Venice, who knew she must bear the main expense of any campaign and meet most of the Turkish reprisals herself, was suspicious of being left in the lurch by the others when the fighting started, and forced to face the enemy alone. The Duke of Burgundy had already made a grandiloquent offer to take the cross himself if another sovereign would. In this, however, he was influenced more by social ambitions than piety: if the offer were accepted (and it almost certainly would not) it would secure acknowledgment of equal status for Burgundy among the kingdoms of Europe. He also insisted on territorial concessions which none of his neighbours was willing to offer. Apart from the zeal of the Pope himself, this seemed to leave only Gjon Hunyadi and the Hungarians, and Scanderbeg and the Albanians. They, however, were already fully committed whether they wished it or not. But what they wanted was money, arms and men to deter the Sultan - not a threatening but powerless alliance which might invite the Turks to strike without providing assistance to resist the attack.

The idea of a Crusade accorded so little with the obvious mood of mid-fifteenth century Europe that many people, both within and outside the Church, did not think that Pius was sincere in proposing it. The most popular view was that he was using the idea of a Crusade as a means of increasing the income of the Papal treasury. Money he certainly sought. In the States of the Church the clergy were to pay a tithe of their possessions and the laity one thirtieth of theirs. A compromise was effected for the Jews, who were to subscribe one twentieth of their possessions towards preparing war on the enemies of Christianity. Even Providence appeared to lay itself under contribution. Alum had long been a Turkish monopoly, but now an alum mine was discovered not far from the papal port of Civitavecchia, and this offered a new source of revenue. Undeterred by the poor response to his overtures, and hoping that everyone else would levy similar taxes on their subjects, Pius gave the monarchs three years in which to prepare for action.

Having thus set his machine of conquest in motion, Pius may have been visited by a memory of the advice he had once given to the Englishman Adam de Moleyn: 'Whatever we do in politics, we do under the persuasion of language.' Was he proposing to conquer the Grand Turk, the infidel of infidels, by the persuasion of language? Moved perhaps by some sense of his inconsistency, some reminder of his past triumphs as a rhetorician, or some prompting of vanity, he decided to write a personal letter to Mehmet the Conqueror asking him to consider abjuring Islam and embracing Christianity. In return, he proposed to acknowledge Mehmet as the legitimate successor of the Byzantine emperors. His own position would be a dazzling one, as spiritual overlord and political arbiter between two Holy Roman Emperors, one in Frankfurt and one in Constantinople. The achievement would be hardly less, though his own role would be less brilliant, if Mehmet had both become a Christian and continued as a conqueror. It is an intoxicating thought that eventually the people of the whole of Europe and the Asian possessions of the Ottoman Empire, from Moray to Mocha and from Portugal to Persia, might have become Romanised Christians and subjects of a Turkish emperor, and that Mehmet and Pius between them might have created a united empire wider than that of Roman days. That would have been the crowning justification of the gospel of Persuasion. Unfortunately the Sultan did not reply to this friendly overture, except by cannon balls on the battlefields of the Balkans. He already possessed the New Rome, whether legitimised or not, and there seemed no reason why he should not take Old Rome as well in due time.

The kings whom Pius had chosen as liberators of the Balkans were at least content with indifference. The people he had decided to liberate went even further. When the Greeks were warned that Islam was to be destroyed in the interests of a papal coalition, they attacked the Latin priests in Crete and helped the Turks to overcome the Pope's garrison in the island of Lemnos. In Serbia, which now consisted merely of the fortress-capital of Smederevo, the ruler had become a Roman Catholic to secure foreign help, whereupon his subjects opened their gates to the Turks rather than engage in a hopeless fight for an alien nominee. Thus the crusading zeal of Rome strengthened the forces it was intended to wipe out, and the loss was not made good by the volunteers who rallied to the Pope from across the dividing line: some Turkish princes who had a grudge against the

Sultan, a Palaeologue recently driven out of his despotate in the Morea, and an ex-Queen of Cyprus who wanted help against the brother who had just usurped her throne.

It was in Bosnia that the consequences of papal policy were soon to be seen most dramatically. Here the Hungarians had installed a Roman Catholic ruler, much against the wishes of nobles and populace, who wanted to be neither Roman nor Orthodox and adopted as a sign of distinction the Bogomilism[4] persecuted by both. Undeterred by the signs of disaffection, desertion and communication with the enemy, the Hungarians demanded certain frontier concessions from Bosnia. On the intervention of Pope Pius, the puppet king was induced to offer a fortress and a sum of money to them, and sign a treaty of alliance. In this way another country was added to the unimpressive list of those willing to support the Crusade. This diplomatic stroke was just the pretext Mehmet was seeking to attack Bosnia. Twelve years earlier, her ruler had undertaken to pay an annual tribute acknowledging the Sultan as overlord. This had been paid only intermittently, and usually under threat of imminent war in the Balkans. Now a formal request was made for payment. King Stefan Tomasevic, the Hungarian protegée, wanted to resist, but could rally no support among his subjects, so he sent ambassadors to Istanbul, offering the money and asking for a fifteen-year truce. Mehmet accepted the money, granted the truce and began to prepare for war.

In Spring 1463 he set out from Skopje and prepared to attack the Bosnian strongpoint of Bobovac. The Turks had often attacked it without success, and it could be expected to endure a long siege. In fact, however, it was handed over without a fight by the governor, a Bogomil forcibly converted to Rome. Unfortunately for him, the Turks had not yet mastered the complexities of Bosnian religion and politics, so they cut off his head. Even so, town after town surrendered in the next few days. Many Bogomil nobles went over to the Turks, who quickly moved to the siege of the capital Jajce, a hill town with a squat, heavy fort above it and magnificent waterfalls below. Here the Turkish cannon demolished large stretches of the walls in a few days, and the army prepared for the assault. The inhabitants, 'fearing that if it were taken by attack they would be destroyed, they sent secret messengers to the Sultan, without the knowledge of their chief, and surrendered themselves and the town. But the chief, on hearing of this, left the town secretly and fled.' The 'chief,' King Stefan, was followed and besieged in his hideout; he finally surrendered on a promise that his life would be spared. He returned to Jajce and in June 1463 authorised a general surrender. The Turks took 100,000 prisoners and enrolled 30,000 young men in their Janissary corps. Mehmet was troubled about the promise given to the king. He had wanted to kill him, but his word had been given on his behalf, and he recalled his father's advice about adhering to the pledged word. A Persian mufti with the army solved the dilemma in both theory and practice. He proved that a safe-conduct must have the direct assent of the Sultan to be valid. He then took up a sword and cut off King Stefan Tomasevic's head himself.

The Sultan's triumph, made possible by the Pope's complaisance towards Hungarian dynastic aims, had brought him to the frontiers of the small coastal republic of Ragusa; and he made up his mind to take possession of this as well, using it as a base for attacks on the opposite coast and on shipping in the Adriatic. If Mehmet had been able to take and keep Ragusa, the threat to Venice and the States of the Church would have been grave. Ragusa called home all her galleys, raised armies from Apulia and from her own hinterland, and prepared to meet the attack with these, the protection of her patron saint Blaise, and her well-tried diplomatic skill. Mehmet first ordered Ragusa to do homage to him. This she did. Then he ordered her to give up all her territory outside the city of Ragusa itself. Ragusa, he was told, was prepared to do as he wished, but would at the same time place the city itself under Hungarian protection and admit a Hungarian garrison. The Sultan had no intention of gratuitously offering his main enemy a second front in the inevitable war against him, so he did not press this demand. Enlightened self-interest had triumphed on both sides, though the popular explanation was that the white-bearded figure of St. Blaise had materialised in front of Mehmet as he marched towards the city. His horse had refused to budge; and, accepting the omen, he had reprieved his chosen victim.

The collapse of Bosnia, even without the threatened loss of Ragusa, was a warning to Venice of the possible fate of her own possessions in Dalmatia. She, too, was evidently in mortal danger; and so her policy, normally indifferent to Turkish attacks unless they were aimed directly at her, was modified to meet the new threat. She was now prepared to create a system of alliances against the aggressor, and this for the first time gave some practical substance to the Pope's plans for a Crusade. Even in adversity, her business sense shone with undiminished light. While still negotiating with her potential allies, Hungary and Albania, she decided to strike at the common enemy on her own account, choosing for terrain the Peloponnese, which she had long wanted for herself and whose conquest by the Turks she had never forgiven. An expedition was sent to Corinth, and there began to build a wall across the narrow isthmus that separates the Peloponnese from the rest of Greece.

The plan was to stop any Turkish relieving forces from the north while mopping up Turkish garrisons to the south, thus adding a sizeable province to the Venetian empire and deflecting enemy attention away from Dalmatia. When the Sultan learned of the attack in Greece he divided his Bosnian forces, leaving one part to police the country and sending the other under one of his generals, Mahmud Pasha, to meet the Venetians. When he arrived, they were still building their wall. Sandwiched between the troops from Bosnia on the one hand and the force built up by the local Turkish commander on the other, the Venetians were either killed or taken prisoner, or escaped to their waiting ships.

This was a severe blow at the Venetian strategic plan, according to which Hungary was to attack in the north and Venice in the south of the Balkans, while Scanderbeg and the Albanians should attack from the west. Unfortunately there had also been difficulties about this latter part of the plan. Relations between Venice and Albania had continued to fluctuate in recent years. After King Alfonso's death in 1458 there had been a rapprochement, and Scanderbeg had handed over a small fortress captured from the Turks as a sign of his goodwill. The Pope had even suggested that Venice might take over the protection of his lands during his absence in Italy. But once the rebellion in Naples had been crushed, and the Aragonese dynasty was back in power, Venetian suspicions of its Balkan aims caused a feeling of indifference or hostility on the part of the Albanians. They, too, had made a provisional truce with the Turks at the very moment that Venice wished to build up her alliance.[5]

When the Sultan arrived at Skopje in 1463 with his forces, the Albanian chieftains met to decide whether they would accept his offer to sign a truce with them. Tanush Thopia insisted on negotiating, and carried the majority with him. A truce was signed on 27th April, which meant that the Turks were free to move into Bosnia without fear of attack from Albania. Scanderbeg is said to have been in the minority, and Tanush was sent to Italy to explain to the Pope at Tivoli why they had bowed for the moment to overwhelming force. He gave assurances that the sovereignty of Albania was unaffected, and that Scanderbeg was prepared to make war on the Turks when the Pope wished it. If the truce was intended to startle the Venetians into giving greater consideration to Albanian purposes than ever they had done in the past, it succeeded perfectly. Negotiations were opened for an alliance, which was signed on 20th August 1463; Gjergj Pellini, Abbot of Rotezo, acted as usual as the main Albanian negotiator.[6] Scanderbeg undertook to resume the war against the Turks if he received subsidies and would be reinforced by Venetian contingents. Venetian warships and auxiliary ships were to be sent into Albanian waters to protect the population, and Venice agreed not to make a separate peace. Scanderbeg's son Gjon was to be made an honorary Venetian nobleman; and he himself was to be given refuge and support in Venetian territory in case of need. Gjon Castrioti became an honorary citizen of Venice and a member of the Grand Council in September, and in October Gabriele Trevisiano arrived in Albania with 1,300 cavalry and infantry, 2,500 ducats towards the expenses of the war, and all the arrears of Scanderbeg's pension.

Even with this help, however, Scanderbeg was in no position to launch a major attack on the Turkish positions in Macedonia. He had throughout the negotiations preserved the right of deciding when he had enough arms and men to embark on war with a reasonable chance of success, and he was not yet satisfied. However, the entire alliance was based on the assumption that he would take part. Hungary, with whom the Venetians made a pact in September, would attack from the north, and the Venetians themselves from the south. Pius II, who had already divided the skin of the Turkish bear before it had been shot, had awarded Greece to Venice and Serbia and Bulgaria to Hungary. If Scanderbeg joined in, he was to be rewarded with Macedonia, like a second conquering Alexander. That was a most attractive bait; and he certainly could not afford to stay out of any coalition that seemed likely to win. At the same time, his absence could condemn the campaign to almost certain defeat. With him, the Turkish armies could be attacked simultaneously on three sides. Without him, the Sultan would be free to occupy the Albanian coast and cut the seaborne communications between the two Christian fronts.

There is no doubt that Scanderbeg wished to see the Turks defeated; but it is equally clear that he realised his own key position in the plans for a Crusade and was determined to turn it to the greatest advantage, if only to make sure that for once he did not have to meet the Turks on such grossly unequal terms as in the past. It was now the turn of the Venetians to show anxiety for the support and goodwill of the Albanians, and the Senate therefore invited the Pope to put pressure on the European sovereigns to provide the missing men and money. They themselves, they declared in a note of 9th September 1463, had done all they could, and they hoped it would prove to have been enough to win Scanderbeg from his truce with the Turks. If only others would do their share, it could reasonably be hoped that he might not only resist an attack but that, attracted by the Promise of territory, he might help to drive the Turks out of Europe altogether. A figure of between 30,000 and 40,000 men should be aimed at for this work – 'so vital and so full of hope for Italy and the faithful' – and the Pope was urged to use his apostolic authority to induce the Powers to do their share by giving them the best possible example himself, and thus shaming the others into following his own generous lead.

For some reason the Senate decided not to send this politely hectoring message, but to stress rather the danger that if Scanderbeg were to renew his truce with the Turks there would be nothing to stop them from moving over into Italy. So when the Apostolic Legate asked for news on 18th September, this danger was dwelt on. Venice, he was told, had forced him from the idea of peace with the enemy as a result of her efforts, and she hoped to have persuaded him back into the Christian camp by the promise of adequate help from the Italians. Accordingly the Senate, 'with filial reverence,' asked Pius to persuade the Duke of Burgundy and the Italian rulers to give what help they could. They had no cause to think that thereby they would be merely helping Venice to expand. They would be contributing only to the triumph of the general Christian interest, and if they played their part a successful outcome might be expected.[7]

Although fear, qualified by cupidity, had induced the Venetians to prepare for war and create their alliance with Hungary and the Albanians, the Pope now saw a belated response to his appeals for a new spirit of disinterested zeal to fight the infidel. In November 1463, two months after the military alliance had been created, Pius declared his Crusade and called for volunteers. It was intended that the Turkish strongpoints should be attacked during the winter, so that Mehmet would be on the defensive when major campaigning was resumed in the spring. On the Albanian front, however, an immediate hitch was apparent in the plans. Some of the chieftains did not want to move. In particular, Trevisiano, the Venetian commander, had failed to induce Lek Dukagjini to join in. Lek's hesitation probably owed something to native caution, for his position on the immediate flank of one of the enemy's main invasion routes was more exposed than Scanderbeg's. But suspicion of campaigns abroad in general, and of Scanderbeg's own ambitions in particular, is likely to have weighed even more strongly with him. He cannot have failed to see that this campaign, if successful, could only complete the process of elevating his great ally and rival to a position of authority over him. Since the Sultan was not at that moment threatening to send an army against Lek Dukagjini, then Lek Dukagjini was in no danger. He was in danger, however, if he did go to war, no matter whether the Albanians won or lost. The Pope intervened through the Archbishop of Durazzo, and agreement was patched up. The Albanians opened their campaign on 27th November by raiding Turkish territory on what proved to be rather a cattle-rustling expedition than a military one. They came back, says one chronicler, with 60,000 cows, 80,000 sheep and goats and 3,000 horses.

The other European powers were less amenable to spiritual sanctions than Lek and his followers. Florence had not changed her view that a long and sanguinary war between Turkey and Venice would be to the good of Italy in general, the States of the Church included. The Duke of Milan, who feared further Venetian encroachments on the mainland, sent an envoy of his own to Albania the following March to study the situation, but took no further action. The King of France said it was no affair of his. The King of Naples retired with the excuse that Venice and Scanderbeg were more than a match for the Turks, and the Duke of Burgundy used this withdrawal as an excuse for following suit. The Neapolitan decision was a moral as well as a material blow to Scanderbeg, who had not hesitated to offer his help when Ferrante needed it. He reacted in characteristic fashion by deciding to cross over to Italy, nominally to render personal homage to the King for the lands at Monte Sant'Angelo and San Giovanni Rotondo which had been given to him in return for his help in the civil war. The visit was at the same time a delicate reminder of the mutual obligations that men of honour owe each other. From Naples he passed on to Rome; and the Venetians, warning the Pope of the coming visit, asked him to show the visitor all possible respect in view of his importance in the coming campaign.

By the time large-scale fighting could be resumed in 1464, King Matthias of Hungary had, as planned, won back many of the Bosnian strongpoints, including the most coveted of them all, Jajce. There the garrison was divided into two parties, one in favour of surrender and the other of resistance, and when these began to fight each other, the town soon fell. The Sultan made straight for Jajce and began the customary preparations for victory: devastation of the countryside so that sorties for food-gathering would be unsuccessful; a trench round the city to protect his army; bombardments with his heavy cannon and attacks in the breaches made by them in the walls.

He was now dealing, however, with Hungarians determined to resist at any cost, not with Bosnians unable to choose between two alien rulers. 'So,' says Kritovoulos, 'a fierce and terrible battle took place there, such as no one ever saw or heard of in a fight at the walls; especially around the point at which the wall had been breached. For, drunken with battle, they yielded entirely to anger and wrath, well-nigh ignoring nature itself. They slaughtered each other and mercilessly cut each other to pieces, charging and being charged, wounding and being wounded, killing and being killed, shouting, blaspheming, swearing, hardly conscious of anything that was happening or of what they were doing, just like madmen.' King Matthias himself tried to raise the siege or at least draw off part of the attacking force by crossing into Bosnia with an army; but the Sultan stayed where he was and merely sent a covering force to keep track of the Hungarian movements. When Matthias saw that the ruse had failed, he sent a message into the city telling the garrison never to surrender, and quietly struck camp in the middle of the night to start operations elsewhere. He did not elude the Turks, however, and the retreating army was hacked and harried, losing arms, equipment and men, some of them killed and nearly two hundred taken alive and sent to Constantinople for execution.

Despite this setback, it seemed a good summer for the Christian forces. Jajce held out, and Mehmet had to leave Bosnia without conquering it. In Albania, Scanderbeg was successfully harassing the local Turkish commanders beyond his own frontiers. On 14th August he beat Sheremet Bey near Ohrida and celebrated the event by dining off *letnica* from the lake: the delicious salmon-trout of a kind found nowhere else in the world, and so highly regarded that it used to be sent in ice to Constantinople every week for the emperor's supper on Fridays. The Crusade was going well, and now Scanderbeg turned back towards the coast to meet the Pope, who was coming over from Italy to lead it in person.

Pius insisted on doing so though he was far from well. In the broiling heat of a Roman summer the sick man and his sceptical retinue began the journey up into the Appenines and across the Adriatic coast to take command of the fleets and armies waiting for him there. The first day, a sailor in the boat that was carrying them along the Tiber fell into the water and drowned; this irruption of sudden death into the Crusade further unnerved him. When the party left the river, he was carried through the mountains in a litter, and from time to time his courtiers drew the curtains so that he should not see the bands of deserters, tired of waiting without pay, and now straggling back towards Rome rather than stay until he came to lead them to victory or death in the mountains of Dalmatia. When he reached Ancona, he found a few small ships waiting in the harbour, and a rabble of hungry, disaffected mercenaries in the town. The Venetians had not yet arrived, because a struggle had broken out between those who wanted to go on with the expedition, and those who wished to abandon it as a self-evident failure. The Pope took to his bed in the bishop's palace on the headland to the south of the bay on which the town stands.

Now came the nemesis of a life devoted to Persuasion above all else. For even his sickness and the efforts he had made to reach the port of departure were not enough to convince his allies that he was completely sincere, and that all this was not a piece of play-acting intended to leave them to do the actual fighting. In fact, he had been prepared if necessary to cross to Ragusa even without the Venetian fleet, using the few ships and wretched land forces available to him. Yet when the Venetian admiral arrived on 13th August, his first care was to find out whether Pius was physically or only diplomatically ill. The Pope answered his question by dying the next day, while Scanderbeg and his men, preparing for the coming invasion that was to make them masters of Macedonia, were eating their victory meal at Ohrida. The Crusade had died with its author. The cardinals handed over the money raised by him to the Venetians and then went home to the more realistic atmosphere of Rome. Scanderbeg and the King of Hungary were left to resist the now thoroughly provoked Sultan as best they might.

Chapter Thirteen

. . . .

A Janissary's Return

Since his conquest of Constantinople the Sultan, like a man claiming his due, had sought to win back the lands over which the great city had once ruled. Each spring he led out his armies to push forward the Ottoman frontiers; each winter he came back to direct the building of an imperial capital worthy of his achievements. As the empire expanded, so the recently declining metropolis was invigorated. The skyline was modified by new palaces and public buildings and softened by trees and gardens, and it assumed a more active and martial appearance as the minarets sprang up around the squat domed Greek churches, like Turkish cavalry lances momentarily at rest.

Towards the end of 1464, as in other years, Mehmet came back from the campaign in Bosnia, repulsed by the Hungarians and Albanians, but knowing that the Crusade against him had collapsed with the death of Pius II. He now resumed his personal supervision of the builders, who had begun his New Palace, the embryo of the later Serai, to replace the hasty wooden structure that had gone up soon after the conquest. Here for the first time he accepted the architectural challenge of the city over which he ruled, and was determined that his work should display a mind as civilised and enlightened as any that had ruled there in the past. Kritovoulos, who wrote his history for the Sultan's eyes in particular and was aware of his personal prides and vanities, is careful to make the point that 'both as to view and as to enjoyment as well as in its construction and its charm, it was in no respect lacking as compared with the famous and magnificent old buildings and sights.

'In it he had towers built of unusual height and beauty and grandeur, and apartments for men and others for women, and bedrooms and lounging-rooms and sleeping quarters, and very many other fine rooms. There were also various out-buildings and vestibules and halls and porticoes and gateways and porches, and bakeshops and baths of noble design.

'There was a grand enclosure containing all this. They were built, as I say, with a view to variety, beauty, size and magnificence, shining and scintillating with an abundance of gold and silver within and without, and with precious stones and marbles, with various ornaments and colours, all applied with a brilliance and smoothness and lightness most attractive and worked out with the finest and most complete skill, most ambitiously. Both in sculpture and in plastic work, as well as in painting, they were the finest and best of all.

'Moreover, all parts were most carefully covered and roofed over with a great quantity of very thick lead roofing. And the whole was beautiful and adorned with myriads of other brilliant and graceful articles.

'Not only this, but around the palaces were constructed very large and lovely gardens abounding in various sorts of plants and trees, producing beautiful fruit. And there were abundant supplies of water flowing everywhere, cold and clear and drinkable, and conspicuous and beautiful groves and meadows. Besides that, there were flocks of birds, both domesticated fowls and song-birds, twittering and chattering all around, and many sorts of animals, tame and wild, feeding there. Also there were many other fine ornaments and embellishments of various sorts, such as he thought would bring beauty and pleasure and happiness and enjoyment. The Sultan worked all this out with magnificence and profusion.'

Such were the surroundings in which the imagination of

later generations was to place the young hostage Scanderbeg, who when it was thus completed was a man of sixty or so, living in his rough patriarchal rock fortress and sleeping when occasion demanded on the bare earth. His enemy lived in luxury indeed; yet there is also in this description the tang and sparkle of a self-assured new regime. It sounds what it was, not the languorous prison of the pale, timid Padishas who later came to rule the empire, but the headquarters of the Napoleon of Islam, a warrior and statesman of supreme ability and almost insolent confidence in his powers, who had conquered one half of the ancient Roman world and was now preparing himself to conquer the other, with every appearance of success.

Scarcely any of the Conqueror's building work now remains, however; fire, earthquake and the conceit of kings have destroyed almost all. Of his new palace only one fragment remains to show how justified Kritovoulos was in his choice of superlatives: the beautiful Tiled Pavilion, colonnaded and decorated with blue mosaic tiles. The mosque that bears his name and houses his body is less than a couple of hundred years old. The covered bazaar has been burned down and rebuilt many times since he first gave it to the people. And the work that he began near the olive-clad headland where the acropolis of ancient Byzantium had stood was taken over by his successors for their own palace and private fortress.

After a pleasant winter working on his palace, Mehmet had intended to resume his campaigning in the spring of 1465, and would no doubt have moved against the Hungarians again. But his army was feeling the strain of regular expeditions to the further corners of the Balkans and Asia Minor, and there seem to have been murmurings, if not of disaffection, at least of discontent: 'he perceived that the soldiers, even including his own bodyguard, were complaining, and felt abused and annoyed, especially because of the frequent long journeys and expeditions and because they were constantly kept on troublesome trips abroad, and since they said that they had lost everything, both their physical health and their money, their horses and donkeys, and were ruined and suffering in everyway, he postponed the start.'

The Sultan also welcomed the excuse for a sabbatical year. He too 'was greatly exhausted and worn out in body and mind by his continuous and unremitting planning and care and indefatigable labours and dangers and trials, and he needed a time of respite and recuperation.' So he disbanded most of the army, giving horses, clothes and money to the men who had served him, offering promotions and even better presents to his own bodyguard. He himself went on with his building plans for the city, gathering round him a group of people with whom he could discuss philosophy, especially the ideas of the Greek peripatetics and stoics. And 'he also ran across, somewhere, the charts of Ptolemy' and found a Greek who was prepared to study the entire work of the old geographer and bring together in a single volume all he had to say about the countries of the world. It is a commentary on the times that a writer of well over a thousand years earlier should serve as authority to a reigning monarch; even more important, perhaps, is the glimpse this commission affords of the Sultan's ambitions.

He had in any case good reason for taking stock of his present position and of the future moves open to him. Having now taken the greater part of Bosnia and Herzegovina he had brought the empire to the mountain ridges almost overlooking the Adriatic Sea; but Venice was still established in Dalmatia and the Albanian highlanders remained unsubdued. The death of the Pope had providentially removed any immediate possibility of an attack against him from these two bridgeheads; but they remained there for use in the future. The most accessible was Albania; and so long as Kruja remained in Albanian hands, it would always be possible to launch armies against him from the coast and through the passes into Macedonia. Mehmet therefore came to the conclusion that his next task must be to dispose of this threat.

However, both he and his father had learned from experience that Albania was a difficult country to subdue at any time because of the lie of the land, and a truly formidable one under its present leader. So, although giving his own main forces a whole summer and a second winter to recover their spirits and prepare more thoroughly for an attack, he had no intention of allowing his intended victim a similar respite. That quarry was to be hunted to a standstill before the Sultan was ready to move in for the kill.

The monotonous defeat of Turkish armies which did not understand Albanian methods of warfare, led by Turkish generals unfamiliar with the ambush-ridden mountains, had taught Mehmet another lesson, and he now entrusted the harrying of Scanderbeg to an Albanian, Balaban Pasha. It was a symbolic and prophetic appointment. Albanians, even Scanderbeg himself, had fought alongside the Turks on occasion in the past, accepting the feudal duties imposed on them by the new conquerors. Even when it seemed that an invading army was too strong to resist, as at the time of the Berat disaster, some chieftains had joined forces with the Turks through fear or calculation, or for purposes of revenge; but when the occasion that gave rise to the defection had passed, they would return to the loose association of the Albanian forces and be accepted by their peers and rivals.

Here, however, was an Albanian not merely handing over a fortress for payment, allowing free passage to invading troops or even sending a hundred or two mercenaries to join them, nor returning home in the train of a foreign army. He was an Albanian, of no standing whatsoever in his own country, in command of a Turkish force of 18,000 men. The appointment was a portent for the future. It showed that the Sultan was entirely without prejudice in the choice of his servants and that an ambitious member of even a conquered nation could hope for greater opportunities in a vast empire than he could ever have in freedom at home. At the same time, there was no risk that Balaban would make common cause with his own people, for his training had effectively cut him off from their beliefs and assumptions. He had had the upbringing that the biographers were to attribute to Scanderbeg, and his reactions were those that Scanderbeg would have shown had he really been subject to the same influences. He had been taken away from his home as a boy and brought up among the Janissaries, a Muslim in religion, and with that training he saw everything, his own native country included, in the light of the Sultan's interests.

Moreover, the appointment was a carefully calculated act of social revolution. Balaban was the son of a shepherd on the Castrioti estates. Had he not been been taken off as a young man he would now have been minding sheep or ploughing the land for Scanderbeg, instead of facing him as an equal in war. This was Mehmet's way of declaring that he was no longer interested, as his father would have been (and as he himself had been as recently as Hamza Castrioti's campaign), in playing the familiar European role of an impotent monarch in a feudal society, set around with powerful barons who wielded the real authority. He did not negotiate with the Serbian despots and *zupans*, he defeated them and annexed their territory. In Albania, where tribalism had hardly yet evolved into the settled hierarchies of feudalism, he was less prepared to compromise. Murad II, expanding his empire in the heart of the Balkans, had been willing to make concessions to secure peace on the Albanian periphery; but to his son, the student of Ptolemy, Albania was not a distant frontier province but a necessary stepping stone to further conquests. Possessing, and personally controlling, the finest army in the world, there was now no reason why he should respect the special privileges of the chieftains who had so long resisted him.

His attacks could be withstood indefinitely only if Scanderbeg were able to give Albania a more modern social and political system, fashioning a nation under his own leadership out of the many disparate tribes. Unfortunately, his weakness in the face of jealousies at home, and his perpetual need to be fighting the Turks when he should have been conducting diplomacy among his own people, not to mention his poverty and need of arms and men, forced him more firmly into the feudal pattern that was already vanishing on both sides of the battle-line between Christianity and Islam. He was forced to take a humiliating step backwards in order to gain the prestige and protection—for what they were worth—of a Neapolitan alliance. Mehmet exploited this moral weakness in his position by the appointment of Balaban, the man best fitted to wound his pride and point the contrast between a dying social order and one that was coming to take its place.

Balaban's campaign did not begin well. He decided to send his army in two parts, one from Skopje and the other from Bitolj, thus escaping the risk of having the whole force ambushed in the passes. They would meet well inside the country and together move on to Kruja. Scanderbeg did not wait for this to happen, but moved in April 1465 against the southern force, under Balaban himself, and broke it up at Valcalia near Ohrid. It was a victory, but a disastrous one.

The Albanian is very brave in war when circumstances are familiar and a quick decisive charge can be made on an enemy unprepared for attack. But he is not trained for those occasions where the tide of battle turns, and an entire army must quickly improvise and carry out a change of tactics. Scanderbeg had harnessed the national élan to the possibilities of light cavalry warfare, bringing to its highest pitch the effects of a reckless charge into the midst of either infantry or heavy cavalry, each prepared only for the familiar exchanges of the orthodox battle line. Under this impetus, the attacked army tended to be seized by panic and to scatter in disorder, so that forces a few hundreds strong could rout thousands. But Balaban, himself an Albanian, was aware of this characteristic. The weapon which had so far enabled between ten and twenty thousand men to hold the Ottoman armies at bay indefinitely was apprehension, and finally panic, heightened by the difficult and unfamiliar surroundings.

Defeat took place, in other words, in the mind of the Turkish soldier, and was in no sense inherent in the weapons or methods employed on either side. Balaban realised, therefore, that it was enough to prevent the initial break down of morale; if that were done, the relative superiority of force could be brought into play at leisure.

The Turkish troops at Valcalia, evidently thoroughly grounded in what to expect, yielded to the first onslaught but did not give way entirely. They allowed the impetus to spend itself, and then themselves closed in to give battle. So the Albanians, long accustomed to breaking up the opposing force in this opening rush, found instead that they were required to fight for their victory. In these unusual conditions, some of the best Albanian officers found themselves taken prisoner, and Scanderbeg's general staff ended in the hands of the Turks. Moses of Dibra, perhaps his best general, was among them once again, together with Vladan Muritza, on whose advice he had greatly relied; Musachi d'Angelina, a nephew who had remained loyal to him throughout; Gino Musachi, Gjon Perlati, Nikola Erisi, Gjergj Kuka and Gino Manershi.

This was a disaster beyond anything that had gone before; but true to the chivalrous rules of mediaeval warfare, negotiations were opened to ransom the captured leaders, after which of course they might be expected to fight as valiantly as ever, and more prudently because of their chastening experience. The defeat would be a blow to their pride rather than a military catastrophe. Scanderbeg was to find, however, that Mehmet's rejection of the Middle Ages was complete. He no longer regarded war, and least of all this particular war, as an elegant game between monarchs, but as a means of imposing his will on the enemy. The eight distinguished captives were sent to Istanbul and there offered inducements to become Muslims and join the Turkish army. When after a fortnight they still refused, they were flayed alive and their corpses thrown into the street for the dogs to eat.

Albania was given up to mourning. The people wore black. The women chanted their wild funeral dirges. The men let their beards grow untended. For days on end the Passing bell tolled from the churches. And in June, when the shock was still fresh, Balaban reappeared in the Ohrida area. Backed by the recent display of power, he now sent gifts to Scanderbeg in the oriental manner, as an overture to peacemaking. Mehmet, in choosing his new general, had shrewdly divined the limitations of his opponent's character. Noble as he was in his loyalties, even to the pitch of quixotry, he could not rise above his inherited prejudices about the social hierarchy. Instead of treating the overture with contempt, or repaying it in kind—say, by sending back a rope with which Balaban could die a traitor's death—Scanderbeg showed that above all his vanity as a chieftain had been offended. He sent back to the son of his father's peasant a hoe and a ploughshare,[1] to remind him of his origin and to suggest how he should be spending his days instead of daring to pretend to the high-born privilege of leading armies. It had seemingly not occurred to Scanderbeg, determined to interpret a symbolic gesture as a mere personal insult, that if the Sultan could take a peasant and make of him a general fit to lead an army of several thousand men, the war between them could move to only one conclusion.

Angered in his turn by the contemptuous gift that had been sent him, Balaban tried to finish the campaign as quickly as he could. He bribed the guards of a nearby Albanian camp at Oranik—an action that already shows the effect of Turkish power on the will to resist—and began to attack it at first light, under the impression that the enemy commander was away to the north in the Dibra area. But Scanderbeg had been warned of the Turkish movements and returned to beat off Balaban, who found the camp expecting him. In this encounter, though, Scanderbeg himself was almost taken prisoner; a soldier called Leveta has gone down in Albanian history as the man who killed the Turk threatening Scanderbeg.

There was to be yet another attack before the campaigning season ended. Balaban's forces were increased to 24,000, and another 16,000 were given to Jakup Arnauti (Jacob the Albanian) who, as his name suggests, was another Turkicised Albanian. Balaban was to move in as usual from Ohrida, and Jakup was to march north from Berat, thus trying to take their opponent in the rear if he tried to forestall the attack this time. There was now a strong movement in the Albanian command, no doubt with the fate of Moses of Dibra and the others in mind, for fighting a purely defensive campaign; but Scanderbeg felt that he must at all costs prevent the two commanders from linking forces and bringing an army of 40,000 men to bear against him. He had received some fresh troops from the King of Naples, and could take the field with about 12,000 men. He decided to attack Balaban first and, escaping an ambush that had been prepared for him, again by bribery, he went on to win a victory in the same plain of Valcalia where his armies had met such a reverse only a few months earlier. Then he turned back to meet the other army that was coming up from the south. It had reached the Tirana area, and there he had the satisfaction of dispersing it and killing Jakup with his own hand.

It had been a triumphal year in that a series of victories had followed each other. All attacks had been repelled, but at what a cost! Scanderbeg had once reminded the Prince of Taranto of the wars Pyrrhus of Epirus had waged against the Romans, and he was now forced by events to show himself a true descendent of that hero in tactics as well as race. He had held at bay comparatively minor Turkish forces only, and they had begun to take his measure as a general and show that there was nothing superhuman about his methods. His people were tiring of incessant war, quite apart from the steady decline in the number of able-bodied fighting men available. Bribery and the desire to attack only when provoked were now factors to be reckoned with. There had been some help in men and arms from abroad during the last campaign, but not enough to free Albania from the threat of invasion. His other potential allies were less willing than ever to help. The King of Hungary was moving towards an uneasy peace with the Turks, and he in any case had never been an unqualified friend of Scanderbeg's, probably because he saw in him an instrument of Neapolitan policy in the Adriatic and on the Balkan mainland. The new Pope, being a Venetian, was in no sense an idealist, and judged policies by whether they could be put into practice and not, as Pius II had done, by whether they were desirable in themselves. His enemy had spent a restful summer building palaces, giving his soldiers money to spend and leave to spend it in, and poring over the geography of the world he intended to conquer. The defender was a man of sixty or so, physically old for his years, with small and diminishing resources which he was forced constantly to employ and dissipate by an opponent hardly more than half his age and possessing unlimited reserves and almost inhuman patience.

After his year of peace, the Sultan returned to war-making in 1466, refreshed in body and mind and in his conceptions of strategy. He now no longer turned towards Hungary and Central Europe in the north, but west towards Albania, where a Sultan had not conducted a campaign in person since Murad II tried to capture Kruja sixteen years earlier. This decision, linked with his rising interest in sea power, showed how his mind was turning towards the need for control of the lower Adriatic coast, with the opportunities that would give him of carrying Turkish power into southern Italy. Before that was possible, however, plans must be made for a permanent occupation of at least central Albania. In the past, Turkish armies had flowed into Albania like a wave, driving the defenders like flotsam to the hills, and had then ebbed back towards Macedonia, leaving only signs of destruction in their wake. They had left no effective authority behind them, so that each successive invasion had to begin again from nothing. Mehmet decided to remedy this state of affairs, and had three ideas for doing so: The narrow passes into the country, which had so often proved death traps for forces attempting to enter or escape, were to be conquered and controlled, and have roads driven through them. Kruja was to be attacked, and if once more it could not be taken, despite the improvements in Turkish artillery fire power since the last attempt, it would be held under close siege and eventually starved out. And to make the other two projects effective, a fortress would be built in the centre of the country to support and provision a local garrison, whose duty would be to prevent the highlanders' depredations and lead to a general pacification.

In the Spring of 1466 he set out from Adrianople with cavalry and infantry that may have numbered more than a hundred thousand men. They moved across Macedonia as speedily as possible, and encamped for a short time at Ohrida, where arrangements were made to split the army in two in order to take Kruja in a pincer movement. One part of the army went down the Black Drin, turning west a little way beyond the fortress of Svetigrad and up the wide, forest-bordered valley of the Bulqizë river; and then, presumably, north and west along the Mat river to cut off any help that might be coming from the Venetians at Scutari and Lezhë. The Sultan himself, with the main bulk of his forces, intended to clear and restore to its old purposes a track that, until the gradual breakdown of Byzantine authority, had been a major international highway for two thousand years or so. From Durazzo on the one hand and Thessaloniki on the other, a trade route had existed into Macedonia from at least the fifth century B.C.; the Romans had adopted, paved, and given it the name of the Via Egnatia. Now it was to be brought back into use by a new conqueror.

At Ohrida the Sultan had now reached the Albanian frontier, and the dark inhospitable mountains rose before him at the far edge of the high plains. To his right, the land rose steadily and distantly to the pasture uplands of Galicnik, green and white with limestone outcrop littered among the grass, and silent but for the bleat of the flocks of sheep that the Albanian marauders so coveted. Overhead the falcons hung in the clear air. On the left was the lake of Ohrid, twenty miles of silver and blue, clear as crystal down to fifty feet or more from the deep springs that forever feed it. On the lake were the primitive boats of the fishermen, looking like hollowed out tree trunks with a rough poop nailed on; beside it, the already old Byzantine churches; and all around orchards, vineyards and market gardens, white oxen and buffalo and flocks of herons.

Turning his back on this type of earthly paradise, Mehmet ordered the light infantry to attack the pass he intended to cross - Qaf e Thanës which lies at nearly 3,000 feet, between Ohrid and the upper waters of the river Shkumbi. A garrison was left behind, and 'then he ordered the woodcutters and part of the infantry to go in and fell trees and clear away the bushes and thickets and impenetrable tangles, and to level and repair the rough and uneven and altogether impassable roads, and make them wide and smooth for the whole army, horse and foot, and for the pack animals and wagons and other means of transport.'

As the parabola of Turkish power declined again centuries later, this road once more disintegrated, and a traveller of the nineteenth century has left a description of the same journey done under very similar circumstances to those met by Mehmet and his army. There came first, says Edward Lear,[2] three hours of 'a dull pass, walled in by low hills covered with stunted oaks,' two hours' descent, then two more hours of 'a narrow dull valley,' all under a hot sun, and then a pause for food on a summit where there was 'literally nothing to be procured, not even a drop of water.' 'A most wild and desolate country does this part of Albania seem, with scarcely a single habitation visible in so great a space; stern-wrinkled hills wall in the horizon, covered midway with oak forests; but after passing another range of low hills we came to the valley of the Shkumbi, and thenceforth the landscape began to assume a character of grand melancholy not to be easily forgotten. About five, the infinitely varied lines of the western heights were most glorious, their giant-rock forms receding into golden clouds as the sun sank down, while below stretched the deep widening valley of the Skumbi, a silvery stream winding through utterly wild scenes of crag, forest and slope as far as eye could see.' And though Lear has no occasion to mention it, at some point in this descent, beyond this row upon row of mountain ranges lying like petrified waves before and below you, lies the glint of the far sea, the ultimate highway of all the conquerors who have broken through these mountains from the east.

Even from here, the descent to the plain took a full day. The track, says Lear, lay 'either along sharp narrow paths cut in the rock, at the very edge of formidable precipices, or by still narrower tracks running on the bare side of a perpendicular clay ravine - or winding among huge trunks of forest trees, between which the baggage mule is at one time wedged - at another loses her load, or her own equilibrium, by some untimely concussion.' The scene combined 'Greek outline—Italian colour—English luxuriance of foliage' with huge walnut and chestnut groves and stupendous precipices. 'Every stony descent, and every toilsome climb up this mountain ridge brought us, if possible, to more vast and wondrously beautiful scenes; far below in the valley the river wound among dark dense oaks, sparkling like a silver thread, while above towered a mountain screen, whose snow-crowned, furrowed summits, frowned over slopes richly clothed with hanging woods. Perhaps the extreme beauty and variety of the colour in these scenes was as attractive as their sublimity . . . after three hours of winding among frightful paths at the edge of clay precipices and chasms, and through scenery of the same character, but gloomier under a clouded sun, we began to descend towards the seaward plains, and were soon effecting a steep and difficult passage between the trunks of oak trees to the purple vale of the Skumbi.'

Chapter Fourteen

. . . .

'A Day of Mist'

RED RATHER THAN PURPLE would be the colour best suited to describe the Shkumbi valley after Mehmet's arrival; for once through the mountain gorges and out into the coastal plain, he and his army committed a deliberate act of terrorism,[1] intended to break any will to resist and to persuade the people to abandon Scanderbeg's hopeless cause. The region of the plains 'he entirely overran and plundered. After that he pitched camp at successive points, and advanced, devastating the country, burning the crops or else gathering them in for himself, and destroying and annihilating. And the Illyrians (the word Kritovoulos uses throughout for the Albanians) took their children, wives, flocks and every other movable up into the high and inaccessible mountain fastnesses. They had their arms also, and they settled down to defend themselves in these difficult strongholds and passes against any attackers.'

Kritovoulos goes on to describe the campaign against them: 'When the Sultan had pillaged and devastated all their lowlands, he made careful preparations, and after putting the whole army in first class condition, moved against the mountains and their passes, and the fortifications in the hills, against the Illyrians and their children and wives and all their belongings. He placed on the van the bowman and musketeers and slingers, telling them to shoot and fire their arrows and sling their stones against the Illyrians and drive them as far away as possible, and get rid of them by firing at the heights.

'Behind them he ordered the light infantry, the spearmen and those with the small shields to go up, and, following them, all the heavy-armed units. These went up slowly and in irregular ranks, up to a certain point, gradually pushing the Illyrians up to the heights. Then with a mighty shout, the light infantry, the heavy infantry, and the spearmen charged the Illyrians, and having put them to flight, they pursued them with all their might, and overtook and killed them. And some they captured alive. But some of them, hard pressed by the heavy infantry, hurled themselves from the precipices and crags, and were destroyed.

'The heavy and light artillery, and in fact the whole army, scattering over the mountains and the rough country and the ravines, hunted out and made prisoners of the children and women of the Illyrians, and plundered all their belongings. Not only this, but they carried off a very large number of flocks and herds. They scoured thoroughly the whole mountain, and hunted out and secured a very enormous booty of prisoners and cattle and other things, and brought it all down to the camp.

'A very great number of the Illyrians lost their lives, some in the fighting, and others were executed after being captured, for so the Sultan ordered. And there were captured in those mountains about twenty thousand children, and women, and men. Of the rest of the Illyrians, some were in the fortresses, and some in the mountain ranges where they fled with their leader Alexander.'

In one case, at least, even the fortresses did not give protection, for the Turks captured Chidna, a strongpoint on the Black Drin, a river which served as an important line of communication for the tribes of the east and north east. Its capture once more reduced Albanian mobility and drew a still tighter chain of steel around them. Its fall was due to treachery, and everyone inside it, old men, women and children as well as soldiers, were massacred.

Kruja was also besieged, and work was begun on the new fortress Mehmet had decided to build for his permanent garrison in central Albania. His site was chosen for him by nature and history. Where the gorges of the road from Ohrida began to open out into the coastal plain, the Romans, no doubt following the example of still earlier settlers, had founded a town called Scampa, from which presumably the river Shkumbi takes its name. The two forks of the Via Egnatia, one from Durazzo and the other from Apollonia, converged here for their onward journey to Constantinople. It kept its importance under the Byzantine empire and had a bishop of its own; and from the new name of Albanon or Albanopolis the country around came to be known as Albania.[2] It was destroyed in a Bulgarian invasion, and as the empire was never again strong enough to maintain the old network of trade and military activity for any length of time, the town remained a ruin, and such population and activity, as revived moved to a fortified Orthodox monastery a mile or two out of the town.

But for an imperial power the advantages of the site were unimpaired; and there were two further reasons why it should appeal to Mehmet. It lay at the edge of one of the most fertile plains of the Balkans, so that the garrison would have plenty to eat while witholding from Scanderbeg and the Albanians their best source of food supplies. In addition, the river Shkumbi was still navigable here, so that for future naval operations there would be no need to warn the Venetians and other Italian powers of their danger by transferring a fleet from the Aegean to the Adriatic. Ships could be built from the timber in the hills and sailed down the river to the sea in complete safety. Mehmet's attention was caught by the ruins of the decayed old town. 'He found traces and foundations of an ancient city in a favourable position, and clearly most desirable and well located in ancient times;' and, as always with any project close to his heart, he personally supervised operations, having decided that this was to be the site of his new garrison town. Into Elbasan,[3] as it was shortly to be known (perhaps as a corruption of the old name Albanon), he brought 'a great abundance of the necessities, of suitable food and of things for their service, and every other suitable and necessary thing in great abundance. He also brought in many weapons and stone-hurling cannon and crossbows and immense quantities of other materials and war supplies.

'And he fitted it out well in every particular, and made it an inhabited town, just as it had been many years before, abounding in every needful and desirable thing. He left in the fortress a considerable garrison, four hundred men from his own bodyguard, of the best fighters and the most healthy men. He appointed as governor of the region and commander of this large force, one of the best men of his suite, a good strategist who was to overrun and ravage all the territory of the Illyrians systematically and unceasingly, and to besiege the town of Kruja.' The 'good strategist' was Balaban Pasha, so that now an Albania governed an area of central Albania in the name of the Sultan from a walled town newly populated by Albanians and garrisoned by Turks. The pattern of a permanent occupation was beginning to show itself.

'Having done this, the Sultan returned in the fall to Byzantium, taking along a very large number of slaves and animals both for himself and for distribution to the army.' There is an air of complacency about this recital, and not without some reason, for it had been a most successful season. At every point he had done what he set out to do: clear the roads, terrorise the population, capture fortresses, tie up the main stronghold of Kruja and build a new town which would eventually ensure control of the whole country. The Albanian problem appeared to be well on the way to a solution, and there had been no reaction from his adversary.

Scanderbeg had not tried to stem this flood of men and materials. A number of skirmishes are recorded as the great armies crossed the border, but no serious attempt to stop their progress was made once they were inside the country. To have done otherwise would have risked complete disaster. On the

Sultan's approach he left Kruja in the care of Tanush Thopia with 4,000 men, and himself withdrew, probably moving between the mountains, to organise their defence, and the Venetian towns where help could perhaps be negotiated. The Venetian Senate, giving instructions on 18th June to their new representative in Scutari, Gian Matteo Contarini, told him that if he had a chance of speaking to Scanderbeg, or if Scanderbeg should happen to be in Scutari, 'we wish you to salute him in our name and give him what consolation you can, letting him know of our great sorrow at the calamity that has come upon his subjects and ours by the arrival of the Turk in that province. And add that if by God's grace and his own skill his excellency has been able to overcome and save himself from the fierce onslaught of such a great adversary, we take heart from such news, and have no doubt about the outcome for us both. In this fashion you will comfort him with the most humane and understanding words you can think of, so that he will make whatever dispositions he can to preserve that province, while we for our part will continue to supply and send to him everything he needs for success.'

As is evident from the warmth of these instructions, the invasion of Albania on such a scale had frightened the Venetians into a new realisation of the value to them of the local mountaineers. On 7th June, in reply to a request from King Ferrante of Naples for news of the war and advice on what he should do, they told him that the affairs of Scanderbeg, Albania 'and consequently of Christianity' were in the greatest possible danger and, if he was in a position to help, he should send infantry and artillery both to Scanderbeg himself and to other points which still held out in Albania. But over the course of the month the Venetians seemed to have realised that the Sultan was not intending to conduct a full-scale assault on Kruja, so on the 23rd they informed Ferrante that the crisis was over, and they did not think any further expense was called for. They had taken Kruja under their wing, provisioned it and sent soldiers there. Only extreme necessity could have induced them to call on their rivals for help, and even then it must have given them pleasure to point out that at Kruja they had usurped the old Neapolitan influence. Aside from their own towns, now nothing in Albania was more important to the Venetians than Kruja. So long as it stood, the Turks would not dare to mount an attack on Scutari or Durazzo. Once they were sure it was in no immediate danger, the old habits of caution and frugality reasserted themselves. They then told Scanderbeg's envoy that they were delighted Kruja had been saved, but were afraid they could spend no more on its defence at the moment. 'We would draw his attention,' wrote the Senate on 7th July, 'to the heavy and burdensome expenses which are flowing in upon us by land and by sea, not only in Albania and Dalmatia, but also in the Morea, Nigroponto and such eastern provinces generally.' However, as a token of goodwill they sent 3,000 ducats and hoped that would be enough to clear the country of the Turks.

The optimist, it has been said, is the man who has not yet heard the news; and the Venetian government supposed that once again a mere punitive expedition had come and gone, killing a few Albanians perhaps, but leaving the most important one unscathed, and changing nothing essential in the situation. Shortly, however, they heard about Elbasan. This, declared the Senate on 16th August, was a most dangerous development, because it was both near their own possessions and also 'well provisioned with materials' for building warships and commercial vessels 'and convenient for sending them down the river and into the sea.' The Venetians might encourage hope in their allies, if only to reduce their financial expectations; but themselves they rarely deluded. They had no doubt what had to be done: Elbasan must be destroyed. Scanderbeg was urged not to rest on his laurels, but to deal with 'this infection, so to speak, in his entrails as in our own,' which was daily becoming graver. The various local governors in Albania were urged to concert ways and means with him. And once again the collecting box was sent around. Ragusa contributed a few victuals. Matthias Corvinus of

Hungary, grateful that the main weight of the Turks had been deflected from him, thought it wisest to send nothing. The Medicis of Florence offered help which they failed to send. Venice herself, though alarmed at the latest developments, still did not wish to commit herself so far in the open that the Turks would be provoked into attacking her possessions in Albania and elsewhere.

Scanderbeg was thus left with three thousand ducats and many good wishes, and told to use these to eject the Turks. At the same time his own assets had diminished. His best lieutenants had been captured and many of his rank and file killed in battle or massacred as prisoners. He probably had no more than 14,000 armed men available at the beginning of the 1466 campaign. They were not enough to prevent defeat; and in addition to more soldiers he needed artillery, since light cavalry and courage were not enough to destroy the walls of Elbasan. He came to the conclusion that he must himself go and see his old friends and supporters, the Pope and the King of Naples, explain the danger in which he (and at one remove, they) found themselves, and beg for the necessary help. So on 12th December 1466 a small train of horsemen reached Rome, led by an old man dressed as an ordinary soldier without marks of rank, as though to symbolise the extremity in which he found himself.

'He came like a poor man,' said an observer; but he was met by the princes of the Church, and great crowds gathered round the house in which he stayed, just below the Quirinale, in order to catch a sight of him. People thought him older than he really was, for his campaigns had aged him. He was a little over sixty, but he looked patriarchal. They saw, to judge from the painting still to be found over the front door of his lodgings, a man with a long white beard, a strongly arched nose and a still stern eye: a man of unbroken will for whom, however, time was growing short. Pope Paul II invested him with a sword of honour and a consecrated helmet at a service in St. Peter's, and then held a consistory to decide what could be done to help. A gift of 7,500 ducats was decided upon. It would have been more, he was told, but unfortunately the Pope was being menaced nearer home. The King of Naples was preparing to attack the States of the Church and money was needed to defend against him. So with sword, helmet, some of the promised ducats and many letters of recommendation to sovereigns who had failed to contribute in the past, Scanderbeg was sent on his way. King Ferrante, on whom he called next, received him with great joy and entertained him lavishly in Castelnuovo in Naples. He also gave him 1,500 ducats and some supplies and ammunition, regretting that it was not more but pleading that this was 'the way things are now.' There was, for example, a war with the Pope to be prepared for, and it would be unwise to denude either the land or its army or the treasury of its resources. With this lavish encouragement and modest practical help Scanderbeg returned home and left his allies to their war with each other.

There he found that the Venetian commanders had assembled some thousands of fighting men, bringing the forces under his command to around 30,000 men. In April 1467 the opportunity for using them arrived. A fresh Turkish force was sent to relieve the one which had been laying desultory seige to Kruja since the previous year under Balaban, and this was led by his brother Yonuzi and by Yonuzi's son Haidan. Scanderbeg attacked them before they could join up with the besiegers and routed them completely, taking the two leaders prisoner and displaying them in full view of Balaban. Stung by the insult, Balaban ordered a fresh assault on the fortress; but Scanderbeg captured a Turkish position on the hill above Kruja, and having thus broken the ring of strongpoints built by the Turks was able to catch their army between his own men and those of Tanush Thopia's garrison. The Turkish army fled to the plains around Tirana, there to regroup and prepare to fight its way back through the passes, which were now in Albanian hands.

Balaban himself was killed by one Gjergj Lleshi, and the other Turkish commanders asked to be allowed to leave the country unmolested. In return, the Albanians could have all the booty that remained, arms, supplies and money. Scanderbeg was in favour of accepting the offer. He knew how the position had worsened at home, and his Italian visit had shown him how little hope there was of adequate foreign help. He had also presumably digested the lessons of 1465, when the Sultan had provoked him into dissipating his strength before what had been intended as the final reckoning of the following year. The aims and methods of Mehmet II were also clear now, and it was unthinkable that he would allow a short-sighted triumph to go unavenged. The important thing was to get the Turks out of the country. They would be only too happy to go without causing trouble, whereas they would fight more bitterly than ever if the offer were to be rejected. 'Men who fear everything are afraid of nothing,' he told his colleagues. He was alone in this view, however. To have in their power part of the army that had caused such miseries in Albania, and to allow it to go free was beyond the range of his colleagues' imagination. Asked for his view, Lek Dukagjini simply used two words: 'Embe ta' - Down with them. The war council supported him, armistice overtures were rejected, and the hunt started. The Turks fought with despairing courage and did for the most part manage to put the river Drin behind them and carried back to Constantinople the story of their humiliation.

With the disappearance of large Turkish forces, Scanderbeg strengthened the garrison of Kruja and stocked the fortress for the further attacks he expected. Then he occupied the lowland area and began to besiege the modest-sized Turkish garrison left behind in Elbasan. 'On hearing this news,' says Kritovoulos understandably, 'the Sultan was very angry. He paid no attention to anything else, but raised a very large army of horse and foot and, after making thorough preparations—for it was already near the end of winter—as soon as Spring set in he marched against him. On arriving in the country of the Illyrians, he ravaged the whole of it rapidly, and subdued its revolted people, killing many of them. He destroyed and plundered whatever he could get hold of, burning, devastating, ruining and annihilating,' though the Albanians had taken away with them every thing they could, even the bells from their churches, when they fled into the mountains.

The Turkish soldiers were given permission to plunder as they would, and to kill their prisoners, and the bulk of the army was sent into the mountains where 'not only did they capture every fortress and all who had fled into them, but they overran every place and took it, and made slaves, and destroyed, for a space of fifteen days,' at the end of which they brought down all their booty into the camp. Once again calculated terrorism was being practised to break the general will to resist; but his anger did not blind the Sultan to the realities of the situation. The key to Albania was Kruja, and it remained true that this was likely to be taken only by sustained siege and starvation. What he could perhaps do to hasten the process was to try and close the routes by which help reached Kruja. He destroyed a fort at a place called Chivril on Cape Rodoni on the Adriatic, which Scanderbeg was building; and which, being just below Kruja, would have been useful for transshipment of supplies. He also made a demonstration against Durazzo, probably as a warning to the Venetians not to provoke him, rather than with any serious hope of conquering it. Until Kruja fell, there was little more he could do than wait patiently, meantime strengthening his own garrisons and leaving a sizeable force around Ohrid to come to the help of his forces in Albania if they should again be in danger. So, having made his dispositions, he returned to Constantinople.

Although at the end of each campaigning season the main body of the Turks retired and the situation seemed to be restored, Scanderbeg's position was worsening all the time. There were now Turkish garrisons permanently in the country and a Turkish walled town in the heart of the plains. The disparity between the forces on the two sides was great, and growing still greater. The Turks had the finest armament in the world, he had not guns strong enough to attack the ring of fortresses they were building around him. His last chance of any honourable accommodation with the Sultan had gone, but resistance offered no hope of victory. If he and his few thousand men went on fighting, it could only be because there was nothing else they could do if they were to be true to themselves.

Scanderbeg decided that the chieftains must be called together, along with representatives from Venice, for a frank statement of the dangers, a discussion on how this Turkish encirclement could be broken so that it did not form again a few months later. On 16th January 1468 the Doge instructed Francesco Capello to go to Albania as quickly as he could to hold discussions with its leader. The League of Princes, formed to begin the struggle twenty-four years earlier, was now coming together again in the same town of Lezhë to face the same problem, though not with the same high hopes.

Scanderbeg reached Lezhë and had an attack of fever, perhaps malaria from some nearby swamp. He was weakened by years of privation, and above all by the last three years of anxieties and disasters, and of victories which were disasters too in their way. So he, who in dozens of battles had scarcely received a scratch, was overcome by a common ailment of the low-lying coastlands, and died on 17th January 1468.

'It was a day of mist, cheerless; and the heavens were ready to weep,' runs the song that his mourning people composed.[4] 'Then the rainwashed dawn broke, and a cry echoed around the hills, throwing every heart and house into mourning.' It was the voice of the chieftain Lek Dukagjin who, beating his forehead with one hand, tore out his hair with the other. 'Arouse yourself, Albania! Come, warriors and women, orphans that you all are, you have lost the father who helped and advised and loved you. No one now will protect the honour of the virgin, the happiness of the citizen, because the Lord of Albania died this morning. Scanderbeg is no more.'

'The houses heard the cry and their foundations trembled. The mountains heard it and were rent asunder. The bells in the churches proclaimed their mourning. Scanderbeg, who had perished, was entering into heaven.'

When the news reached Venice in February the Senate requested the Archbishop of Durazzo and their own local governor there to ask the widow and heir for the right to take over Kruja and the other fortresses and send garrisons to occupy them. This was granted, and for ten years it proved effective, though for most of this period the Sultan was involved in war on his eastern frontier with Venice's Turkoman allies, who had built an empire for themselves in Armenia, Persia and Mesopotamia.

But in 1477 a Turkish army returned to Kruja; and, to keep the spirit of its great commander alive in the hearts of the defenders, choirs of maidens, 'though surrounded by the din of battle and the clang of barbarian arms, assembled regularly every eighth day in the public squares of the cities of the principality to sing hymns for their departed hero.'

On 16th June 1478 the city was finally starved into submission, though it did not surrender without a promise that the lives of the Krujans would be saved. But the Ottomans, who had suffered such humiliations here, went back on their promise when once the population was within their power, massacring the men in cold blood and taking the women and children away to slavery. The same year they conquered the Venetian town of Lezhë and broke into the cathedral of St. Nicholas, where the League of Princes had first met over thirty years earlier, and where its moving spirit lay buried. The soldiers tore open his grave and took fragments of his bones as amulets, hoping thus to share in his valour and success.[5]

In 1479 the Sultan Mehmet II came in person to besiege the Venetian stronghold of Scutari, whose castle lay like a crown on the top of a hill fortified since Illyrian days.[6] Into it he poured over two thousand stone shells; and when it fell, Venice was forced to cede all her Albanian possessions apart from Durazzo, which she managed to retain for twenty years more.

Master of the country at last, Mehmet was now free to turn

his attention across the Adriatic. In July 1480 his fleet crossed the strait, bound for the port of Otranto, the most easterly town of Italy. After a fifteen-day siege it fell on 8th August, and the Ottoman Turks now possessed an Italian bridgehead. The Sultan decided not to extend it immediately, however, for he wanted to dislodge the Knights of St. John from Rhodes, the only island in the Aegean archipelago that had not yet submitted to him. On the way, at his camp on the Asian shore of the Bosphorus, he died on 3rd May 1481, at the age of only 52.

For some months the empire was in disorder, as a short civil war flared up between his sons. The Neapolitans regained the initiative, and the Turks were turned out of Otranto in September 1481. The new Sultan, Bajezid II, inherited his father's taste for poetry and science, but not his desire for conquest. He 'sought to do justice to his duties as a ruler principally through magnificent buildings for public use.' By the time that warriors once more occupied the throne, their attention was diverted to Hungary, Persia and Egypt. Albania was to remain under Turkish rule for more than four centuries, and did not begin to find her national freedom again until 1912; but her resistance, initiated and gloriously sustained by Scanderbeg for a quarter of a century and then continued up to the eve of Mehmet the Conqueror's death, disrupted his ambitious plans and ensured that Italy, and possibly other lands of western Europe, were not called on to share her fate.[7]

Notes

1. Europe's Oldest Society

1 The quotation from Wolfe is in Beckles Willson, Life and Letters of James Wolfe (New York, 1909), pp. 296-7.

2 Taboo on Iron: The quotations are from M.E. Durham, Some Tribal Origins, Laws and Customs of the Balkans,(Allen and Unwin 1928), pp. 298-302. The French traveller was Chaumette des Fooses, who wrote Voyage en Bosnie 1807-8 (Paris 1816).

3 Inducements to murder a brother: The quotation is from Margaret Hasluck, The Unwritten Law in Albania (Cambridge University Press, 1954), p. 210.

4 The Oresteia: The various quotations are - 'a mere quibble', Gilbert Murray, The Complete Plays of Aeschylus (Allen and Unwin, 1952), pp. 261-2; 'an astonishing argument,' H.D.F. Kitto, Greek Tragedy (Methuen, 1939) pp. 90-2; 'a weak argument,' Philip Vellacott, tr. of The Oresteian Trilogy' (Penguin 1956), p. 194.

5 Blood Brotherhood: M.E. Durham, pp. 153-9.;

6 Antigone: The translator is E.F. Watling, whose translation of The Theban Plays was published by Penguin, 1947; his interpretation of Antigone's action appears in a note on p. 167. The other critic is A.J.A. Waldock, Sophocles the Dramatist (Cambridge, 1951), p. 136.

7 A Serbian poem: This is 'A Conjugal Dispute,' in Owen Meredith (Bulwer Lytton), Serbski Pesme,(Chatto and Windus, 1917), pp. 105-9.

8 The wife of Hospodar Gjergj: J.W. Wiles, Serbian Songs and Poems (Allen and Unwin, 1917), p. 69. The title of the poem is 'Greatest Grief for a Brother.'

9 Miss Durham's stories of Ike and the Mirdite woman, and the old ballad, are from her Tribal Origins, pp. 148-51.

10 The Albanian exiles' poem is quoted textually in French translation in Maria Brandon Albini: Calabre (Paris: Arthaud, 1957), pp. 266-9.

11 The traditional law of the mountains is believed to have been codified by one of several chieftains called Lek Dukagjini who headed the tribe of the same name in the fifteenth century. He proved to be 'a law giver of such eminence that what he said is still as sacred as Holy Writ to the mountaineers of Mirditë and all the tribes to the north.' (Hasluck, pp. 12-13).

The law is known as the Kanun, or Canon, of Lek Dukagjini; and the Albanian Franciscan scholar, Father Shtjefen Gjeçov, collected all the items he could find shortly before the First World War. This was published in Albania in 1933 and by the Reale Accademia d'Italia in 1941. The word Kanun comes to Albania from the Greek through Arabic and Turkish, which suggests that the codification may have taken place after the Turkish conquest. The Albanian word for law is 'Ligjë.' (See Hasluck, p. 14)

12 Bone Reading: Durham, pp. 274-8. The shoulder bone of a sheep could also be read; it had the further advantage that having disclosed its secrets it could be used, with a stick attached, for shovelling up the ashes from the hearth, and it was in fact known in Montenegro as lopatica, or 'little shovel.'

2. Emperors, Despots and Chieftains

1 Despotate of Epirus: For the series of events in the early 13th century which gave Kruja its political and national significance, see Donald Y. Nicol, The Despotate of Epiros (Blackwell, 1957).

2 Dante: 'Quello di Rascia, che mal aggiusto il conio di Vinegia' appears in the series of comminations that ends Book XIX of the Paradiso. Dante is referring to the first silver dinars minted by King Uros to finance trade around the middle of the 13th century. Uros was flattering the Venetians as well as 'forging' their coins; where theirs showed the Doge receiving a banner from St. Mark, he showed himself receiving one from St. Stephen.

Stefan Nemanja: He lived for four years at Hilandar under the name of Simeon. Out of his (now empty) sarchophagus grows a vine from which pilgrims take home grapes that are supposed to induce fertility in their womenfolk.

3 The Serbian Renaissance: The brilliance of the Serbian artistic renaissance under the Nemanjas has not yet found a historian who will definitively relate it, in iconography, subject and treatment, to the parallel work of the early Italian Renaissance, and make clear their common relation to the Byzantine work of the same period. Some excellent reproductions of individual frescoes, or details from them, appear in such books as the UNESCO Yugoslavia and the Skira volume on Byzantine Painting.

As to architecture, this has lately received masterly treatment by Cecil Stewart (Serbian Legacy, Allen and Unwin, 1959), who also adds to his analysis of the main buildings a useful outline of Serbia's heroic history. Although Mr. Stewart's treatment of Serbian painting is incidental to his interest in the architecture, he does convey that characteristic feature of the frescoes which, quite apart from their artistic merits, gives them their power to impress: 'It is one thing to look at a picture; it is quite another to find oneself within an encompassment of pictures ... the overwhelming effect of finding oneself within the art itself.' (p. 32)

4 Brocardus: The account of Albania attributed to Brother Brocardus of Mount Sion, a Dominican, was published in French by the Commission Royale d'Histoire of Brussels in 1844. He also wrote a Description of the Holy Land in addition to the Directorium ad faciendum passagium transmarinum, from which the references to Albania are taken.

5 Ottoman Turks: For the significance of the ghazis and the development of Ottoman power in Asia Minor, see G.L. Lewis, Turkey (Ernest Benn, 1957), pp. 18-20; for the various influences on Ottoman architecture in the Bursa period, Behçet Unsal, Turkish Islamic Architecture, Seljuk to Ottoman (Tiranti, 1959)

6 Lazar's Decision: As poetic fiction and plain fact are so hard to disentangle in Balkan history, it should perhaps be said that the flesh and blood Lazar Hrebeljanovic, as distinct from the Tsar Lazar of the poems, did not choose to

be beaten at Kosova. He fought for victory and nearly attained it. He would probably have won had it not been for the desertion of one of his commanders and the untimely excess of zeal of another who, to refute an imputation of treachery, went to the Turkish camp to assassinate the Sultan Murad I, thus inspiring fanatical heroism in the hard-pressed Turkish forces.

7 Scanderbeg's Origins: Since everything in the Balkans has to be turned to political effect, both Greeks and Slavs have claimed Scanderbeg as one of themselves. The Greeks who do so rely on the fact that the name Castrioti probably means that the family originally came from a village with the Greek name of Castrion ('a little castle') of which there were many in the Byzantine empire. This is as scholarly as proving that the Bishop of Chester must be a Roman Catholic, and his ancestors Italians, because 'chester' in a name is proof of Roman occupation.

The claim that Scanderbeg was a Slav was first made by a German who misread a document of 1368 in Serbian. Among the signatories were a Branilo (a Slav Christian name) of Vlora and a Castrioti of Kanina. By overlooking the single letter 'i' (meaning 'and'), he produced Branilo Castrioti as Scanderbeg's Serbian great-grandfather.

3. A Family in Search of a Sovereign

1 Approach to the Venetians: Sime Ljubic, Listine o Odnosajih Izmedju Juznoga Slavenstva i Mletacke Republike (Documents on the Relations between the Yugoslavs and the Venetian Republic), vol. 6 (Zagreb, 1878), p. 51.

2 Gjergj Castrioti's Age: We do not know when he was born. Barletius says he was 63 when he died, but wrongly gives the year of his death as 1466 instead of 1468. It has been assumed that Barletius was probably right about his age, and that 1405 was the year of his birth.

3 Approach to the Venetians: For Gjon Castrioti's dealings with the Venetians in 1422, Ljubic, Listine, vol. VIII (Zagreb, 1886), Pp. 211-14.

4 Ducats: The gold ducat was worth 1,166 grains

5 Gift to Hilandar: Stojan Novakovic, Zakonski Spomenici Srpskih Srednjega Veka (Legal Documents of the Serbian Mediaeval States), (Belgrade, 1912), pp. 467-8.

6 Turks and Castrioti: The evidence for the Turkish approach is quoted from the Venetian State Archives by Nicolae Jorga, Notes et Extraits pour servir a` l' Histoire des Croisades, vol. 1 (Paris, 1899 (PP. 474-6).

7 Gjon Castrioti's Defeat: Ludwig von Thalloczy, etc., Illyrisch-Albanische Forschungen, vol. I (Bunich, 1916), pp. 140-2

4. Birth of a Legend

1 Gibbon: Scanderbeg appears in Chapter 67 of the Decline and Fall

2 Barletius: Scanderbeg's first biographer, an Albanian Roman Catholic priest from Scutari, published his Historia de Vita et Gestis Scanderbegi, Epirotarum

Principis in Rome between 1506 and 1510. About a couple of hundred works on Scanderbeg in various languages between then and now can be traced back to this primary source.

It reached England by way of France, having been translated into French towards the end of the century by Jacques de Lavardin, a Vendome nobleman. Lavardin added an odd detail or two from another short sixteenth century work (Demetrio Franco, Commentario delle Cose dei Turchi e del Signor Giorgio Scanderbeg, Principe di Epyro. Venice, 1545), gave Scanderbeg the title of King and published the book undor his own name.

This was in turn translated into English by 'Z.I. Gentleman,' and appeared under the title of The History of Gjergj Castriot, surnamed Scanderbeg, King of Albanie (London, 1596). There is a panegyric of Soanderbeg for the benefit of the English reader, in which he is likened, not at all to his discredit, to various other historical characters: 'courageous as Hector,' 'bountifull and courteous as Caesar,' 'merciful as Trajan,' 'unpenetrable as Achilles' and 'comely as Edgar Atheling.' Hannibal and Scipio would give the garland to him, and 'it may justly be imagined, that God created him as mirror for the world rather to wonder at, than any way possibly to be matched.' Edmund Spenser, in a sonnet suited to this mood, asked

> Wherefore doth vaine antiquitie so vaunt
> Her ancient monuments of mightie peeres,

when here was a man

> whom later age hath brought to light,
> Matchable to the greatest of those great.
> Great both by name, and great in power and might,
> And meriting a more triumphant feate.
> The scourge of Turks, and plague of infidels,
> Thy acts, O Scanderbeg, this volume tells.

3 Scanderbeg's Brothers: Gjin Musachi, a colleague and contemporary of Gjergj Castrioti who wrote a history of his own family, says that Reposhi Castrioti died at the monastery of Signa in northeastern Albania. (Hopf, Karl: Chroniques Greco-romanes. Berlin, 1873, p. 295)The eldest brother Stanisha was alive in 1445, when he became a citizen of Venice.(Jorge, Notes, v. III, p. 194)

4 Pontano: Giovanni Gioviano Pontano, De Bello Neapolitano, in his Opera Omnia (Venice, 1519), Vol. II, p. 279.

5 Historians and Scanderbeg: The legend of Scanderbeg's training at the Ottoman Court is still active in the mid-twentieth century. Profeseor Arnold Toynbee uses it to help in proving his thesis about 'The Barbarization of the Dominant Minority,' which forms part of 'The Process of the Disintegration of Civilisation' in Book V of A Study of History.In the first act of this barbarisation, the barbarian is used as a hostage and mercenary; in the second act he comes 'unbidden and unwanted as a raider who eventually settles down to stay as a colonist or a conqueror,' and the Dominant Minority is 'decisively and irretrievably' barbariesd in this encounter. Three figures chosen to illustrate this theme are Theodoric, Scanderbeg and Abd-el-Karim (a Rif tribal leader who spent eleven months in a Spanish prison in the 1920s). 'Through tactful handling the young barbarian who becomes a hostage may be induced to stay on as a mercenary; and Theoporic and Scanderbog both completed their apprenticeship ...by

servlng for a time , on a more or less volunta~y footing, in the amy of the empire which they afterwards made it their life-work to combat.' (vol. V, pp. 461-2). Toynbee quotes J. Pisko, Scanderbeg (Vienna, 1894) as his authority. But Pisko was merely repeating the old legend eighteen years after Constantin Jirecek had refused to accept it in his Geschichte Der Bulgaren Prague, 1876). Had Toynbee consulted Jirecek rather than Pisko the Process of the Disintegration of Civilisation might have been arrested.

6 Citizenship ofVenice (and Ragusa):Thalloczy, etc.,Vol I, p. 142; Ljubic, vol. IX, p. 214;V.V. Makushev, Istoricheskia Razyakania o Slavjanah v Albanii v Srednie Veka (Historical Researches on the Slavs in Mediaeval Albania) (Warsaw, 1871) p. 63.

7 Ferocious Rigour: The quotation is from B.A.L. Fisher, A History of Europe (Arnold, 1936), p. 729. The Kiuprili or Köprülü family as their name is spelt in modern Turkey, are still evident in modern Turnish publio life. Mehmet Köprülü, who became premier in 1656, is sometimes referred to as a gardener. This is, however, because the office he held can be literally translated as Head Gardener, though in fact he was captain of the Palace Guard. To call him a gardener is a little like describing the Governor of the Tower of London as a butcher because he is responsible for the beefeaters.

8 Evliya Chelebi: His story appears in A.A. Pallis, In the Time of the Janissaries

9 The Court of Adrianapole: Although one was conquered about a hundred years before the other, it is doubtful whether the distinction between Adrianople and Contantinople was ever very clear in the minds of later generations. Thus the C.I.T. guide Albania (Milan, 1940), p. 47, says that Gjergj was sent as a hostage to the court of Constantinople. Gjergj was 48 years of age at the time Constantinople was conquered by the Turks.

5. The Athlete of Christendom

1 Longfellow: Fan Noli, who translated the poem 'Scanderbeg,' into Albanian (Boston, 1916)'also did some detective work on the sources from which Longfellow learned the story noting, for instance, that the poet referred to Kruja by its Turkish name, Ak-Hissar (White Castle).

2 Athlete of Christendom: Friedrich Kayser, Papst Nicholas V und das Vordringen der Türken, in Historisches Jahrbuch im Auftrage der Görres-Gesellschaft, vol VI (Munich 1885) p.215.

6. War on Two Fronts

1 'Ingrate Foster Son': This, and similar quotations in pungent Elizabethan language later on, are from the 1596 translation of Lavardin's Barletius.

2 Family Rivalries: The suspicion with which Scanderbeg's progress was regarded by some of the older families emerges from Gjin Musachi's family history. (Note on 'Scanderbeg's brothers,' p.50). Musachi, who at one time called himself Despot of Epirus, left Albania in 1479 and wrote his history in Italy in 1510,

when an expedition was being planned to reconquer his native land, in order to tell his three sons what land belonged to them. The expedition never materialised, and the manuscript lay in the Biblioteca Brancacciana in Naples, where Karl Hopf found it in 1863 and later published it in his Chroniques Grecoromanes.

3 Count Vrana: Vrana Altisferi belonged to the same family as Lek Zaharia Altisferi, whose death had led to the war over Dagno. He had served in the army of Alfonso V of Aragon (Gianmaria Biemmi, Istoria di Giorgio Scander-Begh (Brescia, 1742), and as a chieftain received the courtesy title of Conte, or Count, which was the nearest Italian equivalent, just as Gjergj Castrioti received the not dissimilar title of Beg from the Turks.

4 Venetian Diplomacy: The text of the Doge's letter, and details of the subsequent correspondence between Venice and Durazzo, are quoted from the Venetian State Archives, in Alessandro Cutolo, Scanderbeg (Milan, 1940), pp. 71-82. For the terms of the peace treaty between Scanderbeg and Venice, Ljubic, Listine, vol. IX, pp. 282-3.

7. Scanderbeg against The Sultan

1 The Dead Dog of Svetigrad: Fan Noli thinks that 'the Turks succeeded in cutting the water supply and compelled the garrison to surrender.' (Scanderbeg, p. 199, note 95). But one would expect a walled city, willing to accept a siege, to have springs or wells immune from the enemy. Svetigrad, however, stands on porous limestone rock and is just on the edge of an extremely dry region which stretches across Macedonia, so that the failure of the supply seems more likely.(A rainfall chart of Yugoslavia appears in the Collection de Cartes de la Societé de Geographie de Beograd (No. 4; 1935).

8. 'That Furious and Untamed Lion'

1 Offer of Kruja: Cutolo, Scanderbeg, pp. 96-7.

2 An Anonymous Novel: The Great Scanderbeg: A Novel, Done out of French. London, Printed for R. Bentley at the Post-House in Russel-Street in Covent Garden, 1690.

9. Byzantium to Berat

1 Smederevo: For a summary of the story of Smederevo, with a plan, see C. Stewart, Serbian legacy, pp. 87-90. Mr. Stewart points out that though completed in 1456, the fortress was not tested by gunpowder until 1941, when an ammunition carriage on the adjoining railway exploded and brought down a length of wall and one of the great towers. His Plate 61 shows Smederevo from the Danube.

2 Ottoman Architecture: Mr. Cecil Stewart, though so appreciative of the origi-

nality of the Serbian mediaeval architects, is less so of the Turkish. He suggests (Serbian Legacy, p. 97) that after the conquest of Constantinople 'they did not bring a new style with them,' but 'at once adopted the architectural forms of the Byzantine capital.' It has been suggested, however, that Ottoman architects both absorbed many Byzantine achievements before ever reaching Constantinople and retained their own tradition when they had arrived there. Thus the Çinili Kösk (Tiled Pavilion), the only surviving work of Mehmet the Conqueror's, which was built in 1472, nineteen years after the conquest, has been described as 'wholly in the tradition of the Seljuks of Horasan,' who preceded the Ottomans. Behçet Ünsal, Turkish Islamic Architecture (Tiranti, 1959), p. 62. Photographs of this building will be found in Ünsal, Plate 110 (plan on p. 63)' and in Martin Hurlimann, Istanbul (Thames and Hudson, 1958), Plate 21.

3 Gaeta Treaty: Francesco Cerone, La Politica Orientale di Alfonso di Aragona (Archivio Storico per le Provincie Napoletane, vol. XXVIII, Naples, 1903, pp. 172-3) gives the terms of the treaty signed 'fra la Serenissima Maiesta de lo Serenissimo signore don Alfonso Re d'Aragone de Sicilia citra et ultra farum dal una parte e lo vecerablle patre in Xto dommo Stephano Episcopo de Croya e lo religioso Mastro Nicola de Berguzi del ordene de Sancto Domeneco oraturi et ambassiaturi de lo spectabile et magnifico Zorgio Castrioti signore de la dita citate de Croya a de soi parenti baruni in Albania de la parte altra.'

4 Weapons: In close warfare, the archer was still most efficient and lethal. A qualified archer expected to shoot a dozen arrows a minute at a man-sized target and hit it with all of them, and with metal arrowheads chain mail could be pierced or a horse killed at 200 yards. The crossbow had many disadvantages by comparison. It was heavy and slow - six arrows could be discharged in the time ~ it took to fire it once - and it was far from accurate, except at very short range. But it had a decisive advantage over the bow and arrow in that it could be drawn ahead of use, and sighted before the iron 'bolts' were discharged. It could do more damage than the bow; and the larger version - the ballista or arbalest could pierce plate armour and inflict a nasty wound at about 60 yarde. This inhuman object was put under Papal interdict in 1139, as too murderous for warfare; at least among Christians, for it could be used against infidels. The arquebus, a Spanish invention, worked by matchlock and fired a lead ball, and was in effect an early musket. As artillery were also used, the joint Albanian and Aragonese forces were equipped with weapons that in principle spanned the history of war from the earliest to almost contemporary times. (There are interesting summaries and illustratione of these weapons in Edwin Tunis, Weapons, a Pictorial History. Cleveland and New York, 1954.)

11. The Friend of Virtue

1 Excellent concise biographies of the Italian personalities in this chapter - Alfonso, Ferrante, Orsini, Piccinnino, etc. - can be found in the Enciclopedia Italiana.

2 Letters to Orsini and Ferrante: Copies of these letters were given by the archivist of Venice to Vikentij Vasilevich Makushev, a Russian professor at the University of Warsaw, and published by him in his Monumenta Historica Slavorum Meridionalium Vicinorumque Populorum, vol. II (Belgrade, 1882), pp. 117-24.

His idea that Albanians and Greeks are albanised and hellenised Slavs is now probably shared by no one, but it stimulated him to valuable discoveries of this kind on Albanian mediaeval history and economic conditions.

3 Epirots: A modern Albanian would not call himself an Epirot, for since the rebirth of Greece in the 19th century, Ipiros or Epirus has become the name of an administrative region in the north-west corner of Greece; and the area adjoining it beyond the Albanian frontier is claimed from time to time by Greece under the name of Northern Epirus. So 'Epirot' now has a political significance; but in its classical origin, and as Scanderbeg here uses it, it is purely a geographical term. Epirus is 'epeiros,' the mainland or hinterland, as distinct from the truly Greek world of the islands and coastal colonies. (For these modern Greek claims, see E.P. Stickney, Southern Albania or Northern Epirus in European International Affairs, 1912-1923. Stanford U.P., 1926.)

4 A Friend ofVirtue: We should probably be right to assume that whoever drafted this letter thought of virtue in the current Renaissance sense, as including a self-respecting consistency of character and initiative in action: a matter of honour even more than of morality.

5 Machiavelli: Burckhardt, speaking of his Arte della Guerra, calls him 'the greatest dilettante who has ever treated in that character of military affairs,' but thinks more highly than he of the art of war in mid-fifteenth century Italy. (Civilisation of the Renaissance. London, Phaidon, 1944, pp. 62-4) But Burckhardt is comparing Italian artillery and military theory with the rest of Western Europe, and not with that of the Turks.

6 Piccinnino: His shrewdness, however, hardly justifies the chronicler of one of his earlier campaigns who, as Burckhardt mentions, referred to him throughout as Scipio and to his opponent (Francesco Sforza) as Hannibal.

7 Pius II: The quotation is from his Comentarii Rerum Memorabilium (Rome, 1584), p. 302. Pius, or perhaps more properly his secretaries and amanuenses, made a number of 'improvements' to the story of the Italian expedition. Not content with what Scanderbeg had written to Prince Orsini, for example, Pius includes in his version of the letter an insult to the effect that the people of Tarento, Orsini's subjects, were 'a sodden race of people born to catch little fishes.' Orsini is made to tell Scanderbeg that he is no longer 'fighting with effeminate Turks or unwarlike Greeklings,' and that 'no man of Italian blood will fear the dregs of Albania ...We reckon the Albanians as sheep.' Until a few years ago, no English translation of the Commentaries existed, but since 1939 parts of it have appeared in the Smith College Studies in History, in a translation by F.A. Gragg. There are twelve books, of which nine have appeared.

12. The Last Crusade

1 Pius II: The standard biography is in German (by G. Voigt, Berlin, 1856-63; but there is an English biography (by C.M. Ady, London, 1913). The latter was among three books on Pius dealt with in a lively and sympathetic study in the Church Quarterly Review , January, 1910, by E. Armstrong, and reprinted in his Italian Studies (Macmillan, 1934). The Pope's 'bewildering juxtaposition of moral strength and weakness' was the theme of an illustrated article, 'Pius II:

Humanist and Crusader,' by John B. Morrall, in History Today, January 1958.

2 The Children of Aeneas: 'I frankly confess my fault, that I am neither holier than David nor wiser than Solomon,' he wrote to his father, when asking him to bring up one of these children. Continence he described at one point as 'a laudable virtue ... more easily practised in word than in deed, and befits philosophers rather than poets.' (Mandell Creighton, History of the Papacy, vol. II, p. 246.)

3 Boccaccio-style novels: One of these, The Tale of Two Lovers, translated by Flora Grierson, was published by Constable, 1929.

4 TheBogomils: Bogomil ('Beloved of God') is supposed to have been a 10th century Bulgarian priest who founded a puritan sect teaching that the material world was evil, and that virtue thus consisted in practising a rigid asceticism. As a 'heresy' it incurred the hostility of the Roman and Orthodox Churches, and it was equally suspect to the secular authorities because of its contempt for worldly power.In a society where civil and religious authority were both conspicuously oppressive, such a movement was popular. It spread throughout southern Europe, and came to threaten the establishdd order. So it was generally persecuted, and those who remained faithful to it took refuge in the less accessible mountain districts, such as Bosnia (under the name of Patarenes) and southern France (the Albigensians). Where it could be extirpated, it was; and among the instruments used were the new mendicant orders of the Roman Church - the Franciscans and Dominicans - who could not be accused of worldliness. Being disinterested, they proved the ideal instruments of persuasion, especially when the threat of persecution and massacre followed them in the shape of secular armies.

The significance of Bogomilism in Bosnian history is, however, hardly religious at all, but almost wholly political. Hungary, who coveted the country from the north, was Roman Catholic; Serbia, who threatened from the east, was Orthodox, and each of them denied the existence of Bosnia as a separate national unit. But the Bosnians had early experience of independent statehood; and her first ruler, the Ban Kulin - a bon Roi Rene of the Balkans - joined the Patarenes. He was forced to recant in 1203 under papal and Hungarian pressure, but the pattern for the future had been established. After a series of 'crusades' against them by Hungarian armies and prosyletising Dominican priests, Patarenism became the national religion; and when both Roman and Orthodox states went down before the Turks, it was a comparatively simple matter for the Bosnian Patarenes to become converted to Islam, especially as they then became more favoured subjects of the Ottomans than the Christian neighbours who had so long despised and persecuted them.

5 Truce with the Sultan: Biemmi, Istoria, Book VI, pp. 416-9; Pius II, Commentarii, Book XII, p. 607.

6 Peace with Venice: Ljubic, Listine, vol. X, pp. 264-6.

7 Venice and the Pope: Cutolo, Scanderbeg, pp. 179-82.

13. A Janissary's Return

1 Hoe and ploughshare: One may be doing Scanderbeg an injustice here. This symbolic act may have been thought of after the event; but the confrontation of

the two men remains unaffected by its truth or otherwise.

2 Edward Lear: Journals of a Landscape Painter in Albania, Illyria, &c. (London, 1852)

14. *'A Day of Mist'*

1 Terrorism: The Roman reference is to the occupation of Epirus and the sale of 150,000 inhabitabts into slavery

2 Albania: The 'Mount Albius' described by Strabo, who died in 25 A.D., as being inhabited by a mixed Celtic and Illyrian tribe, was much further north on the Adriatic coast.

3 Elbasan: For Venetian diplomacy after the Sultan's construction of his new town and fortress, Ljubic, Listine, v. X, pp. 372-3, and Cutolo, Scanderbeg, pp. 200-6.

4 Dirge for Scanderbeg: This song was heard in the streets of Naples around 1840, sung by an Albanian street singer. See M.B. Albini, Calabre, pp. 266-74, where a French version is given.

5 Turkish soldiers: The cult of Scanderbeg in the West was much less dramatic than this, but it continued until well into the 18th century: until it was evident, that is, that there was no further danger of Turkish expansion. Three plays about him were published in London within fifteen years - William Havard, Scanderbeg, 1733 (which had two performances at Goodmans Fields Theatre); Lillo's Christian Hero, 1735; and Thomas Whincop, Scanderbeg, or Love and liberty, 1747.

6 Siege of Scutari: Barletius, Scanderbeg's biographer, was in Scutari during the siege and wrote an account of it in Latin; this appears in an Italian translation as a section of Francesco Sansovino, Historia Universale dell'Origine et Imperio de' Turchi (Venice, 1568)

7 The Aftermath: After the final conquest of Albania, some of the chieftains, like the Dukagjini, made the best they could of the new conditions and continued their semi-independent way of life under the Turkish overlords.

Others, among them the Castrioti family, went to Italy and founded there the Albanian colonies in Calabria. The Castriotis were given a Neapolitan dukedom, and they were involved in various abortive attempts to mount an invasion of Albania and restore them to their native rights. These continued until about the end of the 19th century. Alexandre Dumas fils was involved in one of them; and another finds its echo in a curious pamphlet (London, 1866), A tribute to the memory of Scanderbeg the Great, by Robert Bigsby LLD, 'Director of the Third Section of the Royal Academy of Palermo' and member, after a long list of similar distinctions, of 'the Literary, and Philosophical and Antiquarian Societies of Newcastle-upon-Tyne.' 'Shall the land of the heroic Scanderbeg continue to groan under the usurping sceptre of the infidel?' he asks, remarking that Byron called him 'the prince of chevaliers in all ages,' and saying that as he is writing his pamphlet Scanderbeg's descendant, Giorgio Castrioti Scanderbeg, Duke of San Pietro in the Kingdom of Naples and Titular Prince of Croia, 'is even now striving with characteristic energy to collect the means of asserting substantially his rightful claims to the sceptre of his race.'

INDEX